How Logic Works

How Logic Works

A User's Guide

Hans Halvorson

PRINCETON UNIVERSITY PRESS

PRINCETON & OXFORD

Published by Princeton University Press
41 William Street, Princeton, New Jersey 08540
99 Banbury Road, Oxford OX2 6JX

All Rights Reserved

First paperback printing, 2024
Paper ISBN 9780691211954
Cloth ISBN 9780691182223
ISBN (e-book) 9780691208718
LCCN: 2020009314

British Library Cataloging-in-Publication Data is available

Editorial: Matt Rohal
Jacket/Cover Design: Layla MacRory
Production: Danielle Amatucci

Jacket/Cover images: Keyhole by Maria Solomakhina;
key by Graphik Designz, IN / The Noun Project

This book has been composed in LATEX

press.princeton.edu

Contents

Preface

THIS BOOK HAS NO SUBJECT MATTER—or, to be more precise, it's about both everything and nothing. For the science of logic has no doctrines or creeds. There is no set of beliefs that distinguishes the logical people from the nonlogical people, not the beliefs of the European Enlightenment, nor the deliverances of contemporary natural science, nor the opinions of some Princeton philosopher. Simply put, learning the science of logic can't be reduced to learning any particular facts at all; it's learning a skill, namely, the skill to discern between good and bad arguments.

There are numerous reasons why you need this skill, no matter what you end up doing with your life. First, being logical will help you reason about how to get what you want. Second, many of our society's best jobs require strong logic skills—whether it be programming computers, buying stock options, curing diseases, prosecuting criminals, discovering alternative energy sources, or interpreting the Constitution. (And that's not even to speak of that all-important task of parenting and raising intellectually healthy children.) Third, regardless of your ideological bent—whether you're religious, atheist, or agnostic—you surely want to do everything you can to ensure that your view aligns with reality. For this task, logic is an invaluable tool, if only to protect you from the plethora of bad arguments you'll hear in your life.

Our goal here is no more or less than to initiate you into the most up-to-date account of what makes an argument good. We'll give you the tools, but it's up to you to decide how you're going to use them.

Note *about how to use this book:* The first six chapters of this book (up through "Quantifying") correspond roughly to a first course in formal logic at an average university in the United States. We cover the material in about a quarter of the number of pages of some well-known logic text-books, which was intentional: logic should organize your already existing thoughts, not add to the jumble of thoughts that need to be organized.

In chapter 7, we gently ramp up to applications of formal logic, and in particular to the application of formal logic to the study of itself (i.e., logical metatheory). In one sense, this material goes beyond a typical first course in logic, but we would like to change that. This material is not intrinsically more difficult than what has gone before. In fact, what can make it seem difficult is that it's less clear what rules of reasoning one is permitted to use. However, we try to explain clearly that the rules of reasoning here are none other than those that were learned in the previous chapters.

Having shown how formal logic can be used to formulate theories, we then begin to use formal logic to formulate a theory about itself. In chapter 8, we use the theory of sets to define the notion of an interpretation of a language and Tarski's rigorous definition of *truth*. In chapter 9, we present a theory about propositional logic, proving both soundness and complete-ness theorems. Finally, in chapter 10, we sketch the outlines of a similar theory about quantifier logic. Thus, the chapters form a natural staircase leading up to the treasure chest of advanced applications of logic, including modal logic, set theory, and Gödel's theorem.

Note *to the instructor, or to the person deciding which logic book to use:* To express a thought, or to make an argument, or to formulate a theory, you have to pick a language to use. Similarly, to become more logical, you have to adopt some particular system of logic. I've made a choice for you here, and here is my rationale.

The first choice point is between "trees" and "arguments." The advantage of trees is that they are really easy and require little mental exertion.

But wait, isn't the goal to become the most excellent logical thinkers that we can be? People don't become better logical thinkers by being taught a recipe that somebody else found and that lets them effectively turn their minds off. But that's precisely the point of logical trees: they give students a *recipe* for evaluating simple arguments. If the goal were to manufacture an army of logical automata, then I might well use trees. But since I'm teaching human beings, I prefer to teach them that distinctively human skill of making and evaluating arguments. Accordingly, this book focuses primarily on how to make rigorous arguments and secondarily on the (nonalgorithmic) skill of detecting bad arguments.

The second choice point is whether to represent arguments using a "Fitch-style" or a "Lemmon-style" system. This is a difficult decision. Fitch style is very intuitive and has a shallow learning curve. Unfortunately, Fitch-style argument is opaque to reflection: it's difficult for students to see why Fitch style works and even more difficult for them to imagine how the rules might have been different (thereby reinforcing an unfortunate perception that there is no human creativity involved in formulating the laws of logic). In contrast, Lemmon-style argument has a steeper learning curve, but it's more flexible and transparent to reflection. It's relatively easy to see why the system works, and it's easy to tweak the rules and see how things would come out different. So, the steeper learning curve of the Lemmon approach is a price I'm willing to pay to enable my reader to become a more clear and creative logical thinker.

There are at least four ways in which this book differs from many other introductory logic books. First, we teach intrinsic methods (e.g., reasoning) prior to teaching extrinsic methods (e.g., checking with truth tables). Here, our philosophical convictions have been reinforced by our pedagogical experience, namely, that an argument-centric approach leads to students gaining a higher level of mastery and confidence and that the skills gained are more easily transferable to other intellectual tasks.

Second, and for similar reasons, we treat formal validity as defined in terms of the inference rules and not in terms of truth preservation. Our issue here is that a precise notion of truth preservation requires a previous understanding of valid reasoning in set theory. So, we want to be forthright with our reader that we, at least, don't have a clear and distinct perception of what truth preservation amounts to, at least not until we explicate the notion in terms of set theory. By taking formal validity as defined by the rules, we emphasize that genuine creativity is required to design rules that both capture and sharpen our intuitions about validity.

Third, in chapter 7, we ease students away from rigid formal proofs and toward "informal rigor." Again, the goal is for the students to be able to transfer their knowledge to other disciplines where rigid formal proofs might not be appropriate or useful. Fourth, in chapter 9, we introduce logical metatheory as "just another theory" by explaining how to formulate the metatheory for propositional with predicate logic and a bit of set theory. Thus, we close the circle of logic back upon itself.

Note *to the reader:* We put an asterisk to the left of exercises that might be perceived as more difficult than the preceding ones. In the case of proofs, it often occurs that a difficult result is basically a version of the law of excluded middle: $P \lor \neg P$. So, if you get stuck, you might try first to prove excluded middle and then to use that to get the result you want.

1

Logic for Humans

You're a curious person, I suspect. You probably already flipped through the pages of this book, in which case you may have run across some unfamiliar symbols. You might have found yourself intrigued—like an archaeologist discovering ancient runes. Or you might have been put off—thinking that this book is for quantitative people.

That's what I assumed at first. I wanted to spend the days of my life thinking about the big questions of human existence—what exists, what we can know, and how we should live. Calculate the derivative of a function? Solve a differential equation? No thank you. I'll leave that to the people who want to build better bridges. I'd prefer to move on to the really meaningful and enriching topics.

But I discovered that it's a false dilemma. In fact, it's not a dilemma at all. Symbolic logic is not only for mathematics, and it's by no means a diversion from the really deep questions of human life. In fact, symbolic logic represents the best account we have of what it means to be *rational*.

Although logic is symbolic, it's not really "mathematical" in any sense that puts it in opposition to humanistic endeavors (such as literature, poetry, history, philosophy, etc.). Yes, mathematics is a human activity that displays logical thinking in a particularly clear way. But logic itself is involved in any type of human thinking that aims at finding the truth. If you've ever argued for a claim or evaluated someone else's argument, then you were using logic—whether you realized it or not and whether or not you did a good job of it.

The goal of this book is simple: it's to make you conscious of how you already use logic and thereby to become even better at it. If you learn to do symbolic logic, then you will become a better thinker, and you will understand better what it means to be a good thinker.

Arguments

Many logic books begin by saying, "The subject matter of logic is...." I think these statements are always a bit misleading. In one sense, logic doesn't have a subject matter at all. Logic isn't *about* something; it's a way of life.

Let's begin by trying to see ourselves from the outside. Just imagine that you are an alien who has landed on earth, and you're trying to understand what human beings are doing when they say that they are thinking logically. Imagine that there are two people, say Anne and Bernt, and that Anne is trying to convince Bernt that something is true. Anne might proceed as follows:

> Of course gay marriage should be legal. Only people with some backward religious view would believe otherwise.

Here Anne is trying to convince Bernt that gay marriage should be legal. But she doesn't try to coerce him with physical force or even with intellectual intimidation. Instead, she offers Bernt a *reason* why he should accept her conclusion. To be more clear, the **conclusion** of Anne's argument is the statement, "Gay marriage should be legal." The reason that Anne gives for this conclusion—"Only people with some backward religious view believe otherwise"—will be called the **premise** of the argument. Thus, the argument consists of a premise and a conclusion that is supposed to be supported by the premise.

Thus, we have three things in play: **argument, conclusion,** and **premise.** The argument itself is made up of the conclusion and the premise.

The conclusion and premise themselves are particular sentences. Notice, moreover, that these sentences are *assertions* (i.e., they make a statement that is either true or false). Thus, an argument is built out of assertions (or statements), some of which are premises and one of which is the conclusion.

The key point about an argument is that it's more than just a disconnected collection of statements. Suppose that I have ten notecards, each of which has a statement on it. If I shuffle them up and hand them to you, then I haven't given you an **argument**. For a collection of statements to be an argument, there has to be some implied sense in which some of the statements stand in a special relation to another one of the statements. In the notecard analogy, I'd have to hand you a first batch of notecards and say, "These are my premises," and then I'd have to hand you another notecard and say, "And this statement is my conclusion—which, I claim, follows logically from those premises."

What is this relation of "following logically" that I claim holds between my premises and my conclusion? We all know it when we see it, and we have many words for it—words such as "supports" or "implies" or "entails" or "shows that" or "grounds." That is, we say things like, "The fact that there are cookie crumbs on the carpet *shows that* my son was eating in the living room."

It's this relation—whatever it is—that we really want to understand. We want to know: when does this relation hold between statements? When does one statement imply another? There is simply nothing more basic to human rationality than the notion of one statement implying another.

We will make a lot of progress in clarifying the notion of implication. But we're not going to make progress by means of a head-on assault. That is, we're not going to offer you a definition of the form:

To say that one statement implies another means that ...

Such a definition would be interesting, but it's not what this book is about. This book is more of a training manual for logic connoisseurs. Just as a wine connoisseur knows a good wine when he tastes one, so a logic connoisseur knows a good argument when she sees one.

Logical Form

The study of logic began in ancient Greece—and possibly in other places at other times, although that history is less well known to us. It all began with a single insight, which you've probably already had yourself. This insight is that whether or not an argument is good depends only on its **form** and not on its **content**. To explain this distinction, we need to back up for a second and explain what we mean by saying that an argument is "good." Consider the following argument:

> All whales are mammals.
> David Hasselhoff is a whale.
> Therefore, David Hasselhoff is a mammal.

Here there are two premises and one conclusion. We've used the word "therefore" to indicate what the conclusion is. But in truth, the word "therefore" isn't part of the content of the conclusion. The conclusion is just the proposition, "David Hasselhoff is a mammal."

Is this a good argument? I hope that your answer is, "it depends." It certainly isn't a perfect argument, because it involves a false statement, namely, that David Hasselhoff is a whale. Or maybe you don't know anything about David Hasselhoff? (Such deplorable lack of cultural knowledge these days!) Suppose that David Hasselhoff were actually a famous whale in a book by an obscure author named Melvin Hermanville. In that case—if Hasselhoff were a whale—then would it be a good argument? Yes, it would definitely be a good argument.

If you're a philosophy type, then you might still be doubtful. You might be thinking, "It all depends on what you mean by 'good.'" If by "good" we mean "interesting, informative, and nontrivial," then that argument might not be very good. However, logic has no use for subjective words such as "interesting." Logic is the *science* of good arguments, and it's interested in isolating an *objective* sense of goodness in arguments.

The insight—passed on to us by the ancient Greeks—is that we can define "good argument" in an objective sense by factorizing goodness into two distinct pieces. The first of the two pieces is easy to understand but difficult to agree upon in practice: are the premises true? The second piece is a bit more elusive but forms the subject matter of logic as an objective science: do the premises support (or imply, or entail) the conclusion? If the premises do imply the conclusion, then we say that the argument is valid.

Definition. An argument is said to be **valid** if its premises imply its conclusion.

The notion of validity isn't concerned with whether the premises or conclusion are true or false. The question, instead, is a conditional one: *if* the premises were true, *then* would the conclusion be true?

You should be able to think of cases where you would agree that the premises support the conclusion, even though you think that the premises are false. It might help to use the phrase, "the premises *would* support the conclusion," the idea being that if they *were* true, then they would imply that the conclusion is also true.

You should also be able to think of arguments where the premises *and* conclusion are true, but the premises do *not* imply the conclusion. For example, the following is a true premise: "I love coffee." The following is also true: "I am over six feet tall." But to make an argument from my loving coffee to my above-average height would be patently invalid. Logical validity is all about the connection between premises and conclusion; it's not directly concerned with the question of whether the premises or conclusion are true.

Sameness of Form

How do we get our hands on this elusive notion of validity and the related notion of implication? Let's begin by looking at obvious cases—where an argument is obviously valid or obviously invalid. For example, the argument above was obviously valid. But the argument below is obviously invalid:

Princeton is a town in New Jersey.
Therefore, God doesn't exist.

Now, you might actually think that both of these statements are true. But that most certainly doesn't mean that the first statement implies the second. Some true statements just don't have anything to do with each other. And that's why this argument is invalid—because the premise doesn't give the right kind of support for the conclusion.

Consider another argument:

All whales are predators.
Bambi is a whale.
Therefore, Bambi is a predator.

Is that a valid argument? Before you answer, remember that validity doesn't have anything to do with whether you believe the premises or the conclusion. It's merely a matter of whether there is the right kind of connection between premise and conclusion.

Imagine for a moment that you just learned English and that you aren't yet familiar with the word "whale" or with the name "Bambi." For all you know, "whale" might mean the same thing as "tiger." And for all you know, "Bambi" might be the name of a tiger at the Philadelphia zoo.

Here's the amazing thing: you don't have to know anything about the meaning of the words "whale," "predator," or "Bambi" to know that this argument is valid. How do you know it's valid? I'm not going to try to answer that question directly. I'm going to assume that you share my intuition that it is obviously valid. If you're still not convinced, let me put it this way:

If all whales were predators, and if Bambi were a whale, then would it follow that Bambi is a predator?

Now it seems pretty obvious, doesn't it?

We said that the validity of that argument doesn't depend at all on what the "content words" mean. In other words, if an argument is valid, then it should remain valid no matter how we interpret the content words or even if we replace the content words with different ones. Thus, given a valid argument (such as the one above), we should be able to create a sort of "mad lib argument" with variables that can be filled in by content words.

All X are Y.

m is an X.

Therefore, m is a Y.

No matter what words you put in for X, Y, and m (provided that the result is a well-formed sentence), you get a valid argument.

The thing above with the variables, it's like a blueprint for constructing arguments. Choose some content words, plug them in, and ta da, you have a valid argument. Let's call it an **argument form**. In this case, it's a valid argument form, because no matter what words you plug in, the argument comes out as valid.

But how did we know that those arguments were valid in the first place? To be honest, it's just our intuition that tells us that these arguments are valid. Nobody found a tablet of stone on a mountain with the argument form above. Instead, that argument form was written down by a human being in an effort to capture what is common in a bunch of arguments that we feel (intuitively) to be valid.

That's how we'll proceed in the first part of this book: we will collect several basic argument forms that seem obviously valid. Then, we'll learn how to string valid argument forms together to create longer valid arguments.

2

Deducing

Let's look at another obviously valid argument.

> Roses are red and violets are blue.
> _____
> Roses are red.

(Here the horizontal line functions as a "therefore" indicator.) The reason this argument is valid is because the conclusion just extracts one of two sentences that are conjoined in the premise. In other words, the argument form looks like this:

> P and Q
> _____
> P

Here we've replaced "roses are red" with the letter P, and we've replaced "violets are blue" with the letter Q. Obviously, the argument would be valid no matter what sentences we put in for P and Q.

The reason why this argument form is valid is because of the way that the word "and" works. It's a special word that connects two statements into one bigger statement that logically implies both of the original statements. Since "and" plays this special logical role, it can be helpful to make it stand out. We'll use the symbol " ∧ " as shorthand for "and," so that "*P* ∧ *Q*" will stand for "*P* and *Q*." In this case, the argument form above looks like this:

$$P \wedge Q$$
$$\overline{}$$
$$P$$

Our arguments are gradually changing from linguistic to symbolic—but simply because we're trying to capture the essence of what makes them valid. The symbol ∧ here is not a new thing. It's just the good old notion of "and," written in compact notation. And that will be the case for *everything* you encounter in this book. In this book, we won't need to introduce new things that you've never encountered before in your life. In this way, logic is quite different from empirical sciences such as biology, chemistry, or physics. In physics, you'll run into things like "quantum fields," which I imagine your mother didn't tell you about. But in logic, we're just going to make precise concepts that you use already in everyday life.

Conjunction Elimination (∧ E)

For any two sentences ϕ and ψ, you are permitted to infer both ϕ and ψ individually from the conjunction $\phi \wedge \psi$.

The Greek letters ϕ and ψ here are meant to emphasize the schematic nature of inference rules. In particular, a Greek letter like ϕ can stand for any sentence whatsoever, whether it be *P* or *Q* or *P* ∧ *Q* or *P* ∧ (*P* ∧ *Q*). So, for example, ∧ E allows one to infer *P* from *P* ∧ *Q*, and it also allows one to infer (*Q* ∧ *P*) from (*Q* ∧ *P*) ∧ *Q*.

In practice, we use the rules (such as ∧ elimination) in a linear format, moving from the top of the page to the bottom. For example, the following is a typical application of ∧ elimination.

(1) *P* ∧ *Q*   A
(2) *P*   1 ∧ E

Here the first line is annotated with "A," which means that it's an assumption of the problem.[1] The second line is annotated with "1 ∧ E," which means that the conjunction elimination rule was used on line 1. In a correctly written (i.e., valid) proof, every line must either be an assumption or be justified by one of the rules of inference.

Here's a slightly more complicated proof of P from $(P \wedge Q) \wedge (R \wedge P)$.

(1)	$(P \wedge Q) \wedge (R \wedge P)$	A
(2)	$P \wedge Q$	1 ∧ E
(3)	P	2 ∧ E

Note that we weren't forced to take the route that we did. We could have peeled off the conjunct $R \wedge P$ instead and used that to get P. In fact, logic never tells you what steps you must take; it only tells you what steps you are permitted to take. It's up to you to decide where you want to go and how you want to get there.

Just as a conjunction can be disassembled into its conjuncts, so a conjunction can be assembled from individual propositions. So we have a rule:

Conjunction Introduction (∧ I)

For any two sentences ϕ and ψ, you are permitted to infer $\phi \wedge \psi$ if you already have both ϕ and ψ.

Schematically: $\dfrac{\phi \qquad \psi}{\phi \wedge \psi}$

So, when you use conjunction introduction, you will cite two lines, one for each conjunct. For example:

(1)	P	A
(2)	Q	A
(3)	$P \wedge Q$	1,2 ∧ I

---

1. In this chapter, assumptions are things that are given to you—as part of the problem you're trying to solve. In the next chapter, we'll explain how you can make your own assumptions.

Note, however, that you can use the same line twice. For example, the following counts as a valid application of conjunction introduction:

(1) P A
(2) $P \wedge P$ 1,1 $\wedge$ I

It also doesn't matter which order the lines occur in. For example, if Q occurs before P, then you can use conjunction introduction to infer either $Q \wedge P$ or $P \wedge Q$.

At this stage, we need to introduce another device. Suppose that you already have one conjunction, say $P \wedge Q$, and you want to conjoin it with yet another statement, say R. In that case, to conjoin the first composite statement with the second simple statement, you first have to put the first sentence into parentheses, as follows:

(1) $P \wedge Q$ A
(2) R A
(3) $(P \wedge Q) \wedge R$ 1,2 $\wedge$ I

You might be thinking that these parentheses aren't really necessary, because it doesn't matter which conjunction gets put in first. There is a sense in which that is correct. But for now, let's be careful to keep track of where things are coming from.

It's also crucial to note that this rule is schematic. In particular, $\wedge$ elimination allows you to derive a conjunct from any conjunction; for example, both P and $Q \wedge R$ may be derived from $P \wedge (Q \wedge R)$. Note, however, that $\wedge$ E does *not* allow you to derive Q immediately from $P \wedge (Q \wedge R)$, because the original sentence isn't a conjunction of Q with something else. Each conjunctive sentence has precisely two conjuncts. In this case, the two conjuncts are P and $Q \wedge R$. The latter is a conjunction, so that the sentence Q is "two levels deep" inside the conjunction $P \wedge (Q \wedge R)$. We'll explain this notion of "levels" inside sentences in chapter 9. But for now, your intuitions should suffice to keep you out of trouble.

With these two rules ($\wedge$ E and $\wedge$ I), you can now start proving some stuff on your own.

Exercise 2.1.

1. Prove that $Q \wedge P$ follows from $P \wedge Q$. That is, write $P \wedge Q$ on line (1), then use the rules ($\wedge$ introduction and elimination) repeatedly until you obtain $Q \wedge P$.
2. Prove that $P \wedge (Q \wedge R)$ follows from $(P \wedge Q) \wedge R$.

In this book, if a concept is really important, then we'll probably invent a symbol for it. The reason we do that is because it makes it easy for us to identify instances where that concept is being used. The most important concept in this book is the concept of a **valid argument** (and the related concepts of when one statement **entails** or **implies** another statement). Since this concept is so central to this book, we'll give it a symbol $\vdash$. Thus, we write $P \wedge Q \vdash P$ as shorthand for "$P \wedge Q$ logically implies P." Or, to be even more precise, $P \wedge Q \vdash P$ means that there is a correctly written proof that begins with $P \wedge Q$ and that ends with P. The entire string $P \wedge Q \vdash P$ is called a **sequent**, which is just a fancy name for a logically valid argument in our symbolic language.

The most general sequent then looks something like this:

$$\phi_1, \ldots, \phi_n \vdash \psi$$

which says that there is a proof that assumes $\phi_1, \ldots, \phi_n$ and derives ψ. For example, using conjunction introduction, you can easily write a three-line proof that establishes the sequent $P, Q \vdash P \wedge Q$. Another four-line proof with conjunction introduction establishes the sequent $P, Q \vdash P \wedge (P \wedge Q)$.

To keep your head clear, it's best not to think of sequents like $\phi \vdash \psi$ as sentences of the artificial language we're describing. Imagine that we're designing an artificial intelligence, and we're programming it with rules for drawing valid inferences. In this case, "P" and "Q" are sentences of the AI's language, and $\wedge$ is a connective that can be used to build more and more complex sentences in the AI's language. However, the symbol $\vdash$ is not of the same kind. It's not part of the AI's language, but part of our design language—which we use to describe the permissible reasoning processes for the AI. In particular, $\phi \vdash \psi$ means that the AI can—by using the rules we've specified—derive ψ from ϕ. But $\phi \vdash \psi$ is not itself one of the sentences that the AI is programmed to assert.

By stating the rules (such as $\wedge$ I and $\wedge$ E), we are gradually building up the relation $\vdash$ that holds between premises and conclusions. We want to build up slowly and carefully so that we don't by accident declare that an argument is valid when, as a matter of fact, it's not really valid.

At the moment, we have only two rules. Now it's time to add some more. Let's start with a rule for introducing disjunctions, that is, sentences that involve an "either …or …" clause, which we'll abbreviate by the symbol " $\vee$." That is, we'll symbolize "either P or Q" as "$P \vee Q$."

Before we state the disjunction introduction rule, note that there are two ways that we use disjunctions in English. In one sense, a disjunction presents you with *exclusive* choices. For example, a person can be born either in the United States or in the United Kingdom (but of course a person cannot be born in both places). In another sense, a disjunction just tells us that at least one of the two options holds. For example, a person can be either a US citizen or a UK citizen—and, as a matter of fact, it's possible to be both. In this case, the disjunction is *inclusive*.

If we take disjunction in the inclusive sense, then a disjunction always follows from either one of its disjuncts. For example, if I tell you that I'm a US citizen, then you know that I'm either a US citizen or a UK citizen. You might not typically have any need to draw such an inference—once you know that one of the disjuncts is true, why would you bother to assert the disjunction? In real life, asserting a disjunction is most useful when you have reason to think that one of the two disjuncts must be true but you don't know which one. For example, you know that I'm either a US citizen or I'm not a US citizen, even if you don't know which of those two is the case.

We hereby stipulate that $\vee$ will behave like inclusive disjunction, and hence the following rule makes sense.

Disjunction Introduction ($\vee$ I)

Given ϕ, you are permitted to infer $\phi \vee \psi$, for any sentence ψ whatsoever. Similarly, given ϕ, you are permitted to infer $\psi \vee \phi$, for any sentence ψ whatsoever. Schematically: $\dfrac{\phi}{\phi \vee \psi}$ $\qquad$ $\dfrac{\phi}{\psi \vee \phi}$

The funny thing about disjunction introduction is that it throws information away. From a stronger premise P, you get to infer a weaker conclusion $P \vee Q$. Why would anyone ever want to do that? In short, weakening premises becomes really useful in contexts where two different premises lead to the same weakening. But we'll get to that maneuver later, in the next chapter. For now, we can start using disjunction introduction in combination with our conjunction rules.

(1)	$P \wedge Q$	A
(2)	P	$1 \wedge E$
(3)	$P \vee R$	$2 \vee I$
(4)	Q	$1 \wedge E$
(5)	$R \vee Q$	$4 \vee I$
(6)	$(P \vee R) \wedge (R \vee Q)$	$3,5 \wedge I$

Notice how we disjoin R on the right in line 3 and on the left in line 5. The disjunction introduction rule allows both of these moves.

Keep in mind that disjunction introduction allows you to disjoin anything you want. So, for example, the following is also valid.

(1)	P	A
(2)	$P \vee P$	$1 \vee I$

The disjunction introduction rule might seem too liberal, because the premise ϕ puts no constraints on the statement ψ that occurs in the conclusion $\phi \vee \psi$. For example, the following argument is valid.

> Klaas is a professor.
> Therefore, either Klaas is a professor or he is a serial killer.

If it seems strange to you that this argument is valid, then I suspect it is because we usually have no good reason to assert a disjunction when we're already in a position to assert one of the disjuncts. For example, if you told somebody (who doesn't know Klaas) that Klaas is either a professor or a serial killer, then they are likely to infer that you are unsure which he is—and, that if you were shown evidence that Klaas is not a professor, then you would conclude that he is a serial killer. But logically speaking, those inferences are not warranted. If you are shown evidence that Klaas is not a professor, when you previously believed that he is, then you're more likely to retract the claim that Klaas is either a professor or a serial killer.

It's time then that we further clarified our methodology. Our aim here is *not* to capture every single intuition we might have about good arguments that are stated in our natural languages. Instead, our aim is to find the best *formal* model of the notion of validity. And the thing about formal models is that they can have two distinct types of virtues. On the one hand, it's good to fit the facts (in this case, our intuitions about which arguments are valid). On the other hand, it's good for our formal apparatus to be be both powerful and manageable. It might be helpful to think of an analogy here. Think of how physics describes the motion of projectiles. One of the first things that a physicist does is to make some idealizing assumptions (e.g., that there is no wind resistance). That assumption won't really hold in real-life applications. But making such an idealizing assumption allows a physicist to bring to bear the powers of abstract reasoning to figure out a lot of information that will be approximately true in many different situations.

Here's another way of putting the same thing. The physicist's model of projectile motion is an *analogy* for projectile motion in the real world. In the same way, symbolic logic is supposed to be an analogy for good arguments in real life. As with any analogy, it breaks down at some point—in this case, it already breaks down in the failure of the logical $\lor$ to capture all the nuances of the natural language "or." However, this disanalogy is the price of constructing a system that is powerful, manageable, and applicable in many different situations in life.

Exercise 2.2. Prove the following sequents.

1. $P \land Q \vdash Q \lor R$
2. $P \land Q \vdash (P \lor R) \land (Q \lor R)$
3. $P \vdash Q \lor (P \lor Q)$
4. $P \vdash (P \lor R) \land (P \lor Q)$

So far, we've found two special logical words that enable valid inferences: "and" and "or." Are there any other logical words besides them? Yes, there are many others. The next one we'll look at is "if ϕ then ψ," which we symbolize as "$\phi \rightarrow \psi$." The sentence $\phi \rightarrow \psi$ is called a **conditional**; the first component sentence ϕ is its **antecedent**, and the second component sentence ψ is the **consequent**.

The statement $\phi \rightarrow \psi$ does not, by itself, imply either ϕ or ψ. It only tells us that, in combination with ϕ, you're entitled to conclude that ψ. Thus, the rule for eliminating $\rightarrow$ requires a second premise as follows:

Modus Ponens (MP)

Given $\phi \rightarrow \psi$ and ϕ, you are permitted to conclude ψ. Schematically: $\dfrac{\phi \rightarrow \psi \quad \phi}{\psi}$

By our earlier convention, we should call this rule "$\rightarrow$ elimination." However, it has an old Latin name **modus ponens**, and we'll follow historical precedent.

As with our previous inference rules, MP is implicitly schematic. That is, it doesn't apply only to the specific conditional $P \rightarrow Q$; it applies to any conditional, such as $(P \vee Q) \rightarrow R$. For example, we can use MP now to derive R from $(P \vee Q) \rightarrow R$ and P.

(1)	$(P \vee Q) \rightarrow R$	A
(2)	P	A
(3)	$P \vee Q$	2 $\vee$ I
(4)	R	1,3 MP

Notice how we used MP on a conditional (line 1) whose antecedent is complex (a disjunction $P \vee Q$). That's perfectly OK, because MP is schematic. In other words, MP works on any conditional sentence, no matter whether its antecedent and consequent are simple or complex. You have to be careful, however, only to apply inference rules to an entire line. For example, you cannot apply MP to the sentences $P \lor (Q \to R)$ and Q, because the first sentence is a disjunction, not a conditional.

Sometimes one conditional is embedded in another, as, for example, if I say, "If you take my class, then if you do the homework you will learn some logic." In such cases, we might have to apply MP twice to detach the consequent of the conditional. Here, then, is a derivation of R from the premises $P \to (Q \to R)$ and $P \land Q$.

(1)	$P \to (Q \to R)$	A
(2)	$P \land Q$	A
(3)	P	2 $\land$ E
(4)	$Q \to R$	1,3 MP
(5)	Q	2 $\land$ E
(6)	R	4,5 MP

Again, you have to be careful only to apply MP when the main sentence on a line is a conditional, and you also have the antecedent of that conditional. For example, given premises $(P \to Q) \to R$ and P, you should *not* infer that Q, or that $Q \to R$. While $(P \to Q) \to R$ is a conditional, its antecedent is $P \to Q$.

Exercise 2.3. Prove that the following argument forms are valid. You may use the rules $\land$ E, $\land$ I, $\lor$ I, and MP.

1. $P \to (Q \to R), P \to Q, P \vdash R$
2. $(A \lor B) \to T, Z \to A, T \to W, Z \vdash W$
3. $(A \to B) \land (C \to A), (C \land (W \to Z)) \land W \vdash (B \lor D) \land (Z \lor E)$
4. $P \to (P \to Q), P \vdash Q$
5. $P \land (P \to Q) \vdash P \land Q$

Our brains are so accustomed to using modus ponens that we sometimes make the simple mistake of trying to apply it in the opposite direction. For example, I've heard more than one person put forward the following argument.

If God exists, then there are objective moral rules.
There are objective moral rules.

God exists.

This argument has the following form:

$P \rightarrow Q$
Q

P

which is like backward modus ponens, since the consequent is the premise, and the antecedent is the conclusion. However, this argument form is invalid. Consider, for example, the following instance of the same form.

If UCLA is in Palo Alto, then UCLA is in California.
UCLA is in California.

UCLA is in Palo Alto.

This argument has obviously true premises and an obviously false conclusion. Therefore, it's invalid, and its form doesn't guarantee validity.

In general, if an argument form is **invalid**, then it admits some instance where the premises are true and the conclusion is false. This instance is called a **counterexample** to the argument form. Historically, invalid argument forms have often been called **fallacies**, especially when people commonly mistake the form for valid. The previous example is an instance of the fallacy of **affirming the consequent**.

Negation

We turn now to negative phrases, such as "it is not the case that ...," which we'll symbolize with ¬. That is, we write "it is not the case that P" as $\neg P$. With this new connective in hand, we can capture another valid argument form using the "if ... then" connective. Consider, for example, the following argument:

If n is divisible by 4, then n is even.

n is not even.

----

n is not divisible by 4.

This argument is valid, and it's an instance of a famous argument form.

Modus Tollens (MT)

Given $\phi \to \psi$ and $\neg \psi$, you are permitted to infer $\neg \phi$.

Schematically: $\dfrac{\phi \to \psi \quad \neg \psi}{\neg \phi}$

As with MP, the new rule applies not just to the conditional sentence $P \to Q$ but to any other conditional, such as $(P \wedge Q) \to R$ or $P \to (Q \wedge \neg Q)$.

Exercise 2.4. Prove that $Q \to (P \to R)$, $\neg R \wedge Q \vdash \neg P$.

Modus ponens can be restated as follows: a conditional $\phi \to \psi$ says that the antecedent ϕ is a **sufficient condition** for the consequent ψ. In other words, the truth of ϕ is a guarantee of the truth of ψ. Modus tollens can then be restated as follows: a conditional $\phi \to \psi$ says that the consequent ψ is a **necessary condition** for the antecedent ϕ. In other words, the falsity of ψ is a guarantee of the falsity of ϕ. To understand the difference between necessary and sufficient conditions, think about the example of rain and clouds. To say that rain is a sufficient condition for clouds does not mean that rain causes clouds but merely that the truth of "it's raining" guarantees the truth of "there are clouds." To say that clouds are a necessary condition for rain means that the falsity of "there are clouds" guarantees the falsity of "it is raining."

It's important also to be totally clear about the relation between the phrase "...if ..." and the phrase "...only if ...." Consider the following examples.

1. Alice is admitted to Harvard Medical School only if she has a high MCAT score.
2. Alice is admitted to Harvard Medical School if she has a high MCAT score.

The first sentence says that having a high MCAT score is a necessary condition for Alice being admitted. The second sentence says that having a high MCAT score is a sufficient condition for Alice being admitted. I would guess that the first sentence is true, no matter who Alice is, and that the second sentence is usually false—because having a high MCAT score is not a sufficient condition for admission to the best medical schools.

To get the full effect out of modus tollens, we need to say something more about the logical role of negation. It turns out that the role of negation is a bit more controversial than you might have thought. But as this is an introductory book, we're going to begin with a simplistic picture of negation.

When I was young, I was taught that it's bad English to use double negations, such as "you don't know nothing." My mother told me that that sentence really means that you do know something, and so I should say "you don't know anything." Now, the goal of this book isn't to teach you to speak better English, and being a living and growing language, English has an enormous amount of subtlety in expression. In particular, two negatives in English don't always mean exactly the same thing as a positive. In contrast, our symbolic language is extremely literal and rigid. We will stipulate in fact that two negations is logically equivalent to no negation at all.

Double Negation (DN)

Given ϕ, you are permitted to infer $\neg\neg\phi$, and given $\neg\neg\phi$, you are permitted to infer ϕ.

Schematically: $\dfrac{\phi}{\neg\neg\phi}$ $\dfrac{\neg\neg\phi}{\phi}$

Among logicians, mathematicians, and philosophers, there has been some skirmishing about whether the second of these rules (i.e., the DN elimination rule) is valid. The thought was: how can proving that something is not true establish that something is true? The foes of DN elimination are typically called *intuitionists*, after an early twentieth-century movement in the philosophy of mathematics. However, our methodology in this book is more empiricist than it is rationalist. In particular, we're not going to stop and search for some Platonic insight into whether or not the rules are valid. Instead, we'll accept the rules as tentative conventions, and then we'll explore their consequences. We believe it's good to ask the deep philosophical question about which are the right rules—but it can be good to keep that question on the back-burner while you're figuring out the consequences of the rules.

As with the other connective symbols, the negation symbol can be applied repeatedly. For example, we can have $\neg P$ or $\neg\neg P$ or $\neg\neg\neg P$, and so on. Of course, DN elimination can be applied whenever there are two or more negation symbols, and it allows us to remove the first two. For example, the following is a valid inference:

$$
\begin{array}{lll}
(1) & \neg\neg\neg P & \text{A} \\
(2) & \neg P & \text{1 DN}
\end{array}
$$

It can also make a big difference which order the connectives are applied. So, for example, $\neg(P \to Q)$ says something very different than $\neg P \to Q$. (The former is a negated sentence, and the latter is a conditional.) We take the negation sign to apply only to what comes immediately after it. So, in the sentence $\neg P \to Q$, the negation applies only to P. In $\neg(P \to Q)$, the negation applies to $P \to Q$. Be careful only to use DN when the entire sentence on a line is negated twice. For example, the sentence $\neg(\neg P \to Q)$ is *not* a candidate for DN elimination, because the first negation symbol applies to the conditional $\neg P \to Q$ and not to the negation $\neg P$. Similarly, you are not permitted to apply DN introduction to a subformula. For example, you may not use DN to infer $\neg\neg P \to Q$ from $P \to Q$, because the former sentence is a conditional, not a twice-negated sentence.[2]

---

2. Later we will show that any subformula ϕ can in fact be replaced by $\neg\neg\phi$. See page 60. But we want to start with a small number of strict rules and then do some work to show that these rules allow us to prove a lot of interesting things.

We can now use all of our deduction rules in combination to prove further validities, such as $P \rightarrow \neg Q, Q \vdash \neg P$.

(1)	$P \rightarrow \neg Q$	A
(2)	Q	A
(3)	$\neg\neg Q$	2 DN
(4)	$\neg P$	1,3 MT

Notice that we needed to infer line 3 before using MT, because Q is not itself literally the negation of $\neg Q$. In formal logic, there are no shortcuts; the rules must be applied exactly as they are stated.

The following more complicated proof shows that $\neg P$ follows from $\neg(P \rightarrow Q) \rightarrow Q$ and $\neg Q$.

(1)	$\neg(P \rightarrow Q) \rightarrow Q$	A
(2)	$\neg Q$	A
(3)	$\neg\neg(P \rightarrow Q)$	1,2 MT
(4)	$P \rightarrow Q$	3 DN
(5)	$\neg P$	4,2 MT

Here we used $\neg Q$ twice over: once to get $\neg\neg(P \rightarrow Q)$, and once to get $\neg P$.

Equivalence

You'll have noticed that some proofs go both ways. For example, you can prove $Q \wedge P$ from $P \wedge Q$ and vice versa. In this case, we'll write $P \wedge Q \dashv\vdash Q \wedge P$, indicating proofs in both directions, and we'll say that the two sentences are **provably equivalent**. There is a strong sense in which provably equivalent sentences are the same "for all logical purposes."

Exercise 2.5. Prove the following sequents.

1. $P \wedge (Q \wedge R) \dashv\vdash (P \wedge Q) \wedge R$
2. $P \dashv\vdash P \wedge P$

Summary

In this chapter, we identified some particularly simple valid argument forms that are based on the special logical words "and," "or," "if ... then," and "not." These argument forms are modus ponens, modus tollens, double negation, conjunction introduction, conjunction elimination, and disjunction introduction.

Exercise 2.6. As we mentioned before, there is only an approximate match between symbolic logic and arguments in the wild. Nonetheless, to develop your intuitions, it helps sometimes to look at an argument in the wild and to try to represent it symbolically. To that end, let's try our hand at representing the logical form of some sentences. Here's how we do it. First of all, identify the overall logical structure of the sentence. Ask yourself: what does the sentence assert? Is it an *atomic sentence* in the sense that there is no internal logical complexity? Does it assert the conjunction of two other sentences? Does it assert the disjunction of two other sentences? And so on.

For example, the sentence, "The cat is on the mat," is atomic. In this case, the best we can do is to represent it with a single letter such as P. On the other hand, "The cat is on the mat, and the dog is in the kennel," asserts a conjunction of two atomic sentences. Thus, it's best represented as something like $P \wedge Q$.

For the following sentences, give the most perspicuous representation you can of their inner logical form. First identify the component atomic sentences and abbreviate each with a (distinct) letter. Then translate the original sentence using the symbols $\vee, \wedge, \neg, \rightarrow$ for the logical words "or," "and," "not," "if ... then...." (We have suggested letters for the atomic sentences at the end of each sentence.)

1. It's not true that if Ron doesn't do his homework, then Hermione will finish it for him. *R, H*
2. Harry will be singed unless he evades the dragon's fiery breath. *S, E*
3. Aristotle was neither a great philosopher nor a great scientist. *P, S*

4. Mark will get an A in logic only if he does the homework or bribes the professor. *A, H, B*
5. Dumbledore will be killed, and either McGonagal will become head-mistress and Hogwarts will flourish, or else it won't flourish. *K, M, F*
6. Harry and Dumbledore are not both right about the moral status of Professor Snape. *H, D*

Exercise 2.7. Prove that the following argument forms are valid. Each line of your proof must either be one of the premises given, or it must be justified from previous lines by one of our rules of inference: MP, MT, DN, $\wedge$ I, $\wedge$ E, or $\vee$ I.

1. $\neg\neg Q \rightarrow P,\ \neg P \vdash \neg Q$
2. $P \rightarrow (P \rightarrow Q),\ P \vdash Q$
3. $(P \wedge P) \rightarrow Q,\ P \vdash Q$
4. $P \vdash Q \vee (\neg\neg P \vee R)$

Exercise 2.8. Demonstrate that the following argument forms are **invalid** by providing a counterexample, that is, give English sentences for P, Q, R such that the premises are obviously true, and the conclusion is obviously false.

1. $P \rightarrow \neg Q,\ \neg P \vdash Q$
2. $P \rightarrow R \vdash (P \vee Q) \rightarrow R$

3

Supposing

OUR OBJECTIVE IS TO FIGURE OUT the difference between valid and invalid arguments. We will break this objective down into two subobjectives. First, we will try to write down enough rules so that we could reproduce any valid argument by chaining those rules together. Second, we will *not* write down a rule that could actually lead to our producing an invalid argument.

We will say that a system of logic is **complete** just in case it has enough rules to reproduce all the intuitively valid arguments.[1] It would be completely easy to produce a complete system of logic if we didn't have any further objective. For example, if you said that "every inference is permitted," then you'd automatically be able to reproduce any valid argument. Obviously, that would be a foolish way of proceeding. But there's also danger in the opposite direction. If we write down too few rules, then there may be some valid argument that our system cannot reproduce. And what a shame that would be if we put on a pair of logical glasses, so to speak, that prevented us from seeing some valid arguments. The consequence of doing that is that we might fail to recognize some important truths, even truths that could change our lives.

In the previous chapter, we wrote down a few rules of inference that we took to be obviously valid. Now the question that faces us is whether we

1. At this stage, we'll have to content ourselves with the vague notion of "intuitively valid." We'll investigate a more precise notion—of truth-preservation—in chapter 9.

wrote down enough rules. In other words, just using the rules from the previous chapter, can we reproduce every valid argument?

That's not such an easy question to answer. Consider the following argument:

(1)	$P \lor Q$	A
(2)	$\neg P$	A
(3)	Q	1,2 ?

Now, this argument seems obviously valid to me.[2] If you know that one of two things is true, either P or Q, and if you know that P is not true, then surely you know that Q is true. But can we prove this argument using the rules from the previous chapter? The answer, in short, is no: we cannot prove this argument using the rules from the previous chapter. One hint is that this argument uses a disjunctive premise—that is, a premise with $\lor$ —and we don't yet have any rule that takes a disjunctive sentence as its input.

(Aside for the ambitious student: You can actually *prove* that the argument above cannot be derived from the rules laid down in the previous chapter. In particular, let's suppose that $P \lor Q$ is always true, no matter whether P and Q are true. It's easy to see, then, that the rules from the previous chapter would always take true sentences to true sentences. However, the argument above could derive a false sentence from two true sentences.)

So, the sequent $P \lor Q, \neg P \vdash Q$ is intuitively valid, but it is not provable from the rules given in the previous chapter. Since our objective is to be able to reproduce all intuitively valid arguments, we need to add some more rules so that we can derive this argument. One thing we could do is whenever we find a new argument that is intuitively valid, we could just add this argument itself as a new rule to our system. However, that would be shortsighted: our system of rules would grow to unwieldy proportions. What's more, the result wouldn't really be a *system*, because a system should

---

2. Most logicians in history shared this opinion. So much so that they invented a name for this apparently valid argument: **modus tollendo ponens**, nowadays usually called **disjunctive syllogism**. But note well: disjunctive syllogism is *not* a basic inference rule of our system.

have some rhyme and reason. We don't want to pick our basic logical rules randomly. We want to pick them on the basis of some principle. The operative principle from chapter 2 is that each special logical word (and, or, if-then, not) corresponds to certain inferences that we are permitted to make. For example, a conjunction $P \land Q$ licenses the inference to P and Q individually.

Now, we have an elimination rule for $\rightarrow$, but no corresponding introduction rule. And we have an introduction rule for $\lor$, but no corresponding elimination rule. So, it would make sense to expand our system by adding the corresponding rules. Let's begin with the idea of arguing for a conditional statement.

Suppose that you want to convince somebody that *if ϕ then ψ*, where ϕ and ψ are some sentences that are either true or false (but you might not know which). For example, you might want to convince somebody that if corporate taxes are reduced, then the budget will not be balanced. Or you might want to convince somebody that if God doesn't exist, then there are no moral rules. Or you might want to convince somebody that if m is a rational number, then m^2 is a rational number. In many such cases, the argument for *if ϕ then ψ* begins with a curious maneuver: the arguer says *suppose that ϕ*. For example, if I wanted to convince you about m^2 being a rational number, I might say:

Suppose that m is a rational number. In that case, $m = a/b$ for two integers, and $m^2 = a^2/b^2$, which means that m^2 is also rational.

Then, I would conclude by saying *therefore, if m is rational, m^2 is also rational.*

The word "suppose" plays a very special role here, and one that might not seem logical at all. You might have thought that being logical boils down to correctly inferring things from a collection of already established facts. However, that is most definitely *not* what is happening in the "suppose" maneuver. When a person says "suppose," she is not deducing anything. Quite to the contrary, she is asking her interlocutor to play a sort of game with her. In fact, she is asking her interlocutor to accept something temporarily that he or she doesn't know to be true.

Now, you might think that allowing suppositions is a recipe for logical disaster. If people can just suppose whatever they want, then how is that logical? Well, it becomes logical when the two discussants keep track of which suppositions they have made.

Imagine then, as an idealized account of what actually occurs in argumentation, that when we sit down to argue, we set out a scorecard. At the beginning of our argument, our scorecard contains a list of agreed-upon premises for our discussion. For example, the two of us might agree to use the word "rational" for numbers of the form a/b, and we might agree that $(a/b)^2 = a^2/b^2$, and so on. During our subsequent argumentation, each of us is allowed to cite any one of these agreed-upon premises. However, besides citing agreed-upon premises, each of us is permitted to "suppose" that something is true—provided that we mark down clearly on the scorecard that we've added a new supposition. Once we've added this new supposition, we can continue drawing inferences; however, it would be a terrible logical mistake to think that the conclusions we derive follow from the *original* list of premises. No, the conclusions we now derive depend on the original list of premises, plus the additional supposition.

So far so good. However, what if we want to see what follows from the original list of premises? Is there a way to go about "unsupposing" things that we supposed during the course of an argument? It's here where a $\rightarrow$ introduction rule could come in handy, because a conditional conclusion is just that: it's *conditional* on something. In particular, if you suppose that ϕ, and then you—perhaps undertaking a long detailed argument—derive ψ, then you are entitled both to conclude that $\phi \rightarrow \psi$ and to forget that you supposed ϕ in the first place. For, when you say that $\phi \rightarrow \psi$, you are now explicitly noting that the conclusion (ψ) depends on a supposition of ϕ.

This then is the idea behind the $\rightarrow$ introduction rule. Fortunately, the implementation of this idea is quite simple. The first thing we need to do is to introduce the "scorecard" to keep track of the suppositions in an argument. We will do so by adding a new column to the left of the line numbers in a proof. This new column will give a running tabulation of the suppositions in force at each stage of the argument. So, now if I ask you to prove something, say, $P \vdash P \lor Q$, then the scorecard begins with agreed-upon premise P. This premise is the supposition that we make together, at the very beginning of the argument. Accordingly, the first line of your proof would read:

1   (1) P A

This line has four columns, one of which is new. The leftmost column contains the number "1," which we call the *dependency number*, and it serves as the "scorecard" of the argument. In other words, the leftmost column tells you which suppositions are in force at that stage of the argument.

So, we are proposing an update in the way we think of proofs. A proof is not a list of sentences, where each sentence is deduced from previous sentences in the list. Instead, a proof is a list of sequents, where each sequent amounts to a statement that some list of sentences implies some other sentence. Correspondingly, the inference rules should be reconceived as telling us which new sequents can be generated from sequents that we have already obtained.

This new way of thinking about proofs is more democratic than the old way from the last chapter. In the last chapter, all proofs began with given premises. From now on, anyone can add new assumptions at any stage of a proof. That is, for any sentence ϕ, you are permitted to write

n (n) ϕ A

which expresses the sequent $\phi \vdash \phi$, since the dependency number "n" points to the sentence ϕ. The official rule for making assumptions is the following:

Rule of Assumptions (A)

At any stage in an argument, you are permitted to suppose anything you want to, as long as you add that supposition to the argument's scorecard.

Here, the schematic statement of the rule of assumptions is strange looking:

$$\overline{\phi \vdash \phi}$$

The horizontal line indicates that one is permitted to infer what lies below the line if one already has what lies above the line. In this case, nothing lies above the line, which means that one is permitted to infer $\phi \vdash \phi$ in any situation.

The above proof might then continue as follows:

1	(1)	P	A
1	(2)	$P \vee Q$	$1 \vee I$

Here the far-right column is the same as the previous chapter: it says that line 2 is justified by application of $\vee I$ to line 1. The far-left column has the number "1" to indicate that the supposition at line 1 is still in force at line 2. In general, for each of the rules that you learned in the previous chapter, the suppositions in force when the premises were asserted will still be in force when the conclusion is asserted. For example, the conjunction introduction rule should be reformulated as saying:

> Given sequents $\Gamma \vdash \phi$ and $\Delta \vdash \psi$, one may derive the sequent Δ, $\Gamma \vdash \phi \wedge \psi$.

Or, written out graphically, $\wedge$ intro appears as follows:

Γ	$(*)$	ϕ	
Δ	$(\star)$	ψ	
Γ, Δ	$(\dagger)$	$\phi \wedge \psi$	$*, \star \wedge I$

In other words, when we use conjunction introduction on lines $*$ and $\star$ to derive line $\dagger$, the dependencies of line $\dagger$ should be the union of the dependencies of lines $*$ and $\star$.

Let's see this use of suppositions in action in the proof of the sequent $(P \vee Q) \rightarrow R, P \vdash R$. Here, we are asked to prove R under the suppositions

$(P \lor Q) \to R$ and P. We begin, then, by writing down those suppositions, giving a new number for each in the left-hand column.

1	(1)	$(P \lor Q) \to R$	A
2	(2)	P	A
2	(3)	$P \lor Q$	2 $\lor$ I
1, 2	(4)	R	1,3 MP

We then proceed as we did in the previous chapter. First we derive line 3 from line 2 using the $\lor$ I rule, and we accordingly carry the supposition from line 2 down to line 3. Then, we derive line 4 from lines 1 and 3 using the MP rule, and we accordingly carry the suppositions from lines 1 and 3 down to line 4.

It would be a good idea now to go back and do a few of the proofs from the previous chapter, but now keeping explicit track of the suppositions in force at each stage. The process may be a bit tedious, but it will be conceptually simple, because whenever you apply a rule, you simply have to copy the suppositions from the lines you cite onto the new line. For example:

1	(1)	P	A
2	(2)	Q	A
1, 2	(3)	$P \land Q$	1,2 $\land$ I
1, 2	(4)	$(P \land Q) \land P$	3,1 $\land$ I

In this example, you can see that the list of suppositions doesn't need to contain duplicate numbers. To derive line 3, we cited lines 1 and 2, and so line 3 depends on whatever lines 1 and 2 depended on. To derive line 4, we cited lines 3 and 1, and so line 4 depends on whatever those lines depended on. However, we don't write "1, 1" in the left-hand column, because it's enough to note that the assumption of 1 is in force. Similarly, it doesn't matter in what order dependency numbers occur. For example, having 1, 2 in the left-hand column is the same as having 2, 1.

Similarly, consider the following proof that uses the other rules from the last chapter.

1	(1)	$P \wedge \neg\neg Q$	A
1	(2)	$\neg\neg Q$	$1 \wedge E$
1	(3)	Q	2 DN
1	(4)	$Q \vee R$	$3 \vee I$

The use of conjunction elimination on line 2 cites line 1, and so we copy the dependencies of line 1 to line 2. The same goes for the use of DN on line 3 and the use of disjunction introduction on line 4.

Now we can come back to the $\rightarrow$ introduction rule. The whole point of keeping track of suppositions is so that *you*, the reasoner, can strategically make new suppositions and then later discharge these assumptions. Hence, the $\rightarrow$ introduction rule, which is also called **conditional proof (CP)**, should look like this:

> If, within context Γ, you suppose that ϕ, and if from Γ and ϕ you derive ψ, then you may assert, in the same context Γ, the conditional $\phi \rightarrow \psi$.

Now we have to see how to implement this general idea concretely in terms of line numbers of a proof. Let's say that you suppose ϕ on some specific line m of your proof:

$$m \quad (m) \quad \phi \qquad A$$

Notice that the dependency number m is the same as the line number, which will always be the case for a supposition (i.e., assumption). Now suppose that you have another line like this:

$$n_1, \ldots, n_k, m \quad (n) \quad \psi$$

The conditional proof rule says that from these two lines, you may infer the line

$$n_1, \ldots, n_k \quad (n') \quad \phi \rightarrow \psi \qquad m, n \text{ CP}$$

Notice how the dependency on m is dropped in the move from line n to line n'. Dropping the dependency signals that we are no longer supposing that ϕ; we are now asserting that *if* ϕ, then ψ.

Here's a simple example of the kind of move permitted by conditional proof. The MT rule says $\neg P$ can be inferred from $P \rightarrow Q$ and $\neg Q$. Now, imagine that everyone agrees that $P \to Q$ but that not everybody agrees that $\neg Q$. Nonetheless, you should be able to convince all logical people that *if* $\neg Q$, then $\neg P$. Your argument could be formalized as follows:

Contrapositive

$P \to Q \vdash \neg Q \to \neg P$

1	(1)	$P \to Q$	A
2	(2)	$\neg Q$	A
1, 2	(3)	$\neg P$	1,2 MT
1	(4)	$\neg Q \to \neg P$	2,3 CP

Our formal system doesn't pick up the nuance that everyone agrees (in this example) to the first assumption (line 1), whereas you made the second assumption (line 2) for the sake of argument. But no matter—the point is just that now we can model this ubiquitous practice of supposing things for the sake of argument.

Conditional Proof (CP)

A proof of ψ from dependencies Γ, ϕ may be converted to a proof of $\phi \to \psi$ from dependencies Γ. Schematically:

$$\frac{\Gamma, \phi \vdash \psi}{\Gamma \vdash \phi \to \psi}$$

Don't try to memorize the CP rule by staring at it. Instead: watch it being used, and use it yourself. Let's begin with a proof that conditionals are transitive (i.e., that if $P \to Q$ and $Q \to R$ then $P \to R$).

1	(1)	$P \to Q$	A
2	(2)	$Q \to R$	A
3	(3)	P	A
1, 3	(4)	Q	1,3 MP
1, 2, 3	(5)	R	2,4 MP
1, 2	(6)	$P \to R$	3,5 CP

The assumption on line 3 is motivated by the idea that we want to prove $P \to R$. So, when we assumed P on line 3, we did so thinking, "All we have to do is derive R, and then we can use CP to get $P \to R$." Notice that as soon as we've made the assumption of P, we are now back in the easy territory of the previous chapter. Now we just deduce and deduce until we get R. Then, at line 6, we remember what we were trying to do: we "discharge" the assumption on line 3 by invoking CP.

In the following proof, we go to a second hypothetical level. That is, we make one supposition and prepare to deduce. But then we see that the conclusion we want is a conditional, so it makes sense to make a second supposition.

1	(1)	$(P \wedge Q) \to R$	A
2	(2)	P	A
3	(3)	Q	A
2, 3	(4)	$P \wedge Q$	2,3 $\wedge$ I
1, 2, 3	(5)	R	1,4 MP
1, 2	(6)	$Q \to R$	3,5 CP
1	(7)	$P \to (Q \to R)$	2,6 CP

On line 2, we suppose P, with the intention of proving $Q \to R$. And then it's like we start all over again. Since we want to prove $Q \to R$, we assume Q. Then, we're back in the gentle territory of the previous chapter, deducing until we get R on line 5. On line 6, we use CP to return from the second hypothetical level to the first. On line 7, we use CP again to return from the first hypothetical level to the zeroth.

Things can become confusing when you try to prove a conditional whose antecedent is a complex sentence. For example, suppose that you want to prove $(P \wedge Q) \to R$ from $P \to (Q \to R)$. Here, you must avoid the temptation to assume P and Q on separate lines and then use $\wedge$ introduction. For then you'd have two dependency numbers, whereas CP only gets rid of one. To use CP properly, you've got to assume exactly the antecedent of the conditional you are trying to prove. Consider, for example, the following proof.

Prefixing

$Q \rightarrow R \vdash (P \rightarrow Q) \rightarrow (P \rightarrow R)$

1	(1)	$Q \rightarrow R$	A
2	(2)	$P \rightarrow Q$	A
3	(3)	P	A
2, 3	(4)	Q	2,3 MP
1, 2, 3	(5)	R	1,4 MP
1, 2	(6)	$P \rightarrow R$	3,5 CP
1	(7)	$(P \rightarrow Q) \rightarrow (P \rightarrow R)$	2,6 CP

Here we're trying to prove $(P \rightarrow Q) \rightarrow (P \rightarrow R)$, which is a conditional whose antecedent is a conditional. Note well: the fact that the antecedent is a conditional makes no difference at all to the fact that *you should assume the antecedent*. You shouldn't try to prove $P \rightarrow Q$, and you shouldn't (yet) assume P, for neither of those would do you any good. Instead, assume $P \rightarrow Q$, and then take up the next problem, that is, of proving $P \rightarrow R$ from $Q \rightarrow R$ and $P \rightarrow Q$.

Before we set you loose on some exercises, we'll explain a method that can make some difficult proofs easier. Consider, for example, the sequent $\neg P \vdash \neg(P \wedge Q)$, which is sometimes called *weakening*. A direct attack on this sequent will only lead to frustration: from an assumption of $\neg P$, there is no amount of conjoining or disjoining that will get you to $\neg(P \wedge Q)$. We recommend, then, that you prove the contrapositive, that is, $P \wedge Q \vdash P$. Of course, that proof is trivially easy, and then you can complete the proof of weakening as follows:

$(P \wedge Q) \rightarrow P$	CP
$\neg P$	A
$\neg(P \wedge Q)$	MT

In summary, you can use MT to transform a proof of a sequent into a proof of its contrapositive.

Exercise 3.1. Prove the following sequents.

    1. $P \vdash Q \rightarrow (P \wedge Q)$
    2. $(P \rightarrow Q) \wedge (P \rightarrow R) \vdash P \rightarrow (Q \wedge R)$

3. permutation: $P \to (Q \to R) \vdash Q \to (P \to R)$
4. suffixing: $P \to Q \vdash (Q \to R) \to (P \to R)$
5. contraction: $P \to (P \to Q) \vdash P \to Q$
6. exportation: $P \to (Q \to R) \vdash (P \wedge Q) \to R$
7. strengthening: $(P \vee Q) \to R \vdash P \to R$
8. weakening: $\neg P \vdash \neg(P \wedge Q)$
9. **DeMorgan's rule (DM):** $\neg(P \vee Q) \vdash \neg P \wedge \neg Q$
    (Hint: prove the individual conjuncts, then use $\wedge$ introduction.)
*10. $P \to \neg P \vdash \neg P$

Proofs without Dependencies

Now that you have a rule for discharging assumptions (namely, conditional proof), you can produce valid arguments that end without *any* assumptions in force. For example, here's a proof of the trivial truth: if P then P.

1	(1)	P	A
	(2)	$P \to P$	1,1 CP

We write this sequent as $\vdash P \to P$, with no premises on the left-hand side of the turnstile; and in this case, we say that $P \to P$ is **provable**. The result, then, is a statement that anybody is permitted to assert in any circumstance whatsoever.

Before we set you loose proving things, we need to warn you of one danger: conditional proof must only be used when the first of the two lines is an assumption. If you don't observe that restriction, then you could prove too much, as in the following argument.

1	(1)	$P \wedge Q$	A	
1	(2)	P	1 $\wedge$ E	
1	(3)	Q	1 $\wedge$ E	
	(4)	$P \to Q$	2,3 CP	$\Longleftarrow$ incorrect

Here we tried to use CP with lines 2 and 3, even though line 2 was not an assumption. But line 2 depends on $P \wedge Q$, which is logically stronger than P, and it's not justified to erase the dependency on $P \wedge Q$ when conditionalizing only on P.

Exercise 3.2. Prove the following sequents.

1. $\vdash (P \wedge Q) \rightarrow (Q \wedge P)$
2. $\vdash (P \wedge Q) \rightarrow P$
3. $\vdash Q \rightarrow (P \rightarrow Q)$
4. $\vdash Q \rightarrow (P \rightarrow P)$
*5. **law of excluded middle (EM)**: $\vdash P \vee \neg P$

Paradoxes of Material Implication

Before we move on to our last two inference rules, we should talk a little bit about something disconcerting that can happen with conditional proof. It will be simplest just to write down two (valid) proofs. If these proofs don't bother you, then there's really no need to read the rest of this section!

We first prove a result known as **positive paradox**: from the assumption that Q, it follows that $P \rightarrow Q$. Since logic is completely general, this result implies, for example, that from the assumption that this match will light when struck, it follows that if we are under water, then this match will light when struck.

Positive Paradox

$Q \vdash P \rightarrow Q$

1	(1)	Q	A
2	(2)	P	A
1	(3)	$P \rightarrow Q$	2, 1 CP

Here the new supposition P occurs on line 2, after the conclusion Q had already been asserted. This maneuver might seem like an egregious abuse of the rule CP, which was intended to capture the idea of making a new supposition in order to derive a certain conclusion. In this proof, the conclusion was already there, and the new supposition wasn't needed to get it. So isn't it quite misleading to conclude that *if P, then Q*? After all, Q had already been supposed before P was supposed.

If you're a bit unhappy that this proof counts as valid, then you are in good company. Ever since the early days of modern symbolic logic, back in the early 1900s, philosophers have wondered whether something has gone wrong. We can't go deeply into that debate here, but it's worthwhile seeing that it's not so easy to fix the CP rule to prevent this kind of argument. The most obvious proposal to fix the CP rule is to require that the antecedent (in this case P) is actually used to derive the consequent. We could try to enforce this requirement by saying that the line on which the consequent occurs must depend on the line on which the antecedent is assumed. The proof above would violate this revised rule, because 2 does not appear among the dependencies on line 1.

Unfortunately, when this revised rule is brought into interaction with the other rules, it proves to be just as liberal as the original rule. Consider the following proof that uses the more conservative rule.

1	(1)	Q	A
2	(2)	P	A
1, 2	(3)	$P \wedge Q$	1,2 $\wedge$ I
1, 2	(4)	Q	3 $\wedge$ E
1	(5)	$P \to Q$	2,4 CP

Here CP is applied to lines 2 and 4, and the supposition made on line 2 is used to get line 4. So, this proof obeys the revised rule, despite the fact that it allows us to derive exactly the same conclusion as the previous proof. In fact, it's not too hard to see that anything that can be derived with the original "liberal CP rule" can be derived with the new "conservative CP rule." So, the new rule is only apparently more conservative than the old, and we might as well allow ourselves to use the old one.

There's another pair of results that are perhaps even more troubling than positive paradox. We'll now write one proof that proves a couple of different paradoxical sequents.

1	(1)	$\neg P$	A
2	(2)	P	A
3	(3)	$\neg Q$	A
2	(4)	$\neg Q \to P$	3,2 CP

1, 2	(5)	$\neg\neg Q$	4,1 MT
1, 2	(6)	Q	5 DN
1	(7)	$P \rightarrow Q$	2,6 CP

The sixth line of the proof demonstrates **ex falso quodlibet (EFQ)**, which, translated loosely, means "from the false, everything follows." This sequent is also sometimes called **explosion**, because it shows that P and $\neg P$ together form a ticking time bomb that, when triggered, ejects all other sentences. The last line proves **negative paradox**, which shows that a conditional follows from the negation of its antecedent.

EFQ has bothered logic students like yourself for well over a thousand years. It seems exactly wrong, you might think, that a person with inconsistent beliefs (such as P and $\neg P$) has "inferential omnipotence," that is, they can infer any sentence Q whatsoever. But that worry stems from an ambiguity in the English verb "to infer that." For example, if you overheard me say that "I infer that the sun will collapse," you might assume that I believe that the sun will collapse. However, there is a weaker sense of "infer" in which it simply means that a person reasons from some claims (which that person need not believe) to other claims (which that person need not believe). For example, I might have inferred that the sun will collapse from a contrary-to-fact supposition about the mass of the sun. I might not actually believe that the mass of the sun is so large, but I nonetheless believe that if its mass were so large, then it would collapse.

So, we should keep it clearly in mind that the typical use of logical reasoning is not to start from a set of premises about which we are completely certain and then to reason to additional conclusions. Much more typically, logic is used to reason from premises that we do not necessarily believe to a conclusion that we don't necessarily believe. In logic, it's not the conclusions that we're interested in, but in the connection between premises and conclusions. And logic doesn't have anything to say about whether one should accept the conclusions of valid arguments from the premises that one already accepts. Indeed, what logic might be telling you is that you ought to reject one of the premises. That's certainly what I would recommend doing if you found yourself with premises that imply both P and $\neg P$.

Reasoning from Disjunctive Premises

Imagine that you're stuck in a dark room and cannot see outside. However, you have a phone, and you can get text messages from your friend, Angelina, who is outside. But Angelina loves to be a bit elusive. If you ask her a question, she tends to reply by asserting a disjunction. For example, if you say, "What's the weather like today?," then Angelina might say something like, "Either it's raining or it's snowing."

Now, Angelina isn't completely useless to you, because you can deduce some helpful information from the things she says. (I'm supposing here that Angelina always tells the truth.) For example, suppose that you're a member of the quidditch club and the club has a rule that practice is canceled on any day that it rains or snows. In this case, Angelina's statement "Either it's raining or it's snowing" is sufficient for you to deduce that there won't be quidditch practice today.

The inference you make is roughly the following:

Either it's raining or it's snowing. (From Angelina)
If it's raining, then there is no quidditch practice. (Club rule)
If it's snowing, then there is no quidditch practice. (Club rule)
Therefore, there is no quidditch practice.

And the form of this inference is

$$\frac{P_1 \lor P_2 \quad P_1 \rightarrow Q \quad P_2 \rightarrow Q}{Q}.$$

This argument form seems obviously to be valid, and hence we will take it as the paradigm case of how to deduce something from a disjunctive premise.

Before proceeding to formalize the rule of disjunction elimination, let's generalize the idea that it needs two conditional premises such as $P_1 \rightarrow Q$ and $P_2 \rightarrow Q$. Let's consider, instead, the possibility that the conclusion Q is based on two *reasoning processes*. In this case, you know that either it's raining or it's snowing because Angelina told you that. Now you reason as follows: First, *if* it's raining, *then* there is no quidditch practice. (Here

$$\boxed{\Gamma \quad (m) \quad P_1 \lor P_2}$$

$$\boxed{\begin{array}{llll} m_1 & (m_1) & P_1 & A \\ & \vdots & & \\ \Delta_1, m_1 & (n_1) & Q & \end{array}} \qquad \boxed{\begin{array}{llll} m_2 & (m_2) & P_2 & A \\ & \vdots & & \\ \Delta_2, m_2 & (n_2) & Q & \end{array}}$$

$$\boxed{\Gamma, \Delta_1, \Delta_2 \quad (n) \quad Q \quad m, m_1, n_1, m_2, n_2 \lor E}$$

Figure 3.1. Disjunction elimination allows you to derive a conclusion from a disjunction by using two subarguments, one based on each disjunct.

you rely possibly on some background information Δ_1, and your reasoning process might be quite long and intricate.) Second, *if* it's snowing, *then* there is no quidditch practice. (Here you might rely on some other background information Δ_2, and you might engage in another reasoning process to arrive at Q.) From your knowledge that either P_1 or P_2 is true, and from your rigorous reasoning on a case-by-case basis, you conclude with confidence that Q. Of course, if you want to produce a valid argument, then you need to keep track of all of the background information you drew upon when reasoning about the two cases. That is, you may assert that Q follows from the disjunction $P_1 \lor P_2$, plus the background information contained in Δ_1 and Δ_2.

The overall argument can be represented visually as in figure 3.1. Here, we've used Γ to represent the original background information from which you derived the disjunction $P_1 \lor P_2$. When the $\lor$ elimination rule is invoked on line n, we have to acknowledge dependency not only on Γ but also on the information in Δ_1 and Δ_2 that might have been used in the two subarguments.

The reason we might need to bring other information into the subarguments is so that we can use disjunctions together with other premises in order to derive conclusions. For example, consider the premises $P \lor Q$ and $Q \to P$. Obviously, these two premises together should imply P. Just consider the two cases: if P, then of course P. In the case of Q, we also have

$Q \to P$ and hence P. But in making the second move here, we cannot forget
the source of our knowledge of $Q \to P$. In other words, that premise needs
to be cited as well. In official, regimented format, the argument would go
like this:

1	(1)	$P \lor Q$	A
2	(2)	$Q \to P$	A
3	(3)	P	A
4	(4)	Q	A
2, 4	(5)	P	2,4 MP
1, 2	(6)	P	1,3,3,4,5 $\lor$ E

The only mystery here is the exact recipe used to calculate the dependencies of line 6. Of course, line 6 should depend on whatever the disjunction
on line 1 depends upon. In this case, line 1 depends only on itself. Then, we
need to look at the two subarguments. The first subargument is completely
trivial: it starts with the assumption of P on line 3, and it ends there. It simply infers P from itself. The second subargument starts with the assumption
of Q on line 4, but then it uses line 2 to get line 5. Thus, the second subargument presupposes line 2 and hence whatever line 2 depends upon. That's
why we need to include line 2 in the dependencies of line 6. But we do *not*
need to include line 3 or 4 in the dependencies of line 6, because those were
purely hypothetical posits, used to see what follows from the disjunction
$P \lor Q$. When we use disjunction elimination, we "forget" that those subproofs ever happened, including the assumptions with which they began.
We only remember the fact that both subproofs led to the same conclusion.

We still need to tell you the *exact* recipe for calculating the dependencies
for a line that is justified by disjunction elimination. We'll do that twice
over, first giving a schematic proof.

Γ	(m)	$P_1 \lor P_2$	
m_1	(m_1)	P_1	A
	$\vdots$		
Δ_1, m_1	(n_1)	Q	
m_2	(m_2)	P_2	A
	$\vdots$		

$$\Delta_2, m_2 \quad (n_2) \quad Q$$
$$\Gamma, \Delta_1, \Delta_2 \quad (n) \quad Q \qquad\qquad m, m_1, n_1, m_2, n_2 \ \vee E$$

That is, $\vee E$ cites five lines: a disjunction (line m), the assumption that begins the first subargument (line m_1), the conclusion of the first subargument (line n_1), the assumption that begins the second subargument (line m_2), and the conclusion of the second subargument (line n_2). The dependencies of line n are to be the union of the following three collections of dependencies:

1. The dependencies Γ of the disjunction $P_1 \vee P_2$ on line m.
2. The dependencies Δ_1 of the conclusion Q on line n_1, except take away m_1 if it happens to occur among them.
3. The dependencies Δ_2 of the conclusion Q on line n_2, except take away m_2 if it happens to occur among them.

In most applications, you'll follow this complicated recipe subconsciously. However, for those of you budding logicians who long for full rigor, the precise set-theoretic calculation of the dependencies on line n is

$$\Gamma \cup (\Delta_1 \backslash \{m_1\}) \cup (\Delta_2 \backslash \{m_2\}),$$

which is just a symbolic representation of the words we said previously.

As we've said before, we recommend that you try to understand abstract rules by working on specific examples. Let's start, then, with a proof that P follows from the disjunction $P \vee (P \wedge Q)$.

1	(1)	$P \vee (P \wedge Q)$	A
2	(2)	P	A
3	(3)	$P \wedge Q$	A
3	(4)	P	$3 \wedge E$
1	(5)	P	1,2,2,3,4 $\vee E$

Here the first disjunct P is assumed on line 2. Of course, it immediately follows from the assumption of P—without drawing any further inferences—that P. For this reason, the application of $\vee E$ on line 5 cites line 2 twice:

once as an assumption of the first disjunct and once as the conclusion drawn from the first disjunct. The second disjunct $P \wedge Q$ is assumed on line 3, and the conclusion P is drawn again on line 4. Thus, the application of $\vee$ E on line 5 cites lines 3 and 4. (Exercise: Suppose that you obtained line 5 from lines 1,2,2,3,2 instead of lines 1,2,2,3,4. What, then, would be the dependencies of line 5?)

We can now give a compact schematic statement of the disjunction elimination rule.

Disjunction Elimination ($\vee$ E)

$$\frac{\Gamma \vdash \phi \vee \psi \qquad \Delta, \phi \vdash \chi \qquad \Theta, \psi \vdash \chi}{\Gamma, \Delta, \Theta \vdash \chi}$$

So, the $\vee$ E rule says that three separate proofs can be converted into one proof. Of course, you're not likely to find those three proofs lying around; you'll usually have to make them yourself.

For example, suppose that you want to show $P \vee Q \vdash Q \vee P$. Then, you'd want to argue that the conclusion follows from each disjunct separately, as follows.

Commutation

$P \vee Q \vdash Q \vee P$

1	(1)	$P \vee Q$	A
2	(2)	P	A
2	(3)	$Q \vee P$	2 $\vee$ I
4	(4)	Q	A
4	(5)	$Q \vee P$	4 $\vee$ I
1	(6)	$Q \vee P$	1,2,3,4,5 $\vee$ E

In this case, the disjunction $P \vee Q$ is an assumption, that is, it hasn't been derived from something else. Thus, the first input to $\vee$ E on line 6 is the proof $P \vee Q \vdash P \vee Q$. The second input to $\vee$ E on line 6 is the sequent on line 3, namely, $P \vdash Q \vee P$. The third input to $\vee$ E on line 6 is the sequent on line 5, namely, $Q \vdash Q \vee P$. In this case, then, $\vee$ E permits us to write $Q \vee P$ on line 6, with the following dependencies: (a) The dependencies Δ of the disjunction $P \vee Q$ on line 1. In this case, Δ is simply $P \vee Q$ itself. (b) The auxiliary assumptions Γ that may have been used to derive $Q \vee P$ from the first disjunct P. In this case, Γ is empty. (c) The auxiliary assumptions Δ that may have been used to derive $Q \vee P$ from the second disjunct Q. In this case, Δ is empty.

For an even simpler—and yet possibly more confusing—application of $\vee$ E, we derive P from the disjunction $P \vee P$.

1	(1)	$P \vee P$	A
2	(2)	P	A
1	(3)	P	1,2,2,2,2 $\vee$ E

Here, the first and second disjuncts are the same sentence, namely, P. Hence, the assumption on line 2 can serve as the assumption for both subproofs. In addition, the desired conclusion is simply P again; hence, line 2 can serve as the conclusion of both subproofs. It's for this reason that the invocation of $\vee$ E on line 3 cites line 2 four times: twice as an assumption and twice as the conclusion of subproofs.

It might also help to see an example where the disjunction elimination rule has been *misapplied*. Intuitively, it shouldn't be possible to prove P from $P \vee Q$. For example, from the fact that the number 2 is either even or odd, you shouldn't be able to deduce that it's odd! But consider the following attempt to prove P from $P \vee Q$.

1	(1)	$P \vee Q$	A	
2	(2)	P	A	
3	(3)	Q	A	
2, 3	(4)	$P \wedge Q$	2,3 $\wedge$ I	
2, 3	(5)	P	4 $\wedge$ E	
1	(6)	P	1,2,2,3,5 $\vee$ E	$\impliedby$ incorrect

Everything in this "proof" is OK except for the dependencies of line 6. The problem is that line 6 should include all the dependencies of line 5 (i.e., the conclusion of the second subproof) except for 3 (i.e., the assumption of that subproof). Thus, line 6 should also include 2 among its dependencies. But in that case, it would be a proof of $P \vee Q, P \vdash P$, which is not so surprising after all.

Exercise 3.3. Prove the following sequents.

1. $(P \rightarrow R) \wedge (Q \rightarrow R) \vdash (P \vee Q) \rightarrow R$
2. association: $P \vee (Q \vee R) \dashv\vdash (P \vee Q) \vee R$
3. disjunctive syllogism: $P \vee Q, \neg P \vdash Q$
4. distribution: $P \wedge (Q \vee R) \dashv\vdash (P \wedge Q) \vee (P \wedge R)$
5. distribution: $P \vee (Q \wedge R) \dashv\vdash (P \vee Q) \wedge (P \vee R)$
6. material conditional: $\neg P \vee Q \dashv\vdash P \rightarrow Q$
7. DM: $\neg P \vee \neg Q \vdash \neg(P \wedge Q)$

In the previous exercises, you proved that $P \vee (Q \vee R)$ is equivalent to $(P \vee Q) \vee R$. Accordingly, in some later discussions, we might allow ourselves to write $P \vee Q \vee R$, when we don't need to specify which of the equivalent sentences we're talking about.

Reductio ad Absurdum

We began the book by stating that logic is a tool to sort between true and false claims. To this point, it might seem that the primary role of logic is to establish which claims are true, by showing that they are logical consequences of claims that we already know to be true. However, logic may be even more effective when applied in reverse: to show which claims cannot possibly be true.

Imagine, for example, that your friend Angelina has a certain belief P that you are quite sure is false. Suppose also that Angelina, like you, is quite good at logic, and she knows the difference between good and bad arguments. Here, then, is a very effective way to convince Angelina to reject P: give her a valid proof that begins with P (and possibly some other agreed-upon background information Γ) and that ends with some conclusion C that Angelina rejects. Since we're supposing that Angelina is completely logical, she'll be forced either to give up P or to change her mind about C.

Now, in the most extreme case, C could be something that not only Angelina, but every rational person, must reject. In particular, C might be a logical contradiction such as $\psi \wedge \neg \psi$. We'll take this extreme case to be paradigmatic of an argumentative strategy called *reductio ad absurdum (RAA)*, which literally means "reducing to absurdity." The idea, again, is that if a statement ϕ leads to an absurdity $\psi \wedge \neg \psi$, then ϕ must be rejected. This argumentative strategy can be formalized as follows:

Reductio ad Absurdum (RAA)

A proof of $\psi \wedge \neg \psi$ from Γ and ϕ can be converted to a proof of $\neg\phi$ from Γ. Schematically:

$$\frac{\Gamma, \phi \vdash \psi \wedge \neg \psi}{\Gamma \vdash \neg\phi}$$

When written in linear format, RAA must cite two lines: (1) an assumption, say of ϕ, and (2) a contradiction, such as $\psi \wedge \neg \psi$. The conclusion of RAA then depends on whatever the contradiction $\psi \wedge \neg \psi$ depends upon, except possibly the assumption of ϕ. As with conditional proof, the contradiction is not required to depend on the assumption of ϕ.

The following is a fairly standard use of RAA.

1	(1)	$P \rightarrow Q$	A
2	(2)	$P \rightarrow \neg Q$	A
3	(3)	P	A
1, 3	(4)	Q	1,3 MP
2, 3	(5)	$\neg Q$	2,3 MP
1, 2, 3	(6)	$Q \wedge \neg Q$	4,5 $\wedge$ I
1, 2	(7)	$\neg P$	3,6 RAA

Here, the assumption of P is used to detach Q and $\neg Q$ from the conditionals in lines 1 and 2. It is, however, acceptable to apply RAA even if the assumption is not used—as in the following alternative proof of EFQ.

1	(1)	$Q \wedge \neg Q$	A
2	(2)	$\neg P$	A
1	(3)	$\neg\neg P$	2,1 RAA
1	(4)	P	3 DN

Here the assumption (line 2) comes after the contradiction (line 1). That might feel like cheating—in the same way that it feels like cheating to use conditional proof in a case where the assumption of the antecedent comes after the derivation of the consequent. However, the RAA rule permits this move. Note also that since the assumption (line 2) wasn't used to derive the contradiction (line 1), the dependencies on line 3 are the same as those on line 1.

As in the previous argument, RAA is frequently used in combination with DN, and this combination makes RAA a powerful tool for proving positive results. In general, to establish a positive result P, all you need to do is to show that its negation $\neg P$ leads to a contradiction. This combination (RAA and DN) can be used to give another proof of EM.

1	(1)	$\neg(P \vee \neg P)$	A
2	(2)	P	A
2	(3)	$P \vee \neg P$	2 $\vee$ I
1,2	(4)	$(P \vee \neg P) \wedge \neg(P \vee \neg P)$	3,1 $\wedge$ I
1	(5)	$\neg P$	2,4 RAA
1	(6)	$P \vee \neg P$	5 $\vee$ I
1	(7)	$(P \vee \neg P) \wedge \neg(P \vee \neg P)$	6,1 $\wedge$ I
	(8)	$\neg\neg(P \vee \neg P)$	1,7 RAA
	(9)	$P \vee \neg P$	8 DN

EM can be a useful auxiliary for proving other things. In fact, EM and RAA are the tools of choice for proving things that have eluded all other methods of attack. Consider, for example, the following valid sequent:

$$\vdash ((P \rightarrow Q) \rightarrow P) \rightarrow P$$

It's not at all obvious how one could prove this sequent. Since it's a conditional sentence, you might try to assume the antecedent $(P \rightarrow Q) \rightarrow P$ and then to derive the consequent *P*. However, since the antecedent is a conditional sentence, there is nothing that you can infer from it, at least until you assume something else. If you go on like this for a while, you might find yourself increasingly flustered. Let's, then, bring out the big guns: first write down a proof of $P \lor \neg P$. Now set up two subproofs, one beginning with the assumption of *P* and the other with the assumption of $\neg P$. The first subproof immediately yields the consequent that you want, namely, *P*. For the second subproof, recall negative paradox: $\neg P \vdash P \to Q$. Hence, from $\neg P$, you could derive $P \to Q$, and then in combination with the assumption $(P \to Q) \to P$, you could derive *P*. The overall structure of this derivation looks like this:

	$\vdots$	
	$P \lor \neg P$	EM
*	P	A
⋆	$\neg P$	A
	$\vdots$	
⋆	$P \to Q$	negative paradox
†	$(P \to Q) \to P$	A
⋆, †	P	
†	P	∨ E
	$((P \to Q) \to P) \to P$	CP

Here the symbols *, ⋆, † stand in for unknown dependency numbers. Of course, if you filled in all the steps, this proof would be quite long. In the next section, we will explain a method for citing one proof inside another so that you can keep your proofs to a manageable length.

Exercise 3.4. Prove the following sequents.

1. material conditional: $P \to Q \vdash \neg(P \land \neg Q)$
2. DM: $\neg(P \land Q) \vdash \neg P \lor \neg Q$
3. material conditional: $\neg(P \to Q) \vdash P \land \neg Q$
*4. chain order: $\vdash (P \to Q) \lor (Q \to P)$
*5. $P \to (Q \lor R) \vdash (P \to Q) \lor (P \to R)$
6. $(P \land Q) \to \neg Q \vdash P \to \neg Q$

Exercise 3.5. People who reject DN elimination also tend to reject the law of excluded middle. This exercise explains why. Use the law of excluded middle and EFQ to re-derive DN elimination. That is, show that $\neg\neg P \vdash P$, without using DN, but where you're allowed to insert $P \lor \neg P$ and where you're allowed to infer anything from a contradiction.

For discussion: Is the law of excluded middle more obviously correct than the DN rule?

4

New Proofs from Old

AS THE OLD SAYING GOES, "Don't work harder, work smarter." You've done the hard work writing a lot of proofs; now it's time to work smarter. In this chapter, we're going to think about how you can reliably take short-cuts with proofs. The key word here is "reliably." That is, we want to ensure that these shortcuts won't cause you to misjudge whether or not something can be proven.

For example, suppose that we ask you to prove the following sequent: $\vdash (P \to Q) \lor \neg(P \to Q)$. You've probably never proved this sequent before. However, you should have—if you've been diligent—proved an instance of the law of excluded middle, that is something like $\vdash P \lor \neg P$. Now suppose that you have the proof of $P \lor \neg P$ saved in a file em.txt and that you run a "find and replace" to swap in $P \to Q$ for P. Then, the result will be a proof of $(P \to Q) \lor \neg(P \to Q)$. That's working smart: take an old proof, run find-and-replace, and ta da, you have a new proof.

What we just did was a case of *substitution*. We'll discuss substitution in the first section. Then, we'll talk about another shortcut method that allows you to splice an old proof into a new one—the method of *cut*. Finally, we'll talk about a third shortcut method that allows you to *replace* a sub-formula with any logically equivalent subformula. If you learn these three methods, you'll be able to prove even the most challenging propositional logic sequents with ease.

Substitution

In this section, we describe the theoretical basis for the "find-and-replace" method of generating new proofs from old. To this end, we first need to define the notion of a *substitution instance*. The idea here is that the find-and-replace operation changes a formula ϕ to a substitution instance ϕ^* and a proof of $\phi \vdash \psi$ to a proof of $\phi^* \vdash \psi^*$.

Each sentence of our symbolic language is either one of the symbols $P, Q, R, \ldots$, or it's built up from those symbols using the connectives $\neg, \wedge, \vee$, and $\rightarrow$. It's time to be a bit more precise about the ways in which we permit sentences to be constructed. We call the capital letters $P, Q, R \ldots$ our *atomic sentences*, the idea being that they have no internal structure. We also stipulate that if ϕ and ψ are sentences, then $\neg \phi, \phi \wedge \psi$, $\phi \vee \psi$, and $\phi \rightarrow \psi$ are also sentences. (To be even more precise, we have to put parentheses around the resulting sentence at each stage of construction. However, we will omit parentheses after applying $\neg$, and we will omit the outermost parentheses from every sentence.) What's more, we stipulate that all legitimate sentences come about from applying a finite number of these construction steps.

We now define a notion of a **translation**. For simplicity, let's suppose that we begin with a list $P, Q, R, \ldots$ of simple sentences. A **reconstrual** is an assignment F of each atomic sentence X to some other sentence $F(X)$. For example, $F(P)$ could be another atomic sentence, such as R, or it could be a complex sentence such as $R \rightarrow \neg S$ or even $\neg P$ or $P \wedge \neg P$. There are no restrictions at all on the assignment F, so long as the result is a legitimate sentence.

Once we have a reconstrual F, we can use it to translate *any* sentence ϕ. In short, we define $F(\phi)$ to be the sentence that results from replacing each atomic sentence X in ϕ with $F(X)$. The resulting string of symbols $F(\phi)$ will always be a legitimate sentence, and we call it a substitution instance of ϕ.

As usual, the definition becomes more clear when we look at examples. Suppose, for example, that we reconstrue P as $Q \rightarrow P$ and Q as $\neg R$. That reconstrual results in the following substitution instances.

$$P \rightarrow Q \quad \rightsquigarrow \quad (Q \rightarrow P) \rightarrow \neg R$$
$$P \vee \neg P \quad \rightsquigarrow \quad (Q \rightarrow P) \vee \neg(Q \rightarrow P)$$
$$Q \rightarrow P \quad \rightsquigarrow \quad \neg R \rightarrow (Q \rightarrow P)$$

It should be clear that there is some sense in which the substitution operation preserves the form of the original sentence or, to be more precise, that $F(\phi)$ is an instance of the form presented by ϕ. However, $F(\phi)$ can have more structure than ϕ itself has; for example, *every* sentence is a substitution instance of the atomic sentence P.

Exercise 4.1. Which of the following formulas is a substitution instance of the formula $P \rightarrow \neg Q$? In cases where you answer affirmatively, show how to reconstrue P and Q to get the resulting formula.

1. $\neg Q \rightarrow \neg P$
2. $(P \rightarrow \neg Q) \rightarrow R$
3. $(P \rightarrow \neg Q) \rightarrow \neg(P \rightarrow \neg Q)$

Recall that our inference rules are schematic, that is, they depend only on the form of the sentences involved. Thus, it should immediately follow that substitution preserves validity, since it preserves form. We will prove that rigorously in chapter 9, with a result known as the **substitution theorem**. But for now, it will suffice to state the upshot, which we can use to generate new proofs from old ones.

Substitution

A proof of $\phi_1, \ldots, \phi_n \vdash \psi$ can be converted to a proof of $F(\phi_1), \ldots, F(\phi_n) \vdash F(\psi)$, where F is a reconstrual of the nonlogical vocabulary.

The **substitution meta-rule** is just a formalization of what you already know: that find-and-replace preserves the validity of proofs (as long as you restrict the finding to atomic sentences, and you replace them with other well-formed sentences). Note that substitution is not a rule in the same sense as, say, modus ponens, which generates new valid inferences. To illustrate this point, imagine that proofs of all valid sequents are saved in some computer file proofs.txt. Each such proof consists of finitely many lines, and in the right-hand column, every line is justified by one of the inference rules: $\wedge I$, $\wedge E$, MP, and so on. None of those lines is justified by some rule called "substitution." Instead, the substitution meta-rule tells us that for any proof in proofs.txt, there is another proof in proofs.txt that looks just like the first, except that the atomic sentences have been replaced by some other sentences.

Exercise 4.2. Do you think the following claims are true or false? Explain your answers.

1. If ϕ is not provable, then no substitution instance of ϕ is provable.
2. The sentence $(P \wedge Q) \to R$ has a substitution instance that can be proven.

Cut

We now introduce a key meta-rule that, if used correctly, can greatly increase your efficiency in proving things. Let's begin with an example.

Suppose that you've been asked to prove that

$$P \to (Q \vee R) \vdash (P \to Q) \vee (P \to R).$$

After many failed attempts, you might decide to bring out the sledgehammer of reductio ad absurdum: to assume the negation of the result you want and derive a contradiction. Now, the negation $\neg((P \to Q) \vee (P \to R))$ doesn't look to be all that useful. However, you might then remember that you've already proven the following version of DeMorgan's rule: $\neg(P \vee Q) \vdash \neg P \wedge \neg Q$. You could then substitute $P \to Q$ for P and $P \to R$ for Q, which gives you a proof of

$$\neg((P \to Q) \vee (P \to R)) \vdash \neg(P \to Q) \wedge \neg(P \to R).$$

But now you've got to figure out how to splice that proof into the proof you're currently working on. The cut meta-rule will allow you to perform this splice, yielding the following lines:

1	(1)	$P \to (Q \lor R)$	A
2	(2)	$\neg((P \to Q) \lor (P \to R))$	A
2	(3)	$\neg(P \to Q) \land \neg(P \to R)$	cut, DM

The basic idea here is that if you've proven a sequent $\phi \vdash \psi$ (such as DeMorgan's), then you can use that sequent to continue a proof from a line with $\Gamma \vdash \phi$ to a line with $\Gamma \vdash \psi$. We state the rule, however, in a more general fashion.

Cut

Suppose that you have already demonstrated that $\phi_1, \ldots, \phi_n \vdash \psi$. Then, in any proof where you have lines $\Gamma_1 \vdash \phi_1, \ldots, \Gamma_n \vdash \phi_n$, you may infer that $\Gamma_1, \ldots, \Gamma_n \vdash \psi$.

As with substitution, cut is not a new inference rule. Instead, it's a promise: if certain proofs exist, then so does another proof. Imagine again a computer file **proofs.txt** that contains all correctly written proofs. The word "cut" does not appear in any of those proofs. However, if **proofs.txt** contains proofs of $\phi_1, \ldots, \phi_n \vdash \psi$, and also of each $\Gamma_i \vdash \phi_i$, then cut promises that **proofs.txt** also has a proof of $\Gamma_1, \ldots, \Gamma_n \vdash \psi$. That latter proof, however, only cites the primitive inference rules such as $\land I$ and MP.

When you write proofs, however, you can cite cut, because you're giving your reader a promise that you could expand it out into a correctly written proof. For example, suppose that you already have a proof of the sequent $\phi \vdash \psi$ (which you named "hocus pocus") and that you've begun a new proof where ϕ appears on line m. Then, on a subsequent line, you can write ψ with a citation of cut.

$$\Gamma \quad (m) \quad \phi$$

$$\vdots$$

$$\Gamma \quad (n) \quad \psi \quad \text{cut, hocus pocus}$$

If somebody then calls you on the cut, you can do the following: take the proof of $\phi \vdash \psi$ and add a line of CP to get a proof of $\vdash \phi \rightarrow \psi$. Then, instead of citing cut on line n, copy in that entire proof, and finish with a step of MP.

$$\Gamma \quad (m) \quad \phi$$

$$\vdots$$

$$(n_1) \quad \phi \rightarrow \psi$$
$$\Gamma \quad (n_2) \quad \psi \qquad\qquad m, n_1 \text{ MPP}$$

So, using cut with an already proven sequent is just a way of indicating that you could write a proof.

Many cases of cut involve the special case $n = 1$, that is, where you've already demonstrated that $\phi \vdash \psi$, and you find yourself with a line like this:

$$\Gamma \quad (m) \quad \phi$$

In this case, cut licenses the following inference:

$$\Gamma \quad (n) \quad \psi \qquad\qquad m \text{ cut}$$

For an example of cut with $n = 2$, suppose that you have proved disjunctive syllogism $P \vee Q, \neg P \vdash Q$ and that you have the following two lines in a proof:

$$\Gamma_1 \quad (m) \quad P \vee Q$$
$$\Gamma_2 \quad (n) \quad \neg P$$

Then cut licenses a subsequent line:

$$\Gamma_1, \Gamma_2 \quad (n') \quad Q \qquad\qquad m, n \text{ cut}$$

The cut rule is also really useful in the case where $n = 0$. In that case, we have already proven a single sequent $\vdash \psi$ that has no premises. The cut rule then says that on any line of a subsequent proof, we may write ψ with no dependencies. So, for example, if we've already proven the law of excluded middle (lem), $P \vee \neg P$, then any time we're writing a proof, we may insert a line:

(n) $P \vee \neg P$ \qquad cut, lem

This invocation of cut goes beyond substitution, because substitution only creates an entire new proof. Cut allows you to paste an old proof in the middle of a new one.

You can, however, use cut together with substitution. For example, if you've proven excluded middle, then substitution gives you a proof of $\vdash (P \to Q) \vee \neg(P \to Q)$. Then, cut permits you to drop this sequent into a proof as follows:

(n) $(P \to Q) \vee \neg(P \to Q)$ \quad cut, lem

Technically speaking, this line n should say something like "substitution + cut." But substitution is so immediate that it can typically be used without mention.

Let's look at one more example of the use of cut. We'll take for granted that you already have proofs of excluded middle $\vdash P \vee \neg P$ and positive paradox $P \vdash Q \to P$. We will use these results to prove the sequent $\vdash (P \to Q) \vee (Q \to P)$.

	(1)	$P \vee \neg P$	cut, lem
2	(2)	P	A
2	(3)	$Q \to P$	2 cut, pos paradox
2	(4)	$(P \to Q) \vee (Q \to P)$	3 $\vee$ I
5	(5)	$\neg P$	A
5	(6)	$\neg Q \to \neg P$	5 cut, pos paradox
2	(7)	$\neg\neg P$	2 DN
2, 5	(8)	$\neg\neg Q$	6,7 MTT
2, 5	(9)	Q	8 DN

5	(10)	$P \rightarrow Q$	2,9 CP
5	(11)	$(P \rightarrow Q) \vee (Q \rightarrow P)$	10 $\vee$ I
	(12)	$(P \rightarrow Q) \vee (Q \rightarrow P)$	1,2,4,5,11 $\vee$ E

On line 2, we have the sequent $P \vdash P$. Positive paradox establishes the sequent $P \vdash Q \rightarrow P$. Hence, cut permits us to combine these two sequents into $P \vdash Q \rightarrow P$, which we write on line 3. We then use positive paradox again to obtain line 6 from line 5. (Note that if we had permitted ourselves to use negative paradox, then we could immediately have obtained $P \rightarrow Q$ from line 5.)

If and Only If

We have one more meta-rule to cover, namely, the replacement rule. However, we pause to define a symbol that will facilitate our discussion of replacement.

If you spend any amount of time hanging around mathematicians or analytic philosophers, you'll pick up the phrase "if and only if." This phrase is meant to express something even stronger than a conditional; it's meant to express a two-directional conditional, or **biconditional**. For example, if I tell you that

You will get an A on the exam if and only if you study

then I'm telling you two things. First, "you will get an A on the exam if you study," which means that studying is a **sufficient condition** for getting an A on the exam. Second, "you will get an A on the exam only if you study," which means that studying is a **necessary condition** for getting an A on the exam.

We will use the symbol $\leftrightarrow$ for the "if and only if" connective. Like a conditional, this connective applies to two sentences; thus, if ϕ and ψ are sentences of propositional logic, then so is $\phi \leftrightarrow \psi$. In order for this new connective to be useful, we now have to specify its inference rules. Fortunately, its meaning is completely transparent, once we already know how to express "if ... then ..." and "and." In particular, $\phi \leftrightarrow \psi$ should be equivalent to $(\phi \rightarrow \psi) \wedge (\psi \rightarrow \phi)$. In fact, we will make this equivalence into a definition of the introduction and elimination rules.

Biconditional Introduction ($\leftrightarrow$I) and Elimination ($\leftrightarrow$E)

$$\frac{\Gamma \vdash (\phi \to \psi) \land (\psi \to \phi)}{\Gamma \vdash \phi \leftrightarrow \psi} \qquad \frac{\Gamma \vdash \phi \leftrightarrow \psi}{\Gamma \vdash (\phi \to \psi) \land (\psi \to \phi)}$$

To check that these are good inference rules, let's first verify that "P if and only if P" is tautologous.

1	(1)	P	A
	(2)	$P \to P$	1,1 CP
	(3)	$(P \to P) \land (P \to P)$	2,2 $\land$ I
	(4)	$P \leftrightarrow P$	3 $\leftrightarrow$I

In technical writing, people often abbreviate "if and only if" to the three letters "iff." Another expression that is sometimes used with the same force is "just in case." In particular, mathematicians often state their definitions by saying something like, "We'll say that a number n is *prime* just in case ...." By this they mean, a number n is prime if and only if ....

Recall that a conditional $P \to Q$ in propositional logic can be asserted in conditions considerably weaker than those that license asserting a conditional in some everyday life contexts. In particular, $Q \vdash P \to Q$, which means that Q itself is a sufficient condition for $P \to Q$. This result also suggests that $P \leftrightarrow Q$ should be assertable in any context where both P and Q are assertable. We verify that fact now.

1	(1)	$P \land Q$	A
1	(2)	Q	1 $\land$ E
1	(3)	$P \to Q$	2 cut, positive paradox
1	(4)	P	1 $\land$ E
1	(5)	$Q \to P$	4 cut, positive paradox
1	(6)	$(P \to Q) \land (Q \to P)$	3,5 $\land$ I
1	(7)	$P \leftrightarrow Q$	6 $\leftrightarrow$I

This proof yields the sequent $P \wedge Q \vdash P \leftrightarrow Q$. A similar proof (see the exercises) shows that $\neg P \wedge \neg Q \vdash P \leftrightarrow Q$. You could then combine these two proofs with a step of disjunction elimination to prove the sequent:

$$(P \wedge Q) \vee (\neg P \wedge \neg Q) \vdash P \leftrightarrow Q.$$

Exercise 4.3. Prove the following sequents. You may invoke cut with any named sequent that you have already proven (e.g., lem, positive paradox, negative paradox).

1. $P \leftrightarrow Q \vdash Q \leftrightarrow P$
2. $\vdash (Q \rightarrow P) \vee (P \rightarrow R)$
3. $P \leftrightarrow Q \dashv\vdash (P \wedge Q) \vee (\neg P \wedge \neg Q)$
4. $\neg(P \leftrightarrow P) \vdash Q \wedge \neg Q$
5. $P \leftrightarrow Q, Q \leftrightarrow R \vdash P \leftrightarrow R$
6. $\neg(P \leftrightarrow Q) \dashv\vdash (P \leftrightarrow \neg Q)$
7. $\vdash (P \leftrightarrow Q) \vee (P \leftrightarrow R) \vee (Q \leftrightarrow R)$

Replacement

The substitution meta-rule permits only transformations that begin with atomic sentences and that propagate through the application of the logical connectives. The **replacement meta-rule** is more flexible: it permits replacement of an entire subformula.

The idea behind this meta-rule is simple. Suppose that you have proven both sequents $\phi \vdash \psi$ and $\psi \vdash \phi$. So, you know then that ϕ and ψ are equivalent, "for all logical purposes." In particular, whatever inferential relations ϕ stands in to any other sentence θ, ψ stands in exactly those same inferential relations to θ. This suggests that in any argument, ψ should be able to play the same role as ϕ.

For example, consider the sequent

$$R \vee ((Q \rightarrow R) \rightarrow P) \vdash R \vee ((\neg Q \vee R) \rightarrow P).$$

This sequent could be proven the long way around by performing disjunction elimination. After assuming the second disjunct of the premise, you could then assume ¬Q ∨ R. Then, plug in the proof of ¬Q ∨ R ⊢ Q → R and so on.

Let θ be the formula Q → R, let θ' be the formula ¬Q ∨ R, and let φ be the formula R ∨ ((Q → R) → P). In other words, φ is the formula R ∨ (θ → P), and the conclusion of the argument is the formula R ∨ (θ' → P).

After doing many proofs, you'll start to get the feeling that a move like this can always be done. That is, if one formula θ occurs as part of another φ, and if θ is provably equivalent to θ', then you'll always be able to find a proof φ ⊢ φ[θ'/θ], where φ[θ'/θ] is the formula you get if you replace θ in φ with θ'.

But can you be sure that it will always work? The answer is yes, that you can be sure, but it takes some patient verification to see why. The key here is simply to check that all of the connectives preserve interderivability of sentences. So, for example, if θ and θ' are interderivable, then no matter what sentence ψ is, the conjunction θ ∧ ψ will be interderivable with θ' ∧ ψ, the conditional θ → ψ will be interderivable with θ' → ψ, and so on. If we apply the same thought again, it follows that χ ∨ (θ ∧ ψ) is interderivable with χ ∨ (θ' ∧ ψ) and so on. In other words, once you have that θ ⊣⊢ θ', then θ can be embedded as deeply as you want in some other formula φ, and it will still be the case that φ ⊣⊢ φ[θ'/θ], where φ[θ'/θ] is the result of replacing θ in φ with θ'.

Our meta-rule of replacement can be made more convenient for proving stuff if we remember that φ ⊣⊢ φ[θ/θ'] implies that if Γ ⊢ φ, then Γ ⊢ φ[θ/θ']. That is, if there's a proof of φ from Γ, then there's also a proof of φ[θ/θ'].

Replacement with an Equivalent (RE)

Given a line Γ ⊢ φ of a proof, and a subformula θ of φ, if θ is equivalent to θ', then you may infer a subsequent line Γ ⊢ φ [θ'/θ], where θ has been replaced by θ'. Schematically:

$$\frac{\vdash \theta \leftrightarrow \theta' \qquad \Gamma \vdash \phi}{\Gamma \vdash \phi[\theta'/\theta]}$$

The replacement meta-rule can be used with any equivalences that have already been proven. If you keep in mind some key equivalences (see page 233), then it can really speed up proofs. Consider, for example, the following alternative proof of Peirce's law.

1	(1)	$(P \to Q) \to P$	A
1	(2)	$\neg(P \to Q) \lor P$	1 RE, mat cond
1	(3)	$(P \land \neg Q) \lor P$	2 RE, mat cond
4	(4)	$P \land \neg Q$	A
4	(5)	P	4 $\land$E
6	(6)	P	A
1	(7)	P	3,4,5,6,6 $\lor$E

On line 2, we used replacement on the entire line with the equivalence $\phi \to \psi \dashv\vdash \neg\phi \lor \psi$. (When replacement is applied to an entire line, we could also have used cut.) On line 3, we used replacement on the first disjunct with the equivalence $\neg(\phi \to \psi) \dashv\vdash \phi \land \neg\psi$.

The replacement meta-rule can be especially helpful if you need to convert a sentence ϕ into an interderivable sentence ϕ' that has some specific form. For example, one particularly nice kind of sentence is one where all negation signs apply only to atomic sentences, all conjunction symbols apply only to atomic or negated atomic sentences, and where there are no conditional or biconditional connectives. (Such sentences are said to be in **disjunctive normal form,** and we will investigate them further in chapter 5.) For example, the following sentence has this form:

$$(P \land Q) \lor (P \land \neg Q) \lor (\neg P \land Q) \lor (\neg P \land \neg Q).$$

We won't provide a detailed recipe here for finding equivalent disjunctive normal form sentences, but instead, we'll just work a couple of examples.

First, we write a proof of the sequent

$$(P \to Q) \lor (Q \to P) \vdash (P \lor \neg P) \lor (Q \lor \neg Q).$$

1	(1)	$(P \to Q) \lor (Q \to P)$	A
1	(2)	$(\neg P \lor Q) \lor (\neg Q \lor P)$	1 RE

1	(3)	$\neg P \vee (Q \vee (\neg Q \vee P))$	2 RE
1	(4)	$\neg P \vee ((Q \vee \neg Q) \vee P)$	3 RE
1	(5)	$\neg P \vee (P \vee (Q \vee \neg Q))$	4 RE
1	(6)	$(\neg P \vee P) \vee (Q \vee \neg Q)$	5 RE
1	(7)	$(P \vee \neg P) \vee (Q \vee \neg Q)$	6 RE

Since the conclusion here is a tautology, it's not surprising that it can be derived from the premise. (It can, in fact, be derived from any premise.) What's interesting is that each step of this proof uses RE, and so the derivation is reversible—hence, the premise and conclusion are logically equivalent.

Exercise 4.4. In the proof above, identify each equivalence that has been used.

Now we convert $P \leftrightarrow Q$ to $(P \wedge Q) \vee (\neg P \wedge \neg Q)$ using a string of equivalences.

$$P \leftrightarrow Q \quad \dashv\vdash \quad (P \rightarrow Q) \wedge (Q \rightarrow P)$$
$$\dashv\vdash \quad (\neg P \vee Q) \wedge (\neg Q \vee P)$$
$$\dashv\vdash \quad ((\neg P \vee Q) \wedge \neg Q) \vee ((\neg P \vee Q) \wedge P)$$
$$\dashv\vdash \quad ((\neg P \wedge \neg Q) \vee (Q \wedge \neg Q)) \vee ((\neg P \wedge P) \vee (Q \wedge P))$$
$$\dashv\vdash \quad (\neg P \wedge \neg Q) \vee (Q \wedge P)$$

In the final line, we used the fact that for any contradiction $\bot$, and for any sentence ϕ, we have $\phi \vee \bot \dashv\vdash \phi \dashv\vdash \bot \vee \phi$. In this sense, a contradiction acts like a zero (i.e., an additive identity) for the $\vee$ operation.

Exercise 4.5. Use replacement-style reasoning to convert the following sentences to disjunctive normal form. You might wish to consult the equivalences on page 233.

1. $(P \rightarrow Q) \vee (Q \rightarrow R)$
2. $(P \leftrightarrow Q) \vee (P \leftrightarrow R) \vee (Q \leftrightarrow R)$

5
Truth

Suppose that you have been trying and trying to prove a sequent, say $\phi \vdash \psi$. Suppose that you've spent ten hours trying to prove it, and nothing seems to be working. At what point would you be justified in concluding that this sequent actually *cannot* be proven—not that it just needs a greater genius than you but that it is literally impossible to use the rules to derive ψ from ϕ?

The short answer is that a failure to prove something never justifies the conclusion that the thing cannot be proven. It doesn't matter how smart you are. You could be the smartest person that ever lived, and still, your failure to prove something is not a proof that it's unprovable. For example, for hundreds of years, the smartest mathematicians in the world tried to prove a result called "Fermat's last theorem." After a while, a lot of people started to think: the reason these mathematicians have failed to prove it is because it must be false! And yet, it turns out that it is true. In 1995, the very patient Andrew Wiles revealed that he had a proof, which, if transcribed into our notation, would be well over a million lines long.

The lesson is, if you want to show that something isn't provable, then you need a different kind of evidence than your—or anyone else's—failure to prove it.

One of the most amazing feats of formal logic has been in explaining how one can prove that something cannot be proven. In this chapter, we explain logicians' method in the special case of propositional logic. It turns out that for propositional logic, it's trivially easy to determine whether or not something can be proven. The trick is to find a simple, *detectable* feature that an argument has if it's provable and that an argument doesn't have if it's not provable. For propositional logic, the relevant feature is **truth preservation**. That feature only becomes detectable when we define "truth" in a simple mathematical way.

Truth Tables

We begin with a metaphor. Imagine that the atomic sentences $P, Q, R, \ldots$ are simple reports about contingent states of affairs. So, for example, P could be the statement, "it rained in Princeton on December 7, 1941." But remember that logic doesn't care at all about what actually is true or false; so, for us, the symbol P is not, in itself, a true claim or a false claim. It only represents the kind of statement that could be true or could be false.

Given this picture, the state of the entire universe would be specified by determining whether each atomic sentence $P, Q, R, \ldots$ is true or false. You could imagine that at creation, God said, "Let P be true, let R be false, etc." We can write all of these possible combinations of truth values in a neat table like this:

P	Q	R
1	1	1
1	1	0
1	0	1
1	0	0
0	1	1
0	1	0
0	0	1
0	0	0

Here we have used 1 for true and 0 for false—merely as a notational convenience. Since there are three atomic sentences, there are eight possible configurations of truth values. The convention we've adopted is for the leftmost sentence (here P) to have four 1s and then four 0s; then, the next sentence alternates truth values twice as quickly, and so on. That pattern ensures that we pick up all possible combinations of truth values.

The idea behind truth-functional (aka Boolean) logic is that once God chooses whether each atomic sentence is true or false, then all His truth-making work is done—because the truth value of the atomic sentences completely determines the truth value of any complex sentence. For example, once God says that P is true, then it automatically follows that $\neg P$ is false. In other words, we should have the following relation between the truth value of P and the truth value of $\neg P$.

P	$\neg P$
1	**0** 1
0	**1** 0

We'll call this the **truth table** for the negation connective. Thus, negation is simply the Boolean "not" that flips 1 and 0. In fact, the truth table for negation is applicable to any negated sentence, not just a negated atomic sentence. Thus, we rewrite the previous table as

ϕ	$\neg \phi$
1	**0** 1
0	**1** 0

We can already get a taste now of how to compute truth values for more complex sentences. Consider, for example, the sentence $\neg\neg P$.

P	$\neg\neg P$
1	**1** 0 1
0	**0** 1 0

Here we use the truth value of P to compute the truth value of $\neg P$, and then we use the truth value of $\neg P$ to compute the truth value of $\neg\neg P$. The **main column** (in bold font) is the column that is filled in *last* as we go through the process. It represents the truth value that the sentence $\neg\neg P$ has in each different situation.

Now we've got to decide on how to compute truth values for conjunctions, disjunctions, and conditionals. The case of conjunction is the most clear: a conjunction is true just in case both conjuncts are true. In particular, for $P \wedge Q$ to be true, both P and Q must be true. If one or both of P and Q is false, then $P \wedge Q$ is false. That yields the following table.

$P\ Q$	$P \wedge Q$
1 1	1 **1** 1
1 0	1 **0** 0
0 1	0 **0** 1
0 0	0 **0** 0

A similarly simple rule allows us to compute the truth value of a disjunction: a disjunction is true just in case at least one of its disjuncts is true. This leads to the following truth table.

$P\ Q$	$P \vee Q$
1 1	1 **1** 1
1 0	1 **1** 0
0 1	0 **1** 1
0 0	0 **0** 0

Now, if you put your critical thinking cap on, you might conclude that this disjunction rule is *bad*, because a disjunction shouldn't be true when *both* disjuncts are true. We think that's a reasonable objection, and it would be good, at some point, to reflect further on other possible options for giving a precise, formal representation of the logical notion of disjunction. But for now, please recall that we are building an *idealized model* of human logic, which means that there may be some mismatch between the model and our intuitions.

The truth value of a complex sentence ϕ can be calculated by working from the inside out. One begins by copying the truth values of atomic sentences $P, Q, R, \dots$ in each row of the truth table over to columns under places where those atomic sentences occur in ϕ. Then, those truth values are used in combination with the tables for $\neg$, $\vee$, $\wedge$ to compute truth values of the more complex subformulas of ϕ, and so on, until we reach the **main connective** of ϕ, which is the last connective that is inserted in the construction of ϕ. For the specific case where ϕ is the sentence $\neg P \lor$ $(Q \land R)$, we computed the full table below.

$P\,Q\,R$	$\neg P \ \lor \ (Q \ \land \ R\,)$
1 1 1	0 1 **1** 1 1 1
1 1 0	0 1 **0** 1 0 0
1 0 1	0 1 **0** 0 0 1
1 0 0	0 1 **0** 0 0 0
0 1 1	1 0 **1** 1 1 1
0 1 0	1 0 **1** 1 0 0
0 0 1	1 0 **1** 0 0 1
0 0 0	1 0 **1** 0 0 0

Let's call this table the **truth table** for the sentence $\neg P \lor (Q \land R)$. To this point, we have been casual with our understanding of what counts as a sentence of propositional logic. However, in order to compute truth tables, it's important to note that any legitimate sentence is built up in a unique way from propositional constants such as P, Q, and R. As a result, if a sentence ϕ is not itself one of these propositional constants, then there is one connective—the so-called **main connective**—that is the last one in its construction. (For more details, see page 177.) The main connective of $\neg P \lor (Q \land R)$ is $\lor$, and we have highlighted the column under that connective in the truth table. The values in this **main column** give the status of the sentence $\neg P \lor (Q \land R)$ in all the different possible situations.

Exercise 5.1. Write the truth table for $P \land \neg P$. How do you interpret the significance of the result?

You can now compute the truth values for any complex sentence built with negation, conjunction, and disjunction. But what about sentences built with the conditional symbol? The table is as follows:

$P\,Q$	$P \to Q$
1 1	1 **1** 1
1 0	1 **0** 0
0 1	0 **1** 1
0 0	0 **1** 0

You'll need to accept this truth table and use it to solve problems. But we want to be upfront about the fact that this truth table does not simply and obviously capture the true meaning of "if…then." For example, "The moon is made of green cheese" is false, and "Caesar crossed the Rubicon" is true; hence, the table suggests that it's true that "If the moon is made of green cheese, then Caesar crossed the Rubicon." That seems rather odd. And the oddness only increases if you cook up examples for rows 1 and 4. The only row that seems obviously correct is the second row.

At this point, symbolic logic comes to a substantial philosophical cross-roads. In short, *there is no truth table that adequately captures the nuance of the "if…then …" connective in natural languages.* In the twentieth century, philosophers spent *a lot* of time worrying about this nasty little connective $\to$, and they came up with many more or less interesting proposals.[1] Meanwhile, there's a strong case to be made that this truth table—and the corresponding rules MP and CP—is the de facto standard used in mathematics and the sciences.

For our current agenda, the important fact is simply that the truth table for $\to$ matches with the inference rules CP and MP in a precise sense that we will explain soon—when we talk about the soundness and complete-ness theorems. What that means is that if you want to change the truth table for $\to$, then you need different inference rules. And if you want different inference rules for $\to$, then you need a different truth table.

Once we've agreed upon the truth table for the conditional, we can compute the truth table for the biconditional.

$P\,Q$	$P \leftrightarrow Q$		
1 1	1	**1**	1
1 0	1	**0**	0
0 1	0	**0**	1
0 0	0	**1**	0

In other words, a biconditional $P \leftrightarrow Q$ is true just in case P and Q have the same truth value.

---

1. You can learn more about these issues in a course or book about **philosophical logic**. For example, "relevance logic" was invented precisely to avoid the paradoxes of material implication. See p. 227 for references.

Exercise 5.2. Compute the truth table for $\neg P \leftrightarrow \neg Q$. How do you interpret the significance of the result?

Truth in the Service of Proof

What can you *do* with these truth tables? What's their cash value? Writing out a truth table is not a particularly challenging exercise—and so it's not a good way to try to build mental muscle. The true utility of truth tables (for us, in this context) is that they can show us what can and cannot be proven.

As you surely have experienced, the process of discovering a proof involves genuine strategic thinking. Especially for the longer and more difficult proofs, you have to choose appropriate intermediate goals. But how do you decide on those intermediate goals? How do you know which intermediate goals are attainable, and how do you know which intermediate goals will get you closer to the destination? Mistakes here can be costly. If you choose an intermediate goal that cannot be proven, then you might waste an enormous amount of time trying to prove it. Conversely, if you choose an intermediate goal that is too weak to obtain the conclusion, then you'll be trapped in a dead end.

To understand how truth tables can be used in the service of proof, you need to know two facts. We will demonstrate these facts in chapter 9, but at present, you'll have to take our word for it. First, a bit of terminology.

Definition. Let $\phi_1, \ldots, \phi_n$ and ψ be sentences. Let's say that the argument from $\phi_1, \ldots, \phi_n$ to ψ is **truth preserving** just in case in the truth table for all $n + 1$ sentences, in any row where each of $\phi_1, \ldots, \phi_n$ is assigned 1, the sentence ψ is also assigned 1.

Here now is the first of the two facts that you need to know:

Soundness theorem. *If $\phi_1, \ldots, \phi_n \vdash \psi$, then the argument from $\phi_1, \ldots, \phi_n$ to ψ is truth preserving.*

The contrapositive of the soundness theorem says that if there's any case where $\phi_1, \ldots, \phi_n$ are true and ψ is false, then ψ cannot be proven from $\phi_1, \ldots, \phi_n$. The upshot is:

If there is a truth table row in which $\phi_1, \ldots, \phi_n$ are true, and ψ is false, then there is no proof from $\phi_1, \ldots, \phi_n$ to ψ.

Such a truth table row is known as a **counterexample** to the validity of the argument.

To take a simple example, consider the argument $P \rightarrow Q, Q \vdash P$, which you know intuitively to be invalid—indeed, it's the notorious fallacy of affirming the consequent. The truth table for this argument looks like this:

$P\,Q$	$P{\rightarrow}Q$	Q	P	
1 1	1 **1** 1	**1**	**1**	
1 0	1 **0** 0	**0**	**1**	
0 1	0 **1** 1	**1**	**0**	$\Longleftarrow$ counterexample
0 0	0 **1** 0	**0**	**0**	

In the first two rows of the truth table, the conclusion P is true—and so those rows don't provide any interesting information about the argument. The third row, however, raises a red flag: here the two premises $P \rightarrow Q$ and Q are both true, and the conclusion P is false. That's a counterexample. Hence, by the soundness theorem, there is no proof from $P \rightarrow Q$ and Q to P.

In the special case of an argument with no premises (i.e., where the conclusion ψ is simply asserted), the truth preservation condition says that whenever all the premises are true (which is always, since there are none of them), the conclusion ψ is true. Hence, the soundness theorem says that the sequent $\vdash \psi$ is provable only if ψ is always true, in every row of its truth table. Contrapositively, if ψ is ever false, then the sequent $\vdash \psi$ cannot be proven. For example, and unsurprisingly, the sequent $\vdash P$ cannot be proven.

Let's see now how the soundness theorem can prevent you from choosing a bad proof strategy. Suppose that you've been asked to prove $\vdash (P \rightarrow Q) \vee (Q \rightarrow P)$. Since the conclusion is a disjunction, you might reasonably think that a good strategy would be to try to prove $\vdash P \rightarrow Q$, then to infer the conclusion by means of $\vee$ I. However, $P \rightarrow Q$ is *not* a tautology, which means that $\vdash P \rightarrow Q$ cannot be proven. Hence, that would be a disastrously bad strategy.

So, the soundness theorem provides a method for proving that something cannot be proven. We already know one way of proving that something can be proven: by producing a proof of it. Amazingly, though, there is another way of proving that something can be proven. The completeness theorem tells us that if a sequent is truth preserving, then it can in fact be proven.

Completeness theorem If the argument from $\phi_1, \ldots, \phi_n$ to ψ is truth preserving, then $\phi_1, \ldots, \phi_n \vdash \psi$.

In the special case of $n = 0$, it follows that if ψ is a tautology, then $\vdash \psi$. For example, it's easy to see that $P \vee \neg P$ is a tautology: if P is true, then $P \vee \neg P$ is true, and if P is false, then $\neg P$ is true, and $P \vee \neg P$ is true. Similarly, a quick truth table test shows that Pierce's proposition is a tautology and hence can be proven.

PQ	$((P{\to}Q){\to}P){\to}P$
1 1	1 1 1 1 1 **1** 1
1 0	1 0 0 1 1 **1** 1
0 1	0 1 1 0 0 **1** 0
0 0	0 1 0 0 0 **1** 0

Exercise 5.3. Write truth tables for $\neg P \vee Q$ and $P \to Q$, and say whether either one implies the other.

Exercise 5.4. Show that P cannot be derived from $P \leftrightarrow Q$.

Exercise 5.5. Explain why $P \wedge \neg P \vdash Q$ is truth preserving.

Shortcuts

The correspondence between proofs and truth tables gives a handy way to classify sentences. We define three mutually exclusive and exhaustive classes of sentences:

- A sentence is an **inconsistency** just in case its truth value is always 0. (Here, "always" means "on every row of its truth table, under the main connective.")

- A sentence is a **tautology** just in case its truth value is always 1. By soundness and completeness, ϕ is a tautology just in case $\vdash \phi$.
- A sentence is a **contingency** just in case its truth value is sometimes 0 and sometimes 1.

You already know paradigm examples of each kind of sentence: $P \vee \neg P$ is a tautology, $P \rightarrow P$ is a tautology, $P \wedge \neg P$ is an inconsistency, P is a contingency, and $P \vee Q$ is a contingency.

We can also give precise definitions for logical relations between sentences.

- Two sentences ϕ and ψ are **logically equivalent** just in case ϕ and ψ have the same value in all rows of their common truth table. By soundness and completeness, ϕ and ψ are logically equivalent just in case $\vdash \phi \leftrightarrow \psi$.
- A set Γ of sentences is **consistent** just in case there is at least one row in their common truth table in which all sentences in Γ have value 1. If Γ is not consistent, then we say it is **inconsistent**.

We previously used the word **interderivable** for two sentences ϕ and ψ when there are proofs $\phi \vdash \psi$ and $\psi \vdash \phi$, which we wrote as $\phi \dashv\vdash \psi$. Clearly, $\phi \dashv\vdash \psi$ just in case $\vdash \phi \leftrightarrow \psi$, and it will be convenient sometimes to write $\phi \equiv \psi$ as shorthand for this relation of interderivability. The soundness and completeness theorems guarantee that ϕ and ψ are interderivable just in case ϕ and ψ are logically equivalent. (On page 233, we've given a list of several pairs of interderivable—hence logically equivalent—sentences.)

Example. We will prove that if $\phi \dashv\vdash \psi$, then $\vdash \phi \leftrightarrow \psi$. Take note: Our proof here is *not* a single formal proof with dependency numbers and so on. Instead, it is a meta-theoretic argument about the existence of certain formal proofs.

We assume, then, that $\phi \dashv\vdash \psi$. This says that there are two formal proofs, one proof of $\phi \vdash \psi$ and one proof of $\psi \vdash \phi$. By the conditional proof rule, these two proofs can be extended to proofs of $\vdash \phi \rightarrow \psi$ and of $\vdash \psi \to \phi$. Then, those two proofs can be concatenated and combined with an instance of conjunction introduction to give $\vdash (\phi \to \psi) \land (\psi \to \phi)$ and an instance of biconditional introduction to give $\vdash \phi \leftrightarrow \psi$.

Exercise 5.6. Show that if $\vdash \phi \leftrightarrow \psi$, then $\phi \dashv\vdash \psi$.

Truth tables are easy ... and also inefficient and potentially mind-numbing. After you've done a dozen of them, you realize that you won't learn anything by doing more. It's time either to find a computer program to do them for you or, better, discover some rules of thumb to find the relevant lines of a truth table without writing out the whole thing. This section is highly pragmatic and nontheoretical. The one and only goal is to provide you with some rules of thumb for finding relevant truth table rows.

Suppose, for example, that you want to know whether the sequent

$$P \lor Q, R \land \neg Q \vdash R \to \neg P$$

can be proven or not. If you write up a full truth table, you'll need eight rows. But notice that the only potential counterexamples are the rows where the conclusion $R \to \neg P$ is false, hence rows where R and P are true. A quick inspection of the premises shows that the first is true whenever P is true, and if R is true, then the second is true when $\neg Q$ is true. So there you have it: The following row of the truth table provides a counterexample to the validity of this argument.

$P\,Q\,R$	$P \lor Q$	$R \land \neg Q$	$R \to \neg P$
1 0 1	1 **1** 0	1 **1** 1 0	1 **0** 01

Each row of a truth table corresponds to an assignment of 0s and 1s to the atomic sentences. We call such an assignment a **valuation**, and we can write it in functional form like this: $v(P) = 1$, $v(Q) = 0$, and $v(R) = 1$. The valuation v here makes the premises of the argument true and the conclusion false. Hence, the argument fails to be truth preserving, and the conclusion cannot be proven from the premises.

This first example shows that when the conclusion of an argument is a conditional, you can immediately narrow focus to the lines where its antecedent is true and its consequent is false. The same kind of rule of thumb applies to a disjunctive conclusion: the only relevant lines are those where both disjuncts are false. Unfortunately, the situation is worse when the conclusion is a conjunction, for there are three different ways that a conjunction can be false.

Consider now a different example: You want to know whether the sequent $P \wedge Q, \neg Q \vee R \vdash R$ can be proven. In this case, the conclusion is an atomic sentence R, so you can focus only on those rows where R is false. Among those rows where R is false, the first premise is true only if both P and Q are true. But that is all the information we need, for if Q is true and R is false, then the second premise is false. In other words, there is no row in which the premises are true and the conclusion is false. This argument is valid, and the sequent can be proven.

What we just did is a lot like playing a game of Sudoku. The key to doing it properly is not to make guesses—you only assign a truth value to a sentence when you are forced to buy the supposition that the conclusion is false and the premises are true. Here, in fact, is how we are arguing:

> Suppose that the argument from ϕ_1 and ϕ_2 to ψ is invalid.
> There is a row in the truth table where ϕ_1 and ϕ_2 are true, but ψ is false.
> If ψ is false, then ...
> If ϕ_1 and ϕ_2 are true, then ...
> [some contradiction]
> Therefore, the argument from ϕ_1 and ϕ_2 to ψ is valid.

To draw such a conclusion, you've got to be careful about the steps "If ψ is false, then ..." and "If ϕ_1 and ϕ_2 are true then...."

In some cases, you simply won't be forced by the suppositions to assign particular truth values; instead, you'll have options. Then, you have to search systematically through the options to see if there is a counterexample to the argument. Consider one more example: you want to know if the argument $(P \wedge Q) \rightarrow R \vdash P \rightarrow (Q \wedge R)$ is valid. If the conclusion is false, then P is true and $Q \wedge R$ is false. But sadly, there are three ways that $Q \wedge R$ can be false. If the premise is true, then sadly we can't say much either. It could be that R is true, or it could be that $P \wedge Q$ is false, and there are three ways that it could be false. At this stage, we can just try out various values for Q and R. Noticing that the premise is true whenever R is true, we can check if the conclusion can be made false in that case. Indeed, if Q is false, then $Q \wedge R$ is false, and the conclusion is false. So there we have it: If P and R are true, and Q is false, then the premise is true and the conclusion is false. This argument is invalid, and the sequent cannot be proven.

This kind of argumentation about truth preservation can sometimes shade into a formal proof, where the only thing that's missing are the dependency numbers and the explicit citation of inference rules. Consider, for example, an argument that if the premise $P \wedge (Q \vee R)$ is true, then so is the conclusion $(P \wedge Q) \vee (P \wedge R)$.

(1) Suppose that $P \wedge (Q \vee R)$ is true.
(2) Then both P and $Q \vee R$ are true.
(3) Since $Q \vee R$ is true, either Q or R is true.
(4) If Q is true, then $P \wedge Q$ is true, hence $(P \wedge Q) \vee (P \wedge R)$ is true.
(5) If R is true, then $P \wedge R$ is true, hence $(P \wedge Q) \vee (P \wedge R)$ is true.
(6) In either case, $(P \wedge Q) \vee (P \wedge R)$ is true.

Here, line 2 is justified by conjunction elimination. Line 3 looks a bit like disjunction elimination, but in fact it's just the statement of the definition of the truth table for $\vee$. The transition from line 1 to line 2 also involves a tacit invocation of the truth table for $\wedge$. Lines 4 and 5 each result from one step of conjunction introduction and one step of disjunction introduction. Line 6 results from disjunction elimination.

Let's write the first bit of this argument again, bringing it even closer in line with complete formalization.

1	(1)	$v(P \wedge (Q \vee R)) = 1$	A
1	(2)	$v(P) = 1$ and $v(Q \vee R) = 1$	def $\wedge$
1	(3)	$v(Q \vee R) = 1$	2 and elim
1	(4)	Either $v(Q) = 1$ or $v(R) = 1$	def $\vee$
5	(5)	$v(Q) = 1$	A
1	(6)	$v(P) = 1$	2 and elim
1, 5	(7)	$v(P) = 1$ and $v(Q) = 1$	5,6 and intro

1, 5	(8)	$v(P \wedge Q) = 1$	def $\wedge$
1, 5	(9)	$v((P \wedge Q) \vee (P \wedge R)) = 1$	def $\vee$

We could continue here by deriving $v((P \wedge Q) \vee (P \wedge R)) = 1$ from the assumption that $v(R) = 1$. Then, we could use $\vee$ elimination to eliminate dependency on the assumptions $v(Q) = 1$ and $v(R) = 1$. The end result would be a proof of the sequent

$$v(P \wedge (Q \vee R)) = 1 \vdash v((P \wedge Q) \vee (P \wedge R)) = 1.$$

To argue in such an explicit fashion can have the advantage of convincing you that you really are using the rules of logic. However, there are also disadvantages to arguing completely explicitly. One disadvantage is simple inefficiency. If your goal is to convince somebody else, then you only need to say as much as is necessary to convince them that a formal proof exists.

Notice also that the conclusion we really want isn't the sequent:

$$v(P \wedge (Q \vee R)) = 1 \vdash v((P \wedge Q) \vee (P \wedge R)) = 1, \qquad (*)$$

it's the general claim:

For every v, $[v(P \wedge (Q \vee R)) = 1 \vdash v((P \wedge Q) \vee (P \wedge R)) = 1]$.

While it's intuitively clear that we have proved the general claim, we don't yet have an inference rule that will let us get from sequent $(*)$ to the general claim. To do that, we need to be able to talk about "all valuations," that is, we need to be able to quantify over valuations. That's the subject of predicate logic, which we take up in the next chapter.

Exercise 5.7. Provide counterexamples to the following invalid argument forms.

1. $P \to Q, Q \vdash P$
2. $P \to R \vdash (P \vee Q) \to R$

   3. $P \to R \vdash P \to (Q \land R)$
   4. $P \to (Q \to R) \vdash (P \to Q) \to R$

Exercise 5.8. Classify each of the following sentences as tautology, inconsistency, or contingency.

   1. $(P \to Q) \lor (Q \to R)$
   2. $(P \to Q) \lor (P \to R)$
   3. $(P \land Q) \lor (P \land \neg Q) \lor (\neg P \land Q)$
   4. $(P \to \neg P) \to P$
   5. $P \to (\neg P \to P)$

Exercise 5.9. Show that the following pairs of sentences are logically equivalent (i.e., always have the same truth value):

   1. $P \equiv \neg P \to P$
   2. $Q \equiv P \leftrightarrow (P \leftrightarrow Q)$
   3. $P \leftrightarrow R \equiv (P \leftrightarrow Q) \leftrightarrow (Q \leftrightarrow R)$

Exercise 5.10. Are the following sequents provable? Explain your answers.

   1. $\vdash (P \to P) \to \neg P$
   2. $P \leftrightarrow Q \vdash \neg P \leftrightarrow \neg Q$
   3. $\vdash (P \leftrightarrow Q) \lor (Q \leftrightarrow P)$
   4. $\vdash (P \leftrightarrow Q) \lor (P \leftrightarrow R) \lor (P \leftrightarrow R)$

Exercise 5.11. Show that the $\to$ connective is not associative. That is, show that $P \to (Q \to R)$ is not equivalent to $(P \to Q) \to R$.

Exercise 5.12. Suppose that you're tutoring another student who is trying to prove the sequent:

$$P \to (Q \lor R) \vdash (P \to Q) \lor (P \to R).$$

That student says that he'll try first to prove $P \rightarrow Q$ and then use $\vee$ introduction to get the result. Do you think his strategy is good?

Exercise 5.13. Suppose that the sentence ϕ is an inconsistency. What can you say about the sentence $\phi \rightarrow \psi$?

Exercise 5.14. Suppose that the sentence $\phi \wedge \neg \psi$ is an inconsistency. Explain how you know that the sequent $\phi \vdash \psi$ is provable.

Propositions as Sets of Possible Worlds

There's another way of thinking about the relation between sentences and truth values—a way that philosophers use to frame many of their discussions. Let's think of a truth valuation (i.e., a row in a truth table) as a "way that things could be." Philosophers sometimes like to use the phrase "possible world" for a way that things could be. Now we can imagine all of these "ways that things could be" to be gathered together into a single collection, a sort of meta-universe of all possible worlds. Imagine, for the sake of this discussion, the point of view of an omnipotent being who might be contemplating the question, "Which world should I create?" As this omnipotent being surveys all of the possible worlds, She might decide that certain things are important to Her—for example, She might decide that She wants a world in which there are colorful flowers. Let P be shorthand for the sentence, "There are colorful flowers." Then She could decide to rule out all worlds where there are no colorful flowers, that is, all worlds in which P is false and $\neg P$ is true. In short, She can use propositions like P to pick out a subcollection of worlds that have a certain feature.

Although we lack the power to create worlds, we do have the power to imagine all possible worlds and to use propositions to differentiate worlds from each other. In fact, it seems that the job of science is to figure out more and more about where we live in the space of all possible worlds. That is, science tries to find which propositions are true, because each such proposition narrows down the set of possible locations of *our* world in the space of all possible worlds.

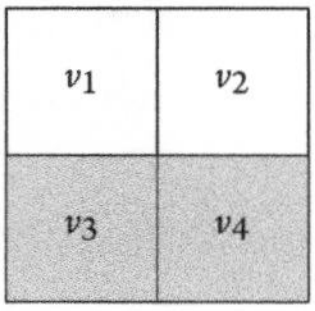

Figure 5.1. The proposition P rules out possibilities v_3 and v_4.

Now let's try to turn this suggestive idea into a useful tool for reasoning. In this section, we'll just look at the case where there are two atomic sentences: P and Q. In that case, there are four truth valuations and hence four possible worlds v_1, v_2, v_3, v_4. (In general, if there are n atomic sentences, then there are 2^n possible worlds, and if there are infinitely many atomic sentences, then there is an uncountable infinity of possible worlds.) Let's imagine these worlds as blocks in a 4×4 grid. The top blocks are those in which $v(P) = 1$, and the left blocks are those in which $v(Q) = 1$.

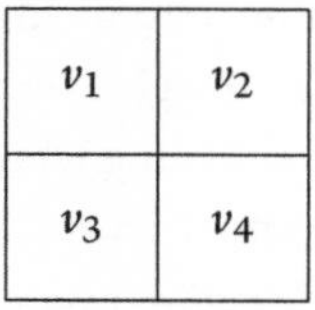

If you don't know anything at all, then all bets are off—you could be in any of the worlds v_1, v_2, v_3, v_4. Furthermore, if you only know a tautology, say $P \vee \neg P$, then you could be in any world. That's what it means to say that tautologies are empty or contentless: they don't rule out any possibilities. If, in contrast, you know that P, then you know that you're not in one of the bottom two worlds. Hence, the proposition P can be represented by graying the bottom row, as in figure 5.1. Similarly, the proposition Q can be represented by graying out the column on the right, the proposition $\neg P$ can be represented by graying out the top row, and the proposition $\neg Q$ can be represented by graying out the column on the left.

Interestingly, this visual representation indicates that there are "missing propositions" that are of the same logical kind as P and Q—that is, other propositions that gray out two squares. Consider, for example, the

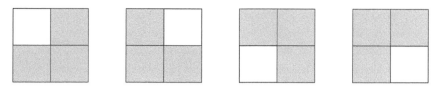

Figure 5.2. Visual representation of truth assignments to two elementary sentences.

case where the top-right and bottom-left square are grayed out. The corresponding proposition ϕ doesn't rule out P, doesn't rule out Q, and doesn't rule out either $\neg P$ or $\neg Q$. What it does rule out are the cross-cases where P is true and Q is false and when P is false and Q is true. In other words, ϕ demands that P have the same truth value as Q. We see then that the proposition ϕ isn't missing after all: it's the proposition $P \leftrightarrow Q$.

Propositions like P and Q leave open more than one possibility. The tautologies, such as $P \vee \neg P$, leave open all possibilities, and the contradictions, such as $P \wedge \neg P$, leave open no possibilities (i.e., they cannot be true). Another interesting kind of proposition are those maximally specific propositions that leave open only one possibility. In this case, there are four maximally specific propositions, represented by $P \wedge Q$, $P \wedge \neg Q$, $\neg P \wedge Q$, and $\neg P \wedge \neg Q$. In figure 5.2, a 4×4 square represents the space of all possible worlds. Each coloring of a 4×4 square represents a proposition, where the grayed-out squares are those worlds that the proposition rules out. A maximally specific, consistent proposition rules out all worlds but one.

We can also use these diagrams to understand better how the logical connectives work. For example, suppose that I assert

$$(P \wedge Q) \vee (P \wedge \neg Q).$$

The first disjunct permits only world v_1, and the second disjunct permits only world v_2. However, as I've asserted a disjunction, I've permitted either v_1 or v_2. Hence, the proposition ϕ I've asserted leaves the top row open, that is, ϕ must be equivalent to P.

If you think through all the possible ways of graying out some subset of possible worlds, you will quickly see that in one sense, there are only sixteen distinct propositions. There is one proposition that rules out all worlds and one that allows all worlds. There are four propositions that permit only one world. There are also four propositions that exclude only one world. And then there are the six propositions that permit exactly two worlds. Of course, each of these propositions can be represented by many different sentences—for example, P and $P \wedge (Q \vee \neg Q)$ represent the same proposition. But it's good to know that every sentence represents one and only one of these propositions.

Before concluding this discussion, we need to warn you about one thing. The preceding considerations might make it seem obviously true that for each possible world w, there is a maximally specific proposition that is true in w and that is false at all other worlds. While that is the case when there are only finitely many atomic sentences, it can fail if there are infinitely many—at least if your propositions are themselves finite strings of symbols. For if a sentence ϕ contains only finitely many symbols, then there might be an atomic sentence X that doesn't occur in ϕ. Then, for any world w in which ϕ is true, there will be a distinct world w' in which ϕ is also true and in which the truth value of X is flipped. Thus, for a language with infinitely many atomic sentences, there are no maximally specific propositions—that is, every proposition is consistent with many different possibilities.

In the case where there are no maximally specific propositions, the study of the collection of all possible worlds becomes more mathematically rich. In fact, there is a entire branch of mathematics—known as *topology*—that studies collections like this, with certain special subcollections (i.e., our propositions), which topologists call "neighborhoods."

Exercise 5.15.

1. Consider two arbitrary sentences that contain only the atomic sentences P and Q. Explain visually the relation between the colorings for ϕ and ψ when ϕ logically implies ψ.
2. Explain visually the relation between the colorings for ϕ and ψ when ϕ is inconsistent with ψ.

3. Use the method of coloring to show that $(P \leftrightarrow Q) \vee (P \leftrightarrow \neg Q)$ is a tautology. Try to use the same thinking to construct an efficient formal proof of the sentence.

4. Let P be any sentence that you wish or hope is true. Here's how to prove that P is true: let ϕ be the sentence "if ϕ is true, then P." Show that ϕ is true, and hence that P is true. (Obviously something fishy is going on here!)

6

Quantifying

THE FOLLOWING ARGUMENT IS INTUITIVELY VALID.

All people are mortal.
Socrates is a person.

Socrates is mortal.

However, the validity of this argument cannot be established by the methods we developed in the previous chapters. In particular, in this argument, none of the sentences is logically complex—that is, none of them is a conjunction, or a disjunction, or a conditional, or a negated sentence. Hence, the proper symbolization of this argument would be $P, Q \vdash R$. That sequent is invalid. Therefore, the methods of the previous chapters would lead you to say that the argument about Socrates is invalid. Apparently, the methods of the previous chapters get this one wrong.[1]

Here's another intuitively valid argument.

Professor Dumbledore believes in magic.

Some professors believe in magic.

---

1. For the über-critical reader: you might translate "all people are mortal" as a very long conjunction, and then the argument would show itself to be valid. We would reply to your objection by presenting an argument with a premise about all natural numbers.

Again, by the lights of propositional logic, the premise and conclusion of this argument are atomic sentences. Hence, the argument should be symbolized as $P \vdash Q$, which is invalid.

We are going to move forward with the assumption that the above arguments are valid. To see *why* they are valid, we need a deeper analysis than that provided by propositional logic. As before, the most important clue is the appearance of certain special words and phrases that connect the "content words" in the argument. In the first argument, the key connecting word is "all," as we can see by replacing the content words (person, mortal, Socrates) with letters.

All P are M.

s is P.

Therefore, s is M.

If you replace these letters with any grammatically suitable words, you'll find that the result is once again a good argument. That's a sign that we've identified a valid argument form. The next step, then, is to decide how to deal with the word "all." Our previous logic words (and, or, if…then, not) played the role of sentence connectives: they construct new sentences out of old ones. The word "all" plays a different role. Here it seems to transform two predicate phrases ("…is a person" and "…is mortal") into a sentence. It doesn't make any sense to think of "all" as combining these phrases in the same way that, say, "and" combines two sentences.

To see how "all" works, let's take a quick detour through another argument.

If Socrates is a person, then Socrates is mortal.

Socrates is a person.

Therefore, Socrates is mortal.

This argument *is* valid in respect to its propositional form—it's just an instance of modus ponens. However, propositional logic would have us use two completely different letters for "Socrates is a person" and "Socrates is mortal," thereby losing track of the fact that those two sentences have the same subject. So now let's write Ps for "Socrates is a person" and Ms for "Socrates is mortal." Then the argument would be symbolized as

$Ps \rightarrow Ms$
Ps
——————
Ms

Keeping your eye on the first premise $Ps \rightarrow Ms$, return now to the question of how to represent the logical form of "all persons are mortal." Let's remove the name Socrates and replace it with a placeholder. We'll use the letter "x" as our placeholder. Then we get "if x is a person, then x is mortal" ($Px \rightarrow Mx$), which isn't exactly a sentence but can be used to create sentences by plugging a name in for x. If we plug in s, we get the sentence $Ps \rightarrow Ms$. Now, the sentence "all P are M" says that no matter what name we plug in for x, the resulting sentence is true, that is, $Pa \rightarrow Ma$ is true, $Pb \rightarrow Mb$ is true, and so on. Thus, the first premise of our original Socrates argument can be partially symbolized as

For any x $(Px \rightarrow Mx)$

Now let's replace "For any x" with a symbol $\forall x$, yielding the following symbolization of the original argument.

$\forall x(Px \rightarrow Mx)$
Ps
——————
Ms

This argument form is valid, and we might want to add it as a basic rule. But that would be a little short-sighted, because it wouldn't capture the full logical power of the concept represented by $\forall x$. For example, the following argument form is also valid:

$$\forall x(Fx \land Gx)$$

$$\overline{\forall x Fx}$$

That is, if everything is both *F* and *G*, then everything is *F*. That's another obviously valid argument, indicating that ∀*x* occurs in many different valid argument forms. Our goal is to find the most basic valid inferences using ∀*x* and then to show that these intuitively valid arguments—and all others— can be reconstructed from those basic valid inferences.

The newly introduced symbol ∀*x* will be called the **universal quanti- fier**. We used symbol *x* as our placeholder and will call it a **variable**, but that doesn't mean that any "varying" is happening here. It's just a symbol. We will also sometimes use other letters at the end of the alphabet for vari- ables, and it will be important sometimes to have more than one variable in play. Suppose, for example, you want to represent the following intuitively valid argument:

∀*x*(*x* is divisible by *a* → *x* is divisible by *b*)
c is divisible by *a*

---

c is divisible by *b*

Here, "*x* is divisible by *y*" is a relation that holds between two things, rather than a property of a single thing. To represent "*x* is divisible by *y*," we can use a symbol such as *Dxy* that has two variables. Then we can represent the preceding argument as follows:

$$\forall x(Dxa \rightarrow Dxb)$$
$$Dca$$

$$Dcb$$

We will also need our inference rules for ∀*x* to explain why this argument is valid. But before we get to that, we need to discuss another special logical notion that plays a key role in many valid arguments.

The following argument is intuitively valid.

All Harvard graduates are hilarious.
Some Harvard graduates are felons.

Some felons are hilarious.

Here, the first premise is again a universally quantified sentence. But the second premise and the conclusion don't say that *all* things have some feature; instead, they say that *some* things have that feature. We introduce a new symbol ∃ corresponding to the phrase "There are some ..." and hence we symbolize "There are some things with feature F" as $\exists x Fx$. In the second premise, we say that there are things that are both Harvard graduates (Hx) and felons (Fx); hence, it could be symbolized as $\exists x(Hx \wedge Fx)$.

The symbol $\exists x$ is called the **existential quantifier** because it expresses that something exists. Like its universal brother, it's always used with some particular variable that connects it to the predicate or relation symbols that follow it. Read somewhat literally, $\exists x Fx$ says that "There is an x such that Fx." Similarly, $\exists x(Fx \wedge Gx)$ says that "There is an x such that Fx and Gx."

In English, we have many phrases that express that something of a certain sort exists. We can say, "There is ..." or "There are some ..." or "Something is ..." and many more like those. In specific conversational contexts, these phrases can have more specific implications—for example, they can indicate that there is more than one or that there are some things with this feature and some things without it. Consider, for example, if somebody asked your logic professor, "Do you have good students?" If he answered, "Some of them are good," then his interlocutor would reasonably conclude that, in addition, some of them are not good. That's because we are often expected to answer by making the (logically) strongest statement that we would be warranted in asserting. If, in fact, your professor believes that all his students are good, then why wouldn't he have said that?

Similarly, suppose that your professor believes that only one student in his class (of say 280 students) is good and that the rest of them are terrible. If he then says that "some of my students are good," one might justly accuse him of concealing the true situation. He could just as easily say, "Strangely,

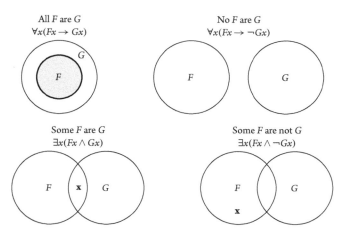

Figure 6.1. The four standard types of quantified statements.

only one of them is good." So, in that case, the phrase "some" wouldn't supply the most accurate answer to the question.

Nonetheless, in symbolic logic, the existential quantifier has no nuanced connotations. The sentence "$\exists xFx$" simply means that there is at least one F. That's consistent with there being only one F, or there being forty-two Fs, or with everything being F. If you wish that symbolic logic could be more nuanced, just remember that what it loses in nuance, it gains in clarity and rigor.

We've seen so far that we can express "there is an F" with $\exists xFx$, and we can express "some F are G" with $\exists x(Fx \land Gx)$. In a similar fashion, we can express "some F are not G" by $\exists x(Fx \land \neg Gx)$. For example, to say "some Wall Street bankers are not evil," we could write $\exists x(Wx \land \neg Ex)$. Combining the expressive power of the existential quantifier with that of the universal quantifier, we can express the four standard sentence types that you might have seen before in reference to Venn diagrams (figure 6.1).

A common mistake that many beginning logic students make is to use $\exists x(Fx \to Gx)$ for "some F are G." But a moment's thought shows that the former symbolic sentence would be a bad translation. The formula $Fx \to Gx$ can be true of an individual a for two different reasons. First, $Fa \to Ga$ would be true if Fa and Ga are true. But $Fa \to Ga$ would also be true if

Fa were false. (Just remember negative paradox, or the truth table for the conditional.) Thus, $\exists x(Fx \rightarrow Gx)$ would be true whenever something is not *F*, which fails to capture the intent to assert the existence of something that is both *F* and *G*.

Similarly, it's easy to mistakenly write $\forall x(Fx \land Gx)$ when you mean to say that "all *F* are *G*." But the sentence $\forall x(Fx \land Gx)$ is way too strong: it says that everything whatsoever is *both F and G*. Yes, it implies that all *F* are *G*, but only for the trivial reason that everything has both features.

As a general rule of thumb, if a natural language sentence is translated to a universally quantified sentence, then the formula inside the quantifier will be a conditional. In contrast, if a natural language sentence is translated to an existentially quantified sentence, then the formula inside the quantifier will be a conjunction.

Exercise 6.1. Represent the form of the following sentences in predicate logic. We've suggested appropriate symbols. (For the sentences about people, you don't need to add an extra predicate for "*x* is a person.")

1. No logicians are celebrities. (Lx, Cx)
2. Some celebrities are not logicians. (Lx, Cx)
3. Only students who do the homework will learn logic. (Sx, Hx, Lx)
4. All rich logicians are computer scientists. (Rx, Lx, Cx)
5. All students and professors get a discount. (Sx, Px, Dx)
6. No logician is rich, unless she is a computer scientist. (Lx, Rx, Cx)
7. Not all logicians are computer scientists. (Lx, Cx)
8. Some logicians are rich computer scientists. (Lx, Rx, Cx)
9. If there are rich logicians, then some logicians are computer scientists. (Rx, Lx, Cx)
10. No pets except service animals are permitted in dorms. (Px, Sx, Dx)
11. If anyone is rich, then Mary is. (Rx, m)

When you're symbolizing sentences, there will occasionally be cases where there seem to be two (or more) possible correct answers. Consider, for example, the sentence "There are no friendly cats." If we use *Fx* for "*x* is friendly" and *Cx* for "*x* is a cat," then any one of the following is a plausible representation of this sentence:

$$\neg\exists x(Fx \wedge Cx) \qquad \forall x(Fx \rightarrow \neg Cx) \qquad \forall x(Cx \rightarrow \neg Fx)$$

The first sentence says that it's false that there is a friendly cat. The second sentence says that every friendly thing is not a cat. The third sentence says that every cat is not friendly. In English, these three statements have slightly different connotations, and yet they would be true in precisely the same circumstance, namely, the circumstance when the class of friendly things does not include any cats. Not long from now, you'll be able to prove that these three sentences are in fact logically equivalent.

There are other cases where a natural language sentence is simply ambiguous between two different ways that we might construe it in symbolic language. Consider, for example, the following sentence:[2]

> Every boy loves a certain girl.

Translating this sentence might seem straightforward. First, the sentence says that every boy has a certain property, hence $\forall x(Bx \rightarrow \phi(x))$, where $\phi(x)$ expresses "x loves a certain girl." For the latter, we could write $\phi(x) \equiv \exists y(Gy \wedge Lxy)$, which says that "there is a girl whom x loves." The final answer then would be

$$\forall x(Bx \rightarrow \exists y Lxy).$$

However, there's another way to interpret this sentence: it might mean that there is some one girl who is loved by every boy. In that case, we want to approach the sentence the other way around, that is, we write $\exists y(Gy \wedge \psi(y))$, where $\psi(y)$ expresses "every boy loves y." Thus, $\psi(y) \equiv \forall x(Bx \rightarrow Lxy)$, and the final answer is

$$\exists y(Gy \wedge \forall x(Bx \rightarrow Lxy)).$$

Unlike the previous example where the different translations were equivalent, these two symbolic sentences are inequivalent—they represent

2. This example was concocted by the logician Peter Geach (1916–2013).

genuine ambiguity in the initial English sentence. In particular, it's possible for the first sentence to be true while the second sentence is false.[3]

The preceding considerations show that, in general, it makes a difference which order you write quantifiers. In fact, a famous philosophical debate turns precisely on this point. Among the many attempts to prove God's existence, the so-called cosmological argument begins from the premise that every event has a cause. It then concludes that there must be a first cause (which, the arguer suggests, we can call "God"). If we were to try to capture the argument in symbolic logic, then we might write the premise as $\forall x \exists y Ryx$, where Ryx means that "y causes x." In that case, the conclusion would be represented as $\exists y \forall x Ryx$. However, the philosopher Bertrand Russell pointed out that the inference $\forall x \exists y Ryx \vdash \exists y \forall x Ryx$ is *not* valid.[4] Indeed, if it were valid, then it would remain so no matter how we interpreted the symbol Ryx. But if we interpret Ryx to mean that "y is the mother of x," then the premise is true of mammals, whereas the conclusion is most definitely not true of mammals.

Exercise 6.2. Represent the form of the following sentences in predicate logic. We've suggested appropriate symbols. (For the sentences about people, you don't need to add an extra predicate for "x is a person.")

1. Mary loves everyone who loves her. (m, Lxy)
2. Mary loves all and only those people who don't love themselves. (Lxy, m)
3. Everyone loves their mother. (Lxy, Mxy)
4. Some people love only those people who love their mother. (Lxy, Mxy)
5. Snape killed someone. (Kxy, s)
6. Snape is a killer. (Kxy, s)

---

3. While it's intuitively clear that the first sentence does not imply the second, you'll first learn to prove that in chapter 8.

4. The Russell-Copleston debate of 1948. An audio recording of the debate can be found on the internet.

7. Someone was killed by Snape. (Kxy, s)
8. Some wizards only marry other wizards. (Wx, Mxy)
9. There is no greatest number. ($Nx, x < y$)
10. c is the least upper bound of a and b. ($a, b, c, x \leq y$)
11. c is the greatest common divisor of a and b. ($a, b, c, Dxy, x \leq y$)

Universal Elimination

We gave a big hint above about the meaning of $\forall x$. We said that somebody who accepts $\forall x \phi(x)$ would be willing to grant that $\phi(a)$, no matter what a names. If that's right, then the first and most obvious inference rule for quantified statements should look like this:

From $\forall x \phi(x)$, it's permitted to infer $\phi(a)$, for any name a.

This rule will be called **universal elimination** (UE) since it permits us to infer something from a universally quantified sentence. Here, we used the notation $\phi(x)$ to stand for any formula that contains the variable x. For example, $\phi(x)$ could be $Px \rightarrow Mx$, or it could be $Px \rightarrow Ms$, or it could be Rx.

The UE rule can be applied to prove Ms from the conjunction of $\forall x(Px \rightarrow Mx)$ and Ps.

1	(1)	$\forall x(Px \rightarrow Mx)$	A
2	(2)	Ps	A
1	(3)	$Ps \rightarrow Ms$	1 UE
1, 2	(4)	Ms	3,2 MP

Universal elimination (UE) is one of those simple rules of inference where we carry down the dependency numbers of the sentence we use. In the above argument, we apply UE to line 1, which depends only on itself. Thus, the resulting line (i.e., line 3), also depends on just line 1.

Here's the precise formulation of the UE rule.

Universal Elimination (UE)

From a universal sentence, you can infer any instance.

Schematically: $\dfrac{\Gamma \vdash \forall x\phi(x)}{\Gamma \vdash \phi(a)}$

Exercise 6.3. Prove the following sequents.

1. $\forall xFx, \forall xGx \vdash Fa \wedge Ga$
2. $\forall x\neg Fx \vdash Fa \rightarrow P$
3. $\forall x(Fx \rightarrow Gx), \neg Ga \vdash \neg Fa$
4. $\forall x(Fx \rightarrow Gx), \neg Ga \vdash \neg\forall xFx$
5. $\forall x\neg Fx \vdash \neg\forall xFx$
6. $\vdash \neg\forall x(Fx \wedge \neg Fx)$

Exercise 6.4. Do the sentences $\forall x(Fx \rightarrow Gx)$ and $\forall x(Fx \rightarrow \neg Gx)$ seem consistent to you?

Universal Introduction

The UE rule won't do much for you on its own. For example, if you're trying to infer $\forall xFx$ from $\forall x(Fx \wedge Gx)$, UE can take you down to $Fa \wedge Ga$, but it can't get you back up to $\forall xFx$. Indeed, to infer a universal sentence from any particular instance is the worst kind of mistake. For example, you cannot conclude that all professors believe in magic from the fact that Professor Dumbledore believes in magic. Thus, in order to get the most out of the UE rule, it needs to be supplemented with a universal introduction rule.

Recall that conditional proof isn't just a rule; it's a strategy for thinking. In short, if you want to prove a conditional, then your first move is to assume the antecedent, which you can use in reasoning toward the consequent. Now, universal introduction (UI) will be like conditional proof in this regard. Only now we have to think about how we come to be convinced of the truth of universal statements.

It is really quite amazing that human beings can ever come to know that a universal statement is true. We are limited in space and time, and none of us will ever be able to survey all possible instances of any generalization. So what could permit us—who can only observe a small finite number of instances—to conclude that something is always true?

The answer is similar to the one we gave for conditional statements. To reason to a conditional statement, we engage in the mental activity of *supposing*, an activity that is not itself aimed at telling the truth. When I say "suppose that *P*," I am not making a claim about what is the case; instead, I'm abstracting away from reality so that I can explore logical connections. When it comes to establishing universal claims, we engage in an even more radical version of abstraction. In essence, we suppose that we can talk about things in general, without talking about any particular thing.

Consider the following dialogue where A and B agree that all Bavarians are German, and all Germans are European, and A is trying to convince B that all Bavarians are European.

A: Suppose that Gretel is some random Bavarian.

B: So the random Bavarian is female?

A: No, I didn't mean that at all. I just meant to choose a Bavarian-sounding name. If I had chosen "Hansel," you might have asked me if the random Bavarian is male.

B: Why don't you just use a letter then?

A: OK, suppose that *X* is some random Bavarian. You agree with me then that *X* is German, right?

B: Yes, certainly.

A: And since all Germans are European, *X* is European.

B: Agreed.

A: Since *X* was an arbitrary Bavarian, it follows that every Bavarian is European.

It's this last step where all the action happens. The letter *X* plays the role of name, but we don't know anything about who it names—except that he or she is Bavarian. So, when we deduce that *X* is European, that licenses us to conclude that *all* Bavarians are Europeans.

We have to beware of a danger here. In the above dialogue, the two parties chose the letter X because there was little danger that the letter would carry connotations that would derail their reasoning process. But there are no guarantees. What if B were obtuse, like this.

> B: Since the arbitrary Bavarian's name is "X," it follows that no Bavarians have the name "Gretel."

Obviously, something has gone very wrong with B's thinking about these issues. Essentially, B forgot that the whole point of choosing a letter "X" was so that nobody would assume they know anything about X. But that's exactly what B has done; she has assumed that X has the feature that its name is "X." She has missed the point completely.

In real-life reasoning, people have common sense to prevent them from making such mistakes. But the goal of formal logic is to make explicit the rules that common sense suggests. We want to forbid this kind of mistake by means of an explicit rule, and here's how we'll do it.

To use an analogy, suppose that the argument or dialogue takes place in a closed room. And suppose that when the two parties enter the room, they each have to declare their assumptions. Once the dialogue begins, they can use those assumptions that they declared upon entering the room. When it comes to reasoning about universal claims, we'll give both parties a stock of new names $a, b, c, \ldots$ that do *not* occur anywhere in their declared assumptions. They may then use these names at any point in their argument. For example, they may use UE to infer $\phi(a)$ from $\forall x \phi(x)$.

With these new regulations in place, we can prevent the parties from making silly mistakes in deducing universal sentences. In short, one may infer a universal sentence $\forall x \phi(x)$ from an instance $\phi(a)$ that contains one of the new names we supplied. Since the two parties didn't bring in any information about a, the only information they can have about a is what they have deduced from universal statements.

Hopefully the analogy helps your intuition. But you won't need the intuition to follow the universal introduction rule, which provides a simple (machine checkable!) syntactic recipe. In short, UI allows you to infer $\Gamma \vdash \forall x \phi(x)$ from $\Gamma \vdash \phi(a)$ whenever there is no information about a in the background assumptions Γ or hidden in the formula $\phi(x)$.

Universal Introduction (UI)

$$\frac{\Gamma \vdash \phi(a)}{\Gamma \vdash \forall x \phi(x)}$$ restriction: a does not occur in Γ or $\phi(x)$.

In general, universally quantified premises can be used together to draw universally quantified conclusions. The strategy is often as simple as applying UE repeatedly to the premises, making sure to use the same name in each case. Then one uses the rules of propositional logic to transform those instances to an instance of the conclusion. Finally, one applies UI to infer the conclusion from that instance.

To prove: $\forall x(Fx \to Gx), \forall x(Gx \to Hx) \vdash \forall x(Fx \to Hx)$

1	(1)	$\forall x(Fx \to Gx)$	A
2	(2)	$\forall x(Gx \to Hx)$	A
3	(3)	Fa	A
1	(4)	$Fa \to Ga$	1 UE
2	(5)	$Ga \to Ha$	2 UE
1, 3	(6)	Ga	4,3 MP
1, 2, 3	(7)	Ha	5,6 MP
1, 2	(8)	$Fa \to Ha$	3,7 CP
1, 2	(9)	$\forall x(Fx \to Hx)$	8 UI

Looking at the conclusion, we realized that we need to show that an arbitrary F is also an H. That is, we need to show that $Fa \to Ha$, depending on no assumptions that mention a. So then on line 3, we suppose that a is an arbitrary F. (There is nothing in line 3 that says "is an arbitrary," but that effect is ensured by choosing a name a that hasn't yet occurred in the proof.) Then we proceed to use the universal premises to infer that a is also an H.

The restriction on the name a corresponds to the idea that a fully general statement cannot be inferred from specific assumptions. To see why we prohibit a from occurring in $\phi(x)$, consider the following attempt to prove $\forall x Rxa$ from $\forall x Rxx$.

1	(1)	$\forall x Rxx$	A	
1	(2)	Raa	1 UE	
1	(3)	$\forall x Rxa$	2 UI	$\Longleftarrow$ incorrect

This argument cannot possibly be valid. Suppose that Rxy is the relation "x has the same net worth as y" and that a is a name for Jeff Bezos. The premise is then obviously true: everybody has the same net worth as themselves. But the conclusion says that everyone has the same net worth as Jeff Bezos, which is as far from the truth as possible. The problem here is line 3, since the formula $\phi(x)$ is Rxa, which contains the name a. In practice, you can ensure that you don't violate this restriction on UI if you follow this rule of thumb: when generalizing $\phi(a)$ to $\forall x \phi(x)$, change all occurrences of a to x. In the case at hand, that would have forced us to generalize Raa to $\forall x Rxx$, which is just what we started with.

The UI rule can be used with any variable. For example, $\phi(a)$ can be quantified to $\forall x \phi(x)$ or $\forall y \phi(y)$ or $\forall z \phi(z)$. You only need to make sure not to get yourself confused by using a variable that already occurs in $\phi(a)$. So, for example, you wouldn't infer $\forall x \forall x Rxx$ from $\forall x Rax$, because the former string of symbols doesn't make sense as a formula.

Using the freedom to apply UI with any variable, it follows that universal statements $\forall x Fx$ and $\forall y Fy$ are equivalent.

1	(1)	$\forall x Fx$	A
1	(2)	Fa	1 UE
1	(3)	$\forall y Fy$	2 UI

The converse proof follows by symmetry, hence $\forall x Fx \dashv\vdash \forall y Fy$. These equivalences—where one variable is switched throughout for another—are known as α-equivalences, and they can be really useful when dealing with sentences that contain more than one variable. For example, by α-equivalence, $\forall x Fx \rightarrow \forall y Fy$ is a tautology, and we'll soon see that

$\forall xFx \rightarrow P$ implies $\exists x(Fx \rightarrow P)$. Thus, substituting $\forall yFy$ for P shows that $\exists x(Fx \rightarrow \forall yFy)$ is a tautology.

Exercise 6.5. Prove the following sequents.

1. $\forall x(Fx \rightarrow Gx) \vdash \forall xFx \rightarrow \forall xGx$
2. $\forall x(Fx \rightarrow Gx) \vdash \forall x\neg Gx \rightarrow \forall x\neg Fx$
3. $\forall xFx \wedge \forall xGx \dashv\vdash \forall x(Fx \wedge Gx)$
4. $\forall xFx \vee \forall xGx \vdash \forall x(Fx \vee Gx)$
5. $\neg Fa \vdash \neg\forall xFx$
6. $\forall x\neg Fx \vdash \forall x(Fx \rightarrow Gx)$
7. $P \vdash \forall x(Fx \rightarrow P)$, where P is any sentence that doesn't contain the variable x.
8. $P \rightarrow \forall xFx \dashv\vdash \forall x(P \rightarrow Fx)$
9. $\forall x\forall yRxy \vdash \forall xRxx$
10. $\forall x\forall yRxy \vdash \forall y\forall xRxy$

Exercise 6.6. What's wrong with the following attempted proof?

1	(1)	Fa	A
	(2)	$Fa \rightarrow Fa$	1,1 CP
	(3)	$\forall x(Fa \rightarrow Fx)$	2 UI
	(4)	$Fa \rightarrow Fb$	3 UE

Exercise 6.7. Start to try to write a proof of

$$\forall x(Fx \vee Gx) \vdash \forall xFx \vee \forall xGx,$$

and explain where the restriction on UI prevents you from continuing.

Existential Introduction

It's not too uncommon that we know that there is something or other with a certain feature, but we don't know who or what it is that has that feature. For example, we know that somebody murdered eleven women in London in the years 1888 to 1891, but as of today, the identity of the murderer is still unknown.

We can also use such knowledge to infer other things, although we have to be careful when using knowledge that "something is ϕ" without knowing who or what it is that is ϕ. For example, if you know that something is ϕ, and you know that all ϕ are ψ, then you also know that something is ψ. In contrast, you might know that something is ϕ and that something is ψ, but those two facts do *not* entitle you to conclude that something is both ϕ and ψ.

What, then, is the logic of "something is ϕ"? As with our other key logical notions, we are looking here for typical inferences to such statements (an introduction rule) and typical inferences from such statements (an elimination rule).

Let's look first for an existential intro rule—that is, a paradigmatic inference to a statement of the form "something is ϕ." In real life, our reasons for believing existential statements are frequently not *guaranteeing* reasons, in the sense that the existential statement is a logical consequence of what we know. For example, in the Jack the Ripper case, the reason that I believe that somebody killed eleven women is because I read or heard about it on TV. But of course, the documentary evidence doesn't guarantee—in a logical sense—that the event actually happened. So this kind of evidence is not what we're looking for in a deductively valid rule of existential introduction.

However, there was at least one person who had guaranteeing evidence for the claim that someone killed eleven women. In particular, Jack the Ripper—if he existed—knew that "I killed eleven women," and so he would have been entitled to infer that "somebody killed eleven women." There is *no way* that the premise could be true and the conclusion false, indicating the presence of a valid argument form. Thus, Jack the Ripper's valid inference could be represented as follows:

$$\frac{\phi(a)}{\exists x \phi(x)}.$$

Here a is Jack's name for himself, and $\phi(x)$ represents "x murdered eleven women." Thus, the inference goes from "I murdered eleven women" to "somebody murdered eleven women." We'll take this inference to be the paradigm way that an existential statement can be inferred from another statement.

Existential Introduction (EI)

If an instance $\phi(a)$ of $\exists x \phi(x)$ follows from Γ, then $\exists x \phi(x)$ follows from Γ. Schematically: $\dfrac{\Gamma \vdash \phi(a)}{\Gamma \vdash \exists x \phi(x)}$

Here, $\phi(x)$ is a formula in which the variable x occurs, and $\phi(a)$ is the formula that is obtained by replacing all the instances of x in $\phi(x)$ with a. However, there is no requirement that a does *not* occur in $\phi(x)$. For example, it's perfectly legitimate to infer that somebody killed Ernest Hemingway from the fact that Ernest Hemingway committed suicide. That is, $\exists x Kxa$ can be inferred, by existential intro, from Kaa.

Like disjunction intro, existential intro actually throws away information—and so it's dangerous to use it without knowing where you want to go. Remember that disjunction intro is most useful in cases where you want to show that two different premises have the same conclusion. We'll soon see that the same sort of intuition applies to existential intro, that is, it's most effective in the search for a common conclusion from several different premises.

Nonetheless, there are some cases where EI by itself is useful. In the following, we show that a negated existential sentence implies a universal sentence.

To prove: $\neg \exists x Fx \vdash \forall x \neg Fx$

1	(1)	$\neg \exists x Fx$	A
2	(2)	Fa	A
2	(3)	$\exists x Fx$	2 EI
1, 2	(4)	$\exists x Fx \wedge \neg \exists x Fx$	3,1 $\wedge$ I
1	(5)	$\neg Fa$	2,4 RAA
1	(6)	$\forall x \neg Fx$	5 UI

(Note that since line 5 depends only on line 1, and line 1 does not contain *a*, the invocation of UI on line 6 is legitimate.) Here, our strategy is not completely straightforward. The premise $\neg\exists xFx$ is not in itself useful: it's a negated sentence, and none of our rules will let us do something with a single negated sentence. We then have to work our way backward from the conclusion, which is $\forall x\neg Fx$. Since it's a universal sentence, it would suffice to obtain an instance $\neg Fa$, so long as that instance doesn't depend on any assumptions about *a*. In frustration, one might decide (as we did) to try to obtain $\neg Fa$ by reductio ad absurdum. Indeed, as soon as we assumed *Fa*, it was obvious that it conflicts with the premise on line 1.

Notice that if we run through the preceding proof, replacing *Fx* with $\neg Fx$, then line 5 would become $\neg\neg Fa$. We can then perform a step of DN elimination to get *Fa* and then $\forall xFx$. Thus, we also have a proof of the sequent $\neg\exists x\neg Fx \vdash \forall xFx$.

Exercise 6.8. Prove the following sequents.

    1. $\neg\exists x(Fx \wedge Gx) \vdash \forall x(Fx \to \neg Gx)$
    2. $\forall xFx \vdash \exists xFx$
    3. $\forall x(Fx \to Gx), Fa \vdash \exists xGx$
    4. $\neg Fa \vdash \exists x(Fx \to P)$
    5. $\neg\forall xFx \vdash \exists x(Fx \to P)$
    6. $\neg\exists xFx \vdash \forall x(Fx \to Gx)$
    7. $\forall x\forall yRxy \vdash \exists xRxx$
    8. $P \to Fa \vdash P \to \exists xFx$
    9. $\exists xFx \to P \dashv\vdash \forall x(Fx \to P)$
   10. $\neg\exists xFx \vdash \forall x(Fx \to P)$
   11. $\neg\exists x(Fx \to P) \vdash \forall xFx \wedge \neg P$
 *12. $\forall xFx \to P \vdash \exists x(Fx \to P)$

Existential Elimination

The real power of existential intro comes when it's combined with an existential elimination rule. But let's slow down, because existential elimination is the most conceptually challenging rule in this book.

To understand the conceptual challenge of existential elimination, let's first note what the rule could *not* be. The following inference is definitely invalid.

$$\frac{\exists x \phi(x)}{\phi(a)}.$$

For example, from the fact that somebody killed eleven women, you cannot validly conclude that Lewis Carroll killed eleven women.

If you think about it, it's hard to see how one could derive anything of interest from an existentially quantified statement. The problem is that $\exists x \phi(x)$ just doesn't tell you which thing is ϕ. So, how can you *use* that statement when it is so unspecific? Well, the strategy here will be quite similar to the strategy we used for UI. The sentence $\exists x \phi(x)$ doesn't tell us that Richard or Connie or Albert is ϕ, but it tells us that something is ϕ. So, you could then grab a new name a off the shelf and use it for this ϕ. Then, you can explore logical space, seeing what conclusions you can reach—without assuming any further knowledge about the identity of a. The idea, then, is that whatever conclusion ψ you reach, as long as it doesn't mention a, follows from $\exists x \phi(x)$.

For example, let's take it as given that somebody killed eleven women in London between 1888 and 1891. We can call this person "Jack the Ripper," or a for short, and then we could start drawing conclusions by means of standard logical reasoning. We could infer that a was a serial killer in London in the late 1800s and hence, by existential intro, that there was a serial killer in London in the late 1800s. Since that conclusion doesn't beg any questions about the identity of the person, we have reliably deduced that there was a serial killer in London in the late 1800s.

That's how existential elimination will work. In this case, let's use the rule before properly explaining it. We will derive $\exists x Fx$ from the premise $\exists x (Fx \wedge Gx)$.

1	(1)	$\exists x(Fx \wedge Gx)$	A
2	(2)	$Fa \wedge Ga$	A
2	(3)	Fa	2 $\wedge$E
2	(4)	$\exists x Fx$	3 EI
1	(5)	$\exists x Fx$	1,2,4 EE

The first four lines use rules that you've seen before, but the second line isn't deduced from the first; it's a new assumption. You might want to gloss line 2 as saying "let *a* be a name for one of these things that is *F* and *G*." Line 5 is where all the action happens. Line 4 shows that $Fa \wedge Ga \vdash \exists x Fx$, and that conclusion would have followed no matter what name *a* we had chosen on line 2. Thus, $\exists x Fx$ follows simply from the fact that *something* is *F* and *G*, which is what allows us to replace the dependency on 2 with dependency on 1 in line 5. Here, our EI rule cites three lines: line 1 where the existential sentence occurs, line 2 where an instance of that sentence occurs, and line 4 where we've drawn a conclusion from that instance. The second two lines mark off a subproof, namely, the derivation of $\exists x Fx$ from $Fa \wedge Ga$. So, while EE officially cites three lines, it's best to think of EE as citing one line (with an existential sentence) and then a subproof that begins with an assumption (of an instance of the existential) and that ends with the desired conclusion.

Now we're ready for a fully precise description of the EE rule, along with all of its restrictions.

Existential Elimination (EE)

If an instance $\phi(a)$ of $\exists \phi(x)$ implies ψ, and the name *a* does not occur in ψ, then $\exists x \phi(x)$ implies ψ. More precisely,

$$\frac{\Gamma \vdash \exists x \phi(x) \qquad \Delta, \phi(a) \vdash \psi}{\Gamma, \Delta \vdash \psi}$$

restriction: *a* does not occur in $\Gamma, \Delta, \phi(x)$, or ψ.

In this picture, we have three things:

1. A derivation of $\exists x \phi(x)$ from some premises Γ. That corresponds to a line in a proof on which an existential sentence occurs, with dependencies Γ.
2. A derivation of ψ from an instance $\phi(a)$, plus possibly some auxiliary assumptions Δ. These auxiliary assumptions cannot say anything

about *a*. In a proof, this derivation begins with an assumption of $\phi(a)$ and ends on a line with ψ that depends on nothing but Δ and $\phi(a)$.

3. When the first two things are in place, we are permitted to infer ψ by EE, where the dependencies are the union of Γ and Δ.

Here's a simple example of all the different bits in play.

To prove: $\forall x(Fx \rightarrow Gx), \exists xFx \vdash \exists xGx$

1	(1)	$\forall x(Fx \rightarrow Gx)$	A
2	(2)	$\exists xFx$	A
3	(3)	Fa	A
1	(4)	$Fa \rightarrow Ga$	1 UE
1, 3	(5)	Ga	4,3 MP
1, 3	(6)	$\exists xGx$	5 EI
1, 2	(7)	$\exists xGx$	2,3,6 EE

Here, our Γ is simply $\exists xFx$ itself, and the first part of the EE is just line 2 (i.e., the derivation of $\exists xFx$ from itself). The second part of the EE is the subproof that begins on line 3 (the assumption of the instance Fa) and that ends on line 6 (the conclusion $\exists xGx$). This subproof shows $\forall x(Fx \rightarrow Gx), Fa \vdash \exists xGx$, that is, our auxiliary assumption Δ is simply $\forall x(Fx \rightarrow Gx)$. All the restrictions on EE are respected, and so line 7 is correct.

The legalistic restrictions on EE might seem hard to remember, but they all flow from the same idea that an existential sentence $\exists x\phi(x)$ doesn't give any information about who or what is ϕ. Of course, it would be blatantly invalid to argue from an existential claim $\exists xFx$ to the claim that Fa.

1	(1)	$\exists xFx$	A	
2	(2)	Fa	A	
1	(3)	Fa	1,2 EE	$\Longleftarrow$ incorrect

Here, the application of EE on line 3 violates the restriction that the name *a* may not appear in the conclusion of the subproof.

In practice, the best way not to run afoul of the restrictions on EE is to choose a completely new name *a* for the assumed instance $\phi(a)$ and then not to make any further assumptions about *a*. The *only* fact that you should use about *a* is that it is one of the things that makes $\exists x \phi(x)$ true. Consider, for example, what would happen if we tried to derive $\exists x(Fx \wedge Gx)$ from $\exists xFx$ and $\exists xGx$.

1	(1)	$\exists xFx$	A	
2	(2)	$\exists xGx$	A	
3	(3)	Fa	A	
4	(4)	Ga	A	$\Longleftarrow$ bad idea
3, 4	(5)	$Fa \wedge Ga$	3,4 $\wedge$ I	
3, 4	(6)	$\exists x(Fx \wedge Gx)$	5 EI	

If we tried to perform EE on lines 1, 3, and 6, we would have the following setup:

$$\frac{\exists xFx \vdash \exists xFx \qquad Ga, Fa \vdash \exists x(Fx \wedge Gx)}{\exists xFx, Ga \vdash \exists x(Fx \wedge Gx)}.$$

The problem here is that the auxiliary assumption Δ is Ga, which mentions something specific about *a*. That's not allowed, so lines 1, 3, and 6 cannot be used for EE.

The problem with the preceding argument is clear if you just use some common sense. Suppose that you know someone who loves logic and someone else who hates logic. Then it would be a bad idea to say "suppose that *a* loves logic" and, in the next breath, "suppose that *a* hates logic." There's nothing logically illegal with making both suppositions—logic places no restrictions on supposing things—but the logic police won't let you use these suppositions together to infer something from an existential premise.

In Exercise 6.5, you showed that the universal quantifier commutes with conjunction, that is,

$$\forall x(Fx \wedge Gx) \dashv\vdash \forall xFx \wedge \forall xGx.$$

While the existential quantifier doesn't commute with conjunction, it commutes with disjunction. We prove one direction here and leave the other to the exercises.

To prove: $\exists x(Fx \lor Gx) \vdash \exists xFx \lor \exists xGx$

1	(1)	$\exists x(Fx \lor Gx)$	A
2	(2)	$Fa \lor Ga$	A
3	(3)	Fa	A
3	(4)	$\exists xFx$	3 EI
3	(5)	$\exists xFx \lor \exists xGx$	4 $\lor$ I
6	(6)	Ga	A
6	(7)	$\exists xGx$	6 EI
6	(8)	$\exists xFx \lor \exists xGx$	7 $\lor$ I
2	(9)	$\exists xFx \lor \exists xGx$	2,3,5,6,8 $\lor$ E
1	(10)	$\exists xFx \lor \exists xGx$	1,2,9 EE

It may seem strange that the sentence $\phi \equiv \exists xFx \lor \exists xGx$ occurs four times in this proof. However, in each case, it occurs with different dependencies, and so it says something different. The first instance, on line 5, says that ϕ follows from Fa. The second instance, on line 8, says that ϕ follows from Ga. Those two subderivations show that ϕ follows from the disjunction $Fa \lor Ga$, and since the name a was arbitrary, ϕ follows from the existential sentence $\exists x(Fx \lor Gx)$.

Some applications of existential elimination are a bit more subtle. Consider, for example, the following derivation of $\neg \forall xFx$ from $\exists x \neg Fx$. If you ignored the conclusion and tried to extract some information from the premise, you wouldn't get very far. Being an existential sentence, the premise is weak. However, since the conclusion is a negated sentence $\neg \phi$, it makes sense to assume ϕ and to try for reductio ad absurdum. That's what we've done here.

To prove: $\exists x \neg Fx \vdash \neg \forall xFx$

1	(1)	$\exists x \neg Fx$	A
2	(2)	$\forall xFx$	A
3	(3)	$\neg Fa$	A
2	(4)	Fa	2 UE
2,3	(5)	$Fa \land \neg Fa$	4,3 $\land$ I
3	(6)	$\neg \forall xFx$	2,5 RAA
1	(7)	$\neg \forall xFx$	1,3,6 EE

Once we assume "everything is *F*," it's clear that it contradicts "something is not *F*." It's just a matter of thinking how explicitly to demonstrate their incompatibility. The only way we'll be able to show their incompatibility is by choosing a name *a* for an arbitrary ¬*F* and then using ∀*xFx* to infer that *Fa*. That's a contradiction (*Fa* ∧ ¬*Fa*), but this contradiction doesn't follow from premises 1 and 2, because it depends on the assumption of *Fa*. So then we use the fact that a contradiction can be leveraged to derive the negation of any assumption, in particular, the assumption we made on line 2. Since the negation of that assumption doesn't contain *a*, we can finish by a step of EE.

The definitions of the EI and EE rules have been fine-tuned so that we can prove the arguments that are intuitively valid and cannot prove those that are intuitively invalid.

To prove: ∃*xRxx* ⊢ ∃*x*∃*yRxy*

1	(1)	∃*xRxx*	A
2	(2)	*Raa*	A
2	(3)	∃*yRay*	2 EI
2	(4)	∃*x*∃*yRxy*	3 EI
1	(5)	∃*x*∃*yRxy*	1,2,4 EE

(To see that this argument is intuitively valid, remember that ∃*x*∃*y* doesn't say that there are two *distinct* things.) In contrast, suppose that we tried to prove ∃*x*∃*yRxy* ⊢ ∃*xRxx*, which is intuitively invalid. The following might be the first few steps of our attempted proof.

1	(1)	∃*x*∃*yRxy*	A
2	(2)	∃*yRay*	A
3	(3)	*Raa*	A
3	(4)	∃*xRxx*	3 EI

But now we are stuck. We cannot apply EE to lines 2, 3, and 4 because the arbitrary name "*a*" already occurs in the sentence on line 2.

Exercise 6.9. Explain what's wrong with the following attempted proof.

1	(1)	$\forall x \exists y Rxy$	A
1	(2)	$\exists y Ray$	1 UE
3	(3)	Raa	A
3	(4)	$\exists x Rxx$	3 EI
1	(5)	$\exists x Rxx$	2,3,4 EE

Exercise 6.10. Which line of the following attempted proof is wrong and why?

1	(1)	$Fa \wedge Gb$	A
1	(2)	Gb	1 &E
1	(3)	$\exists x Gx$	2 EI
4	(4)	Ga	A
1	(5)	Fa	1 &E
1, 4	(6)	$Fa \wedge Ga$	5,4 &I
1, 4	(7)	$\exists x(Fx \wedge Gx)$	6 EI
1	(8)	$\exists x(Fx \wedge Gx)$	3,4,7 EE

Exercise 6.11. Prove the following sequents.

1. $\exists x Fx \vee \exists x Gx \vdash \exists x(Fx \vee Gx)$
2. $\forall x(Fx \to Gx), \neg\exists x Gx \vdash \neg\exists x Fx$
3. $\forall x(Fx \to Gx) \vdash \exists x\neg Gx \to \exists x\neg Fx$
4. $\forall x(Fx \to P) \vdash \exists x Fx \to P$
5. $P \wedge \exists x Fx \vdash \exists x(P \wedge Fx)$
6. $\exists x(Fx \to P) \vdash \forall x Fx \to P$
7. $\exists x(P \to Fx) \vdash P \to \exists x Fx$
8. $\exists x \forall y Rxy \vdash \forall y \exists x Rxy$
9. $\exists x \forall y Rxy \vdash \exists x Rxx$

Chapter Six

Relations between Quantifiers and
Boolean Connectives

In this section, we undertake a more systematic exploration of how the quantifiers interact with the Boolean connectives. Some of the most useful sequents show how quantifiers interact with negation. In particular, any negated quantified sentence is provably equivalent to the sentence that begins with the other quantifier and is followed by a negation symbol. It might help you to think of a dynamic analogy: if you move a negation sign across a quantifier, it changes to the other quantifier.

$$\neg\exists x\phi \quad \dashv\vdash \quad \forall x\neg\phi \qquad \neg\forall x\phi \quad \dashv\vdash \quad \exists x\neg\phi$$

We call these four sequents the **qn**. We already proved $\neg\exists x\phi \vdash \forall x\neg\phi$ on page 101 and $\exists x\neg\phi \vdash \neg\forall x\phi$ on page 107. We now sketch a proof of $\neg\forall x\phi \vdash \exists x\neg\phi$.

$\neg\exists x\phi$	$\vdash$	$\forall x\neg\phi$	already proven
$\neg\exists x\neg\phi$	$\vdash$	$\forall x\phi$	substitute $\neg\phi$ for ϕ, DN
$\neg\forall x\phi$	$\vdash$	$\neg\neg\exists x\neg\phi$	contraposition
$\neg\forall x\phi$	$\vdash$	$\exists x\neg\phi$	DN

Exercise 6.12. Sketch a proof that $\forall x\neg\phi \vdash \neg\exists x\phi$.

We also established the following equivalences:

$$\forall x(\phi \wedge \psi) \quad \dashv\vdash \quad \forall x\phi \wedge \forall x\,\psi$$
$$\exists x(\phi \vee \psi) \quad \dashv\vdash \quad \exists x\phi \vee \exists x\,\psi$$

Just remember: universal commutes with conjunction, and existential commutes with disjunction. In contrast, there are no such equivalences for the $\rightarrow$ connective. First of all, $\forall xFx \rightarrow \forall xGx$ does not imply $\forall x(Fx \rightarrow Gx)$. You'll be able to *prove* that this implication doesn't hold after chapter 8, but for now, here's an intuitive counterexample: let Fx be "x has net worth over \$100M," and let Gx be "x lives in a society without poverty." It's true that if everyone has net worth over \$100M, then everyone lives in a society without poverty, but it's false that everyone who has net worth over \$100M lives in a society without poverty. (By the lights of formal logic, the truth of the first sentence is guaranteed by the falsity of its antecedent.)

The implication from $\exists x(Fx \rightarrow Gx)$ to $\exists xFx \rightarrow \exists xGx$ fails for a similar reason. In particular, imagine that Fx is a property that some things have and some other things don't, and imagine that Gx is a property that nothing has. Then there could be some thing that is not F, but such that *if* it were F, then it would be G. For example, suppose that Fx is the property of winning the 2018 soccer World Cup and that Gx is the property of having won six soccer World Cups. Then it's true that if Brazil had won the 2018 World Cup, then Brazil would have won six World Cups. Hence, $\exists x(Fx \rightarrow Gx)$ is true. It's also true that $\exists xFx$, that is, somebody won the 2018 World Cup. But it's false that $\exists xGx$, that is, that some country has won six World Cups.

There are further equivalences in cases when one of the two formulas does *not* contain the variable that appears in the quantifier. We've seen many of these equivalences in previous sections and exercises, and we summarize them here.

$\forall x(\phi \lor \chi)$	$\dashv\vdash$	$\forall x\phi \lor \chi$		$\exists x(\phi \land \chi)$	$\dashv\vdash$	$\exists x\phi \land \chi$
$\forall x(\chi \rightarrow \phi)$	$\dashv\vdash$	$\chi \rightarrow \forall x\phi$		$\exists x(\chi \rightarrow \phi)$	$\dashv\vdash$	$\chi \rightarrow \exists x\phi$
$\forall x(\phi \rightarrow \chi)$	$\dashv\vdash$	$\exists x\phi \rightarrow \chi$		$\exists x(\phi \rightarrow \chi)$	$\dashv\vdash$	$\forall x\phi \rightarrow \chi$

Here, it's required that χ is a sentence and, in particular, that the variable x does not occur free in χ. There are twelve sequents here to prove, and most of them are straightforward. (You were asked to prove a few of them in exercises 6.5, 6.8, and 6.11.) The more challenging ones are the bottom two in the right column, in particular, the ones with the existential conclusions. The problem there is that the premises don't contain any information about something existing. You were asked to prove $\forall x\phi \rightarrow \chi \vdash \exists x(\phi \rightarrow \chi)$ in exercise 6.8. For $\chi \rightarrow \exists x\phi \vdash \exists x(\chi \rightarrow \phi)$, we might recommend using excluded middle with $\exists x\phi \lor \neg\exists x\phi$ and arguing by cases. In the former case, positive paradox leads to $\exists x(\chi \rightarrow \phi)$. In the latter case, MT with the premise gives $\neg\chi$, and negative paradox leads to $\exists x(\chi \rightarrow \phi)$.

We turn, finally, to the relations between quantifiers. You've already proven the following equivalences:

$$\forall x \forall y \phi \quad \dashv\vdash \quad \forall y \forall x \phi \qquad \exists x \exists y \phi \quad \dashv\vdash \quad \exists y \exists x \phi$$

As a summary, universal quantifiers commute with each other, and existential quantifiers commute with each other. It might be tempting to think that universal quantifiers also commute with existential quantifiers. However, the implication from $\forall x \exists y \phi$ to $\exists y \forall x \phi$ fails. For example, let $\phi(x, y)$ represent the statement that "x is the biological mother of y," and let the quantifiers range over mammals. Then it's true that every mammal has a biological mother, but it's false that there is some particular mammal that is the biological mother of all others.

Exercise 6.13. Prove the following sequents.

1. $P \rightarrow \exists x Fx \vdash \exists x (P \rightarrow Fx)$
2. $\exists x (Fx \rightarrow P) \vdash \forall x Fx \rightarrow P$
3. $\forall x (Fx \rightarrow P) \dashv\vdash \exists x Fx \rightarrow P$

New Tautologies

Every propositional logic tautology is also provable in predicate logic. By this we mean that if you take a propositional tautology, say $P \vee \neg P$, and replace the atomic sentences (in this case, P) with predicate logic sentences, then the result is also provable. For example, if we uniformly replace P with $\forall x Fx$, then a proof of $P \vee \neg P$ would be transformed into a proof of $\forall x Fx \vee \neg \forall x Fx$. Similarly, if we replaced P with $\exists x Fx$, then we would get a proof of $\exists x Fx \vee \neg \exists x Fx$. The fact we've just mentioned is an extension of the substitution meta-rule that we introduced in chapter 4.

Predicate logic has some additional tautologies that are not substitution instances of propositional logic tautologies. For example, the sentence

$\forall x(Fx \lor \neg Fx)$ can be proven without any premises.

(1) $Fa \lor \neg Fa$ cut, lem
(2) $\forall x(Fx \lor \neg Fx)$ 1 UI

Here, on line 1, we allowed ourselves to use cut/substitution from propositional logic. Since line 1 has no dependencies, we're permitted to invoke UI, resulting in $\forall x(Fx \lor \neg Fx)$.

Exercise 6.14. Prove the following sequents.

1. $\vdash \forall x(Fx \rightarrow Fx)$
2. $\vdash \forall xFx \lor \exists x\neg Fx$
3. $\vdash \forall x\neg(Fx \land \neg Fx)$
4. $\vdash \neg\exists x(Fx \land \neg Fx)$
5. $\vdash \forall x\exists y(Rxy \rightarrow Rxx)$
6. $\vdash \forall x\exists y(Rxy \rightarrow Ryx)$
*7. $\vdash \exists x(Fx \rightarrow \forall yFy)$
*8. $\vdash \exists x\forall y(Fx \rightarrow Fy)$
*9. $\forall x\exists y(Fx \rightarrow Gy) \vdash \exists y\forall x(Fx \rightarrow Gy)$
*10. $\vdash \forall x\exists y(Rxy \rightarrow \forall zRxz)$

Exercise 6.15. Consider the following attempted proof. Which step is wrong and why?

1	(1)	Fa	A
	(2)	$Fa \rightarrow Fa$	1,1 CP
	(3)	$\forall y(Fa \rightarrow Fy)$	2 UI
	(3)	$\exists x\forall y(Fx \rightarrow Fy)$	3 EI

Exercise 6.16. Symbolize the following sentence and prove that it leads to a contradiction.

There is a person who loves all and only those people who don't love themselves. *Lxy*

Thinking Fast but Carefully

Suppose that you want to prove the following sequent.

$$\forall x(\exists y Rxy \rightarrow \forall z Rzx), \exists x \exists y Rxy \vdash \forall x \forall y Rxy.$$

Sometimes it helps to think syntactically, that is, about the form of the sentences, and how the rules can be used to move from premises to conclusion. Other times, it's more helpful to think about "what the formulas are actually saying." In this particular case, we have found it helpful to think about what the formulas are actually saying.

The conclusion says that any two things stand in the relation R. The second premise says that some two things stand in the relation R. (But recall that "two" here doesn't necessarily mean distinct.) The first premise says something a bit funny, which we find helpful to construe in terms of an analogy. Let's imagine that our sentences are talking about airports and that Rab means that there is a direct flight from a to b. Then the first premise says:

> If an airport offers departing flights, then you can fly to it direct from any other airport.

Now we want to show that there is a direct flight between any two airports a and b. From the second premise, there are airports c and d and a direct flight from c to d. Then, by the first premise, every airport has a direct flight to c in particular, airports a and b. So we now have the following picture:

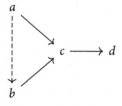

The dashed line indicates our realization that since b offers departing flights, you can get there directly from any other airport, including from a. Since there is a direct flight from a to b, and those were arbitrarily chosen airports, it follows that $\forall x \forall y Rxy$.

The reasoning we just went through could easily be converted now into a fully regimented proof. It would be good practice to write up such a proof yourself.

Exercise 6.17. Prove the following sequent. You might want to try first coming up with an intuitive argument before you try writing a regimented proof.

   1. $\forall x(\exists z Rxz \rightarrow \forall y Rxy), \exists x \exists y Rxy \vdash \exists x \forall y Rxy$

7

Theories

EVERYONE USES LOGIC EVERY DAY—albeit usually without thinking twice about it. In the sciences, logic gets used more explicitly. I'm thinking especially here about the all-important task of formulating theories. Theories are interesting creatures, because they aren't just a bunch of truths. Instead, a theory is like a network of truths with a lot of logical structure between them.

In this chapter, then, we're going to talk about how to use logic to represent the structure of a theory. We'll focus on one particular theory that is beloved among philosophers and mathematicians: the theory of sets. In the following chapter, we'll use the theory of sets to get a better handle on what can and cannot be proven with predicate logic.

Theory of Equality

In previous chapters, we used symbols to represent predicates (such as Px) and to represent relations (such as Rxy). We also used other symbols to represent names (such as a, b, c). At this point, we need to add one special relation symbol, which you already know quite well: the symbol "$=$." This symbol is binary, that is, it needs two variables, or two names, to form a meaningful formula. But unlike our other relation symbols, people tend to write "$=$" as an infix, rather than as a prefix. Following standard practice, we'll write formulas such as $x = y$, or $a = b$, and so on. Notice that it makes sense to write $a = b$, even though a is not b. The idea here is that a and b are distinct names, and "$a = b$" means that a and b name the same thing. We then stipulate as our first axiom that a and a name the same thing.

Equality Introduction (=I)

For any name a, one may write $a = a$ without any

dependencies. Schematically: $\dfrac{}{a = a}$

Equality Elimination (=E)

From $a = b$ and $\phi(a)$, one may infer $\phi(b)$. Schematically:

$$\frac{\Gamma \vdash a = b \qquad \Delta \vdash \phi(a)}{\Gamma, \Delta \vdash \phi(b)}$$

While this second rule looks complicated, it just says that when you have established $a = b$, then you can convert $\phi(a)$ to $\phi(b)$, as long as you remember to gather all the dependencies together.

We can illustrate these new rules by proving that the relation $=$ is symmetric and transitive.

To prove: $a = b \vdash b = a$

1	(1)	$a = b$	A
	(2)	$a = a$	=I
1	(3)	$b = a$	1,2 =E

When we apply =E in line 3, we are thinking of line 2 as $\phi(a)$, where the name to be replaced is on the left side of the $=$ symbol. Since we have $a = b$ in line 1, we may infer $\phi(b)$, which is $b = a$.

To prove: $a = b, b = c \vdash a = c$

1	(1)	$a = b$	A
2	(2)	$b = c$	A
1, 2	(3)	$a = c$	1,2 =E

Here we are thinking of $a = b$ as $\phi(b)$. Then applying $b = c$, we get $\phi(c)$, which is $a = c$.

We can also show the unsurprising result that everything is equal to something.

(1)	$a = a$	=I
(2)	$\exists y(a = y)$	1 EI
(3)	$\forall x \exists y(x = y)$	2 UI

The use of UI on line 3 is permitted, because line 2 doesn't depend on any assumptions in which a occurs, and since all occurrences of a are replaced by x and then bound by $\forall x$. Note that this maneuver would *not* work to prove $\forall x \forall y(x = y)$. If one tried to apply UI to line 1, then one would be required to replace both instances of a with y and bind with $\forall y$, yielding $\forall y(y = y)$.

Being able to express equality claims greatly expands the expressive power of our logic. For example, consider the following sentence:

$$\forall x \forall y((Px \wedge Py) \rightarrow x = y).$$

This sentence says that for any two things, if both are P, then they are the same thing. (The English phrase "for any two things" typically carries an implication of distinctness. However, $\forall x \forall y$ should be thought of on the analogy of drawing marbles from a jar, where we return each marble after it has been drawn.) In other words, this sentence says, "There is at most one P." We can also assert the unconditional numerical claim as follows:

$$\forall x \forall y(x = y) \quad \equiv \quad \text{There is at most one thing.}$$

The sentence $\forall x\forall y((Px \land Py) \to x=y)$ does *not* tell us that there is a P. We now claim that the following two sentences are equivalent:

$$\exists zPz \land \forall x\forall y((Px \land Py) \to x=y) \; \equiv \; \exists x(Px \land \forall y(Py \to x=y)).$$

To write out a full numbered proof of this equivalence would be a bit tedious. In the following "proof sketch," we play a bit fast and loose.

1	(1)	$\exists zPz \land \forall x\forall y((Px \land Py) \to x=y)$	A
1	(2)	$\exists zPz$	1 $\land$ E
3	(3)	Pa	A
4	(4)	Pb	A
1	(5)	$(Pa \land Pb) \to a=b$	1 $\land$ E, UE
1, 3, 4	(6)	$a=b$	3,4,5 $\land$ I, MP
1, 3	(7)	$Pb \to a=b$	4,6 CP
1, 3	(8)	$\forall y(Py \to a=y)$	7 UI
1, 3	(9)	$Pa \land \forall y(Py \to a=y)$	3,8 $\land$ I
1, 3	(10)	$\exists x(Px \land \forall y(Py \to x=y))$	9 EI
1	(11)	$\exists x(Px \land \forall y(Py \to x=y))$	2,3,10 EE

On line 5, we've combined an application of $\land$ E with an application of UE. On line 6, we combined an application of $\land$ I with an application of MP. If you decompressed these steps, you'd have a proof that follows the letter of the law. The important thing, however, is to grasp the thought process behind the formal proof. The premise tells us two things: first, that something is a P, and second, that any two things that are P are identical. We now need to show that there is a P with the feature that any other P is identical to it. So take any P, say a, whose existence is guaranteed by the premise. What features does this P have? Well, if there were some other P, say b, then a and b would be identical. Hence, a has the feature that $\forall y(Py \to a=y)$. Thus, there is some P (namely a) with this feature, that is, $\exists x(Px \land \forall y(x=y))$.

Exercise 7.1. Prove the following sequent.

1. $\exists x(Px \land \forall y(Py \to x=y)) \vdash \exists zPz \land \forall x\forall y((Px \land Py) \to x=y)$

This sentence, $\exists x(Px \land \forall y(Py \to x = y))$, is one of the most famous of symbolic logic. It says that there is a P, and that any other P is identical to it. In short, it says,

$$\exists x(Px \land \forall y(Py \to x = y)) \quad \equiv \quad \text{There is a unique } P.$$

For convenience, one sometimes abbreviates this sentence as $\exists! x Px$, the exclamation mark indicating the uniqueness clause. As proven above, the sentence on the left can be broken up into two components: (1) an existence clause and (2) a uniqueness clause. For this reason, when mathematicians (or computer scientists, or physicists, etc.) prove that there is a unique such and such, they have two tasks to carry out. They have to prove that such a thing exists, and they have to prove that there is at most one such thing. For example, mathematicians will tell you that there is a unique group of order p, where p is a prime number. To validate that claim, they construct these groups (proving existence), and they prove that any two such groups are isomorphic (proving uniqueness).[1]

In terms of natural language, uniqueness claims are often signaled by the word "only." For example, suppose that I say that the number 2 is the only even prime number. Here I am asserting both that 2 is an even prime number and that anything else with this feature is identical to the number 2. Hence, I might represent this statement as follows.

$$Fa \land \forall x(Fx \to (x = a)) \quad \equiv \quad \text{2 is the only even prime number.}$$

Here we've used Fx for the compound predicate "x is an even prime number." The sentence on the right tells us that a is an F and that any F is identical to a. This reading suggests that the sentence on the right is equivalent to $\forall x(Fx \leftrightarrow (x = a))$, which is indeed the case.

Exercise 7.2. Prove the equivalence of $Fa \land \forall x(Fx \to (x = a))$ and $\forall x(Fx \leftrightarrow (x = a))$.

---

1. The advanced reader might note that it's not *strict* uniqueness that is claimed here but only uniqueness up to isomorphism. The idea is the same, only strict identity has been replaced by isomorphism.

As we've just stated, there is only one even prime number. It would make sense, then, to talk about *the* even prime number. In contrast, it wouldn't make sense to talk about the prime number less than four, since there are two such prime numbers. It also wouldn't make sense to talk about the largest prime number, because there is no such thing.

In one of the most famous uses of symbolic logic in philosophy, Bertrand Russell explained what it means to say that something does not exist.[2] The puzzle here is that if I say, "There is something that does not exist," then it's dangerously close to saying that "there exists something that does not exist." Russell pointed out, however, that when we assert nonexistence, all we are saying is that nothing fits a certain description. For example, to say "Santa Claus does not exist" might mean something like, "There is no being who lives at the North Pole and delivers gifts to children at Christmas," which can be symbolized simply as $\neg \exists x \phi(x)$. Accordingly, a phrase such as "Santa Claus loves me" might appropriately be symbolized as

$$\exists x(\phi(x) \land \forall y(\phi(y) \to y = x) \land Lxa).$$

Here, the first two conjuncts assert that Santa Claus exists, and the third conjunct asserts that this guy loves a, the name I've chosen for "me." If we simply wrote

$$\exists x(\phi(x) \land Lxa)$$

then we would have "some Santa-like figure loves me," but no implication that this figure is unique.

I myself think that there is something slightly suspicious with Russell's analysis. For example, if I say that Santa Claus has a round belly, then I don't mean to be saying that Santa Claus exists. And if you told me that Santa Claus has a white beard, then I wouldn't judge that what you said is false on the basis that Santa Claus doesn't exist. So, if my intuitions are right, then fictional discourse has a kind of logic of its own, and one might wonder whether this logic can be illuminated by formal methods.[3]

---

2. "On denoting" *Mind* (1905).

3. The subject called **free logic** studies questions like this one.

Phrases such as "the ϕ" are called **definite descriptions**. Russell's proposal, then, is that definite descriptions can be symbolized as a conjunction of existence and uniqueness claims. Consequently, to say that "the ϕ is not ψ" can mean two different things: it can mean that there is no unique ϕ, or it can mean that there is a unique ϕ, but it is not ψ.

The equality relation can also be used to express superlative claims. Suppose, for example, that you want to express the following sentence:

Mette is the fastest runner in the class.

For this, we could use the relation symbol Rxy to express that x is at least as fast as y. Then the sentence $\forall y Rmy$ says that Mette is at least as fast as anyone, but it doesn't rule out the possibility that somebody else is as fast as her. If we wanted to say that Mette was the unique fastest runner, then we could add a further clause saying that Mette is the only person who is as fast as herself, namely, $\forall x(Rxm \rightarrow x = m)$.

Note, however, that in using Rxy to represent "x is as fast as y," we tend to implicitly incorporate some other assumptions that are not explicitly captured in the formalism. For example, it's trivially true that everyone is as fast as herself; however, it's not trivially true—for an arbitrary relation symbol Rxy—that $\forall x Rxx$. Thus, if we wanted to capture all the relevant facts about the relation "as fast as," then we would have to add some other assumptions about Rxy.

We've already seen how to express the claim that there is at most one P. It's easy to extend this method to expressing claims of the form

At most n things have property P.

Consider, for example, how we might say that there are at most two Ps. Imagine again that you're drawing marbles out of a jar, replacing each marble after it's drawn. If there are at most two marbles in the jar (i.e., there are none, one, or two), then if you draw three times from the jar, you are guaranteed to draw the same marble twice (supposing that there are any marbles to be drawn). Hence, for any three draws x, y, z, either $x = y$ or $x = z$ or $y = z$. Written symbolically,

$$\forall x \forall y \forall z (x = y \lor x = z \lor y = z).$$

This sentence will serve as our official translation of the phrase, "There are at most two things." To say that there are at most two Ps, we need only conditionalize on the things being P. In particular, the sentence

$$\forall x \forall y \forall z ((Px \land Py \land Pz) \rightarrow (x = y \lor x = z \lor y = z))$$

says that for any three Ps, at least two of the three are identical.

It should be easy to see how to generalize from the case of "at most 2" to the case of "at most n." Thus, for any number n, we can express the fact that there are at most n things. We'll now see that we can also express that there are at least n things. Beginning again with the case of 2, the sentence $\exists x \exists y (x \neq y)$ is sufficient to express the fact that there are at least two things.[4] Similarly, the sentence $\exists x \exists y \exists z (x \neq y \land x \neq z \land y \neq z)$ expresses the fact that there are at least three things. As before, to say that there are at least three Ps, we need only conditionalize on the fact that the things are P. In this case, since we're using an existential quantifier, we want to conjoin with the claim that the things are P, hence

$$\exists x \exists y \exists z (Px \land Py \land Pz \land x \neq y \land x \neq z \land y \neq z).$$

Now, obviously if there are at least n things and at most n things, then there are exactly n things. Similarly, if there are at least n Ps and at most n Ps, then there are exactly n Ps. Thus, to express the claim "there are exactly n Ps," we could simply conjoin the two sentences above. However, there is a more compact and elegant way to express the same thing. We claim, for example, that the following two sentences are equivalent.

$$\exists x \exists y (x \neq y) \land \forall x \forall y \forall z (x = y \lor x = z \lor y = z),$$
$$\exists x \exists y (x \neq y \land \forall z (x = z \lor y = z)).$$

4. Here we use $x \neq y$ as shorthand for $\neg(x = y)$.

The second sentence says that there are two distinct things, and everything is identical to one of these two things. Intuitively, that sentence captures the claim that there are exactly two things. We'll leave it to you to prove that this sentence is equivalent to the conjunction of the sentences saying that there are at least, and at most, two things.

Exercise 7.3. Represent the logical structure of the following sentences using the equality relation "$=$" when appropriate.

1. Maren is the only student who didn't miss any questions on the exam. (m, Qx, variables are restricted to students)
2. All professors except a are boring. (Px, a, Bx)
3. a is the best of all possible worlds. (Rxy, variables are restricted to possible worlds)
4. There is no greatest prime number. (Px, $x < y$, variables are restricted to numbers)
5. The smallest prime number is even. (Px, Ex, $x < y$)
6. For each integer, there is a unique next-greatest integer. ($x < y$, variables are restricted to integers)
7. There are at least two Ivy League universities in New York. (Ix, Nx)
8. For any two sets a and b, there is a largest set c that is contained in both of them. ("y is at least as large as x" $\equiv$ "y contains x" $\equiv$ $x \subseteq y$)
*9. The function f achieves its least upper bound on the domain $[0, 1]$. (f, $x \leq y$, 0, 1)

Exercise 7.4. Consider the following lyric from the jazz musician Spencer Williams:

Everybody loves my baby, but my baby don't love nobody but me.

Represent the logical form of this sentence, and show that it implies that the speaker is his own baby. (Hint: use a as a name for the speaker and b as a name for the speaker's baby, and restrict variables to people.)

Ordering

We have many occasions for ranking things, or putting them into some kind of order. Famously, each year *US News and World Report* publishes a ranking of universities in the United States, which looks something like this:

$$\cdots \longrightarrow a \longrightarrow b \longrightarrow c$$

where c is ranked number one, b is ranked number two, and so on. Let's look at this as logicians, ignoring the content and focusing on the form. We note that this ranking validates the sentence

$$\forall x(x \leq y \wedge y \leq z \rightarrow x \leq z),$$

that is, the ordering is transitive. It would be pretty weird if it weren't: that would suggest that c might be both more excellent than b, which is more excellent than a, but c is not more excellent than a. We also note that this ranking validates the sentence $\forall x \forall y(x \leq y \vee y \leq x)$, that is, *US News and World Report* tells us that for any two universities, either the one is better than the other, or the other way around.

Logicians don't have any business opining about the quality of universities, but between us, I'm suspicious about whether the latter sentence is actually true. To be more concrete, let's suppose that there are two different virtues that a university can have—let's call them F-ness and G-ness. Suppose further that c has more F-ness than b but that b has more G-ness than c. Suppose, furthermore, that we lack public consensus about whether F is more important than G or about how much more important it is. In that case, if we try to build the $\leq$ ordering based on F-ness and G-ness, then the situation might more accurately be portrayed as follows:

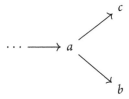

This picture says that both c and b are better than a but that c and b are incomparable with each other. That is, neither $c \leq b$ nor $b \leq c$. In that case, the axiom $\forall x \forall y(x \leq y \lor y \leq x)$ fails, and the ordering is not linear.

Quantifier logic is particularly good at describing structural features of orderings. Let's first specify a very general notion of an ordering, a so-called **partial order**. Any time we construct a theory, the first thing we need to do is to choose some **nonlogical vocabulary**, that is, some relation symbols or function symbols. For the theory of partial order, it will suffice to choose one binary relation symbol, say $\leq$, which we will use in infix notation.

The second step in defining a theory is to write down some **axioms** that specify what the theory says about its nonlogical vocabulary. For the theory of partial order, we have the following axioms:

Reflexive	$x \leq x$
Antisymmetric	$(x \leq y \land y \leq x) \rightarrow (x = y)$
Transitive	$(x \leq y \land y \leq z) \rightarrow x \leq z$

(Here we have, for convenience, allowed ourselves to drop outermost universal quantifiers. Each of these axioms is meant to be universally quantified over all the variables that occur in it.) A lot of different orderings meet these criteria. The above two orderings of universities meet these criteria.

We get another kind of ranking that meets these criteria if we stick two rankings side by side and simply say that they have nothing to do with each other. For example, consider the collection that consists of (a) all US universities and (b) all single scullers who competed in last year's rowing world championship. Let's say that $x \leq y$ just in case either x and y are universities, and y was ranked higher than x in the *US News and World Report* poll, or x and y are scullers such that y finished ahead of x at the world championship. Then this heterogeneous collection also satisfies the axioms of a partial order.

To say that an order is not heterogeneous in this way—that is, that everything is comparable to everything else—we might try adding an axiom such as

Total	$x \leq y \lor y \leq x$

But this axiom is awfully strict; for example, it doesn't permit the second sort of university ranking we entertained above, where two different universities are better than all the others but cannot be directly compared with each other.

We might then add the following weaker axiom:

Directed $\quad \forall x \forall y \exists z (z \leq x \wedge z \leq y)$

This axiom would ensure that any two things are at least indirectly related; in particular, either one is worse than the other, or there is some other university that is worse than both of them. However, the Directed axiom wouldn't permit the possibility that there could be two distinct universities that are both the worst in their own special way. That scenario would look like this:

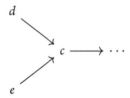

(Imagine, for example, that d has the least rigorous admissions standards and that e has the worst postgraduation job placement record.) You could go on trying various other axioms, but it should be clear enough now that there's a lot you can say about order using quantifiers and Boolean logical connectives.

Exercise 7.5. Show that if a partial ordering satisfies the Total axiom, then it satisfies the Directed axiom.

Exercise 7.6. A relation R is said to be symmetric just in case $\forall x \forall y (Rxy \rightarrow Ryx)$. Show that if R is symmetric and transitive, then it's reflexive.

Exercise 7.7. Write down a sentence about linear orders that is true in the integers (i.e., whole numbers) but false in the rational numbers (i.e., fractions).

Functions

In earlier chapters, we applied predicates to variables, such as x, and to names, such as a. Let's use the word **terms** as a common description of these variables and names. Syntactically speaking, terms are whatever comes after predicate symbols or relation symbols.

We now need to introduce another kind of symbol that builds more complex terms. To see what we're going for, consider first, as an example, the phrase, "The biological father of...." That phrase, of course, doesn't name anyone in particular. Interestingly, though, it has the feature that whenever you plug in a name that denotes a unique individual, the phrase also denotes a unique individual (supposing, for simplicity, that each such individual has a unique biological father). This phrase, then, acts as a **function**, taking denoting terms (e.g., names) and returning other denoting terms.

Mathematicians have long recognized the value of functions, and some of their favorites are binary functions such as $+$. If you give me two number names, say 4 and 17, then $4 + 17$ is a name for another number. Thus, $+$ takes as input two denoting terms, and it returns a denoting term as output.

In the abstract, we'll typically use symbols like $f, g, h, \ldots$ for functions. These functions can be unary (i.e., take one term as input), binary (i.e., take two terms as input), or n-ary (i.e. take n terms as input). Besides allowing function symbols to be applied to names, we also allow function symbols to be applied to variables. Thus, if f is a unary function symbol, then $f(x)$ also counts as a legitimate term (although not a name). What this means is that $f(x)$ can itself be put in any slot where terms are allowed to go. For example, if R is a binary relation symbol, then $Rf(x)y$ is a legitimate formula. More intuitively, since $=$ is a binary relation symbol, we may place $f(x)$ on its left- or right-hand side. For example, $f(x) = y$ is a perfectly good formula; hence, $\forall x \exists y (f(x) = y)$ is a perfectly good sentence. In fact, because of the rules for equality, that last sentence is provable.

(1)	$f(a) = f(a)$	$=$I
(2)	$\exists y(f(a) = y)$	1 EI
(3)	$\forall x \exists y(f(x) = y)$	2 UI

Since the first step invokes =I, there are no dependencies at any stage of the proof. This proof shows that for each input, a function always assigns some or other output. It does *not* follow, however, that every possible output corresponds to some input. That additional condition can be formulated as

$$\forall y \exists x (f(x) = y),$$

and in this case, it is said that f is **onto** or **surjective**. Another important condition a function can satisfy is having different outputs for different inputs or, contrapositively, having the same input for the same output. Symbolically, this condition amounts to

$$\forall x \forall y (f(x) = f(y) \rightarrow x = y),$$

and in this case, it is said that f is **one-to-one** or **injective**.

As mentioned before, mathematics is chock-full of binary function symbols such as $+$, $\times$. It also uses unary function symbols, although their presence is sometimes difficult to detect. Consider, for example, that little superscript $^{-1}$ that you learned to use when talking about the inverse of a number. Well, you can think of that little superscript as a function symbol that is applied to the right side of a term but where no parentheses are added. In particular, given the name of a number, say 2, the symbol 2^{-1} names another number, namely, the multiplicative inverse of 2. You might also remember that there is one number that doesn't have a multiplicative inverse, namely, 0. What this means is that the symbol 0^{-1} doesn't make sense, and $^{-1}$ is only a function when restricted to nonzero numbers.

When you learned how to reason about functions (e.g., in your precalculus class), there were some moves you probably came to take for granted. For example, if $a = b$, then $f(a) = f(b)$. It's illuminating to see that this fact can be derived from the inference rules for equality.

1	(1)	$a = b$	A
	(2)	$f(c) = f(c)$	=I
1	(3)	$f(a) = f(b)$	1,2 =E
	(4)	$a = b \rightarrow f(a) = f(b)$	1,3 CP

Since the last line has no dependencies with a or b, the result holds for arbitrary a and b.

With the expansion of the class of terms, we should also expand the range of the equality introduction and elimination rules. In particular, for any term t, the $=$E rule allows us to write the sentence $t = t$ on a line without any dependencies. Similarly, if t and s are terms, then $\phi(s)$ can be derived from $\phi(t)$ and $t = s$. The latter permits the following sort of substitution:

1	(1)	$1 + 1 = 2$	A
2	(2)	$2 + 1 = 3$	A
1, 2	(3)	$(1 + 1) + 1 = 3$	1,2 $=$E

Or similarly,

1	(1)	Sinned(adam)	A
2	(2)	adam $=$ father(cain)	A
1, 2	(3)	Sinned(father(cain))	1,2 $=$E

Exercise 7.8. Suppose that f and g are functions such that $\forall x(g(f(x)) = x)$. Show that f is one-to-one.

Exercise 7.9. A function f is said to be an *involution* just in case $\forall x$ $(f(f(x)) = x)$. Show that if f is an involution, then f is one-to-one and onto.

Exercise 7.10. Suppose that $\circ$ is a binary function symbol, that i is a unary function symbol, and that e is a name. Assume the following as axioms:

A1. The function $\circ$ is associative:

$$\forall x \forall y \forall z((x \circ y) \circ z = x \circ (y \circ z))$$

A2. The name e functions as a left and right identity:

$$\forall x(x \circ e = x = e \circ x)$$

A3. The function i gives left and right inverses:

$$\forall x(x \circ i(x) = e = i(x) \circ x)$$

Prove that:

1. Inverses are unique: $\forall x \forall y((x \circ y = e) \rightarrow (y = i(x)))$.
2. Inverse is an involution: $\forall x(i(i(x)) = x)$.
3. Inverse is anti-multiplicative: $\forall x \forall y(i(x \circ y) = i(y) \circ i(x))$.

Exercise 7.11. Suppose that f is one-to-one but not onto. For each number n, it can be shown that there are more than n things. Show here that there are more than two things.

Arithmetic

At an early age, children learn basic facts about addition and subtraction. In the process, they become comfortable with the idea of negative numbers. Some time later, children learn facts about multiplication and division, and in doing so, it becomes apparent that for division always to make sense, there must be further numbers beyond the whole numbers—namely, the fractions, which can also be expressed in terms of decimal expansions. At this stage, a student may become vaguely aware that fractional numbers correspond to repeating decimals and hence that nonrepeating decimals are a new kind of number.

With the introduction of each new type of number, students learn new bits of vocabulary. Addition corresponds to a function symbol $+$, and subtraction corresponds to a function symbol $-$. The introduction of multiplication and division comes with two new function symbols: $\times$ and $\div$. The introduction of exponents provides a new binary function symbol x^y and so on. The new function symbols are given meaning by the axioms they are assumed to satisfy. For example, addition is tacitly assumed to be commutative and associative:

$$x + y = y + x, \qquad x + (y + z) = (x + y) + z.$$

Furthermore, the number 0 is tacitly assumed to be the additive identity: $x + 0 = x = 0 + x$.

Multiplication is then assumed to be related to addition in certain ways; for example,

$$a \times b = \underbrace{a + \cdots + a}_{b \text{ times}},$$

which implies that multiplication distributes over addition and (as a limiting case) that $a \times 0 = 0$.

Most students tacitly accept these facts—or, rather, axioms—and use them when they reason about numbers. It takes a special kind of mind to ask, "Could the axioms be written down explicitly, so that whenever a student reasons validly about numbers, she could cite the relevant axiom?"

Let's try to write down a sufficient set of axioms to capture all of the facts about addition and multiplication of the nonnegative whole numbers $0, 1, 2, \ldots$. The first thing we need is to introduce the basic vocabulary: we let $+$ and $\cdot$ be binary function symbols, and we let 0 and 1 be names. The theory **Peano arithmetic (PA)** has six primary axioms:

P1. $x + 1 \neq 0$	P2. $x + 1 = y + 1 \rightarrow x = y$
P3. $x + 0 = x$	P4. $x + (y + 1) = (x + y) + 1$
P5. $x \cdot 0 = 0$	P6. $x \cdot (y + 1) = x \cdot y + x$.

For the sake of readability, we drop the outermost universal quantifiers from the axioms. The function $s(x) = x + 1$ is called the **successor function**. Note that P2 says that the successor function is one-to-one, and P1 says that the successor function is not onto. (As we will see later, this means that P1 and P2 imply that there are infinitely many things.)

Peano arithmetic also comes equipped with an **induction schema**, which consists of one axiom for each formula $\phi(y, \vec{x})$.

$$(\phi(0, \vec{x}) \land \forall y(\phi(y, \vec{x}) \rightarrow \phi(y + 1, \vec{x}))) \rightarrow \forall y \phi(y, \vec{x}).$$

Here, the vector variable $\vec{x}$ is just shorthand for an n-tuple $x_1, \ldots, x_n$ of variables. Although they might look strange, the induction schema represents a well-known strategy for proving things about the natural numbers.

In short, they say that if you can prove that 0 has some feature ϕ, and if you can prove that whenever y is ϕ then $y + 1$ also is ϕ, then you may conclude that every number is ϕ.

Here's a classic case of the inductive reasoning strategy: define a function σ by

$$\sigma(x) = 1 + 2 + \cdots + (x - 1) + x.$$

In other words, $\sigma(x)$ is the result of adding together all the numbers up to x. We'll use induction to show that $\forall x \phi(x)$, where $\phi(x)$ is the formula

$$\sigma(x) = \frac{x(x+1)}{2}.$$

First check that $\phi(0)$, that is, that $0 = 0(0 + 1)/2$. Now let a be a fixed natural number and suppose that $\phi(a)$, that is, $\sigma(a) = a(a + 1)/2$. Then,

$$\sigma(a+1) = \sigma(a) + a + 1 = \frac{a^2 + 3a + 2}{2} = \frac{(a+2)(a+1)}{2},$$

which means that $\phi(a + 1)$ is true. We've shown then that $\forall x(\phi(x) \rightarrow \phi(x+1))$, and hence by induction, $\forall x \phi(x)$.

The preceding proof sketch assumes several facts about arithmetic that we haven't yet proven. For example, it assumes that addition is associative and commutative. So let's back up a step, and take up an argument where each step is explicitly justified by the axioms of Peano arithmetic.

Consider, for example, the claim that every nonzero number has a predecessor, that is, that $\forall y(y \neq 0 \rightarrow \exists x(x + 1 = y))$. This fact follows almost immediately from the induction axioms. By negative paradox, it's true that if $0 \neq 0$, then $\exists x(x + 1 = 0)$. Furthermore, for any number $a + 1$, it's true that there is an x such that $x + 1 = a + 1$. Thus, it's trivially true that if the claim holds for a, then it holds for $a + 1$.

Let's now formalize the argument. We use the induction schema with the predicate

$$\phi(y) \equiv y \neq 0 \rightarrow \exists x(x + 1 = y).$$

The variable vector $\vec{x}$ here is the trivial zero-length vector. The argument then proceeds like this:

$$
\begin{array}{lll}
(1) & 0 = 0 & =\text{I} \\
(2) & 0 \neq 0 \rightarrow \exists x(x+1=0) & \text{neg paradox} \\
(3) & a+1 = a+1 & =\text{I} \\
(4) & \exists x(x+1=a+1) & \text{3 EI} \\
(5) & a+1 \neq 0 \rightarrow \exists x(x+1=a+1) & \text{pos paradox} \\
(6) & \phi(a) \rightarrow \phi(a+1) & \text{pos paradox} \\
(7) & \forall y(\phi(y) \rightarrow \phi(y+1)) & \text{UI} \\
\text{IS} \quad (8) & \forall y \phi(y) & \text{2,7 induction}
\end{array}
$$

If we plug in the definition of $\phi(y)$, then line 2 is $\phi(0)$, and line 5 is $\phi(a+1)$. Then on line 6, we apply positive paradox to get $\phi(a) \rightarrow \phi(a+1)$. Note that induction is the only axiom of PA that we used in the argument. We included a dependency IS on line 8 to indicate that the result is not a tautology, in the strict sense; it is a consequence of an axiom of PA.

Exercise 7.12. We use the abbreviation $\text{PA} \vdash \phi$ to indicate that there is a proof from the Peano axioms to ϕ. Prove the following:

1. Prove that addition is associative. We'll give an informal argument and ask you to write something that looks more like a formal proof. We use induction on the formula $\phi(z) \equiv \forall x \forall y(x + (y+z) = (x+y)+z)$. By two applications of P3, we have $y+0=y$ and $(x+y)+0=x+y$. Hence, $x+(y+0)=x+y=(x+y)+0$. That is, $\phi(0)$. Now let a be an arbitrary natural number, and suppose that $\phi(a)$, that is, $x+(y+a)=(x+y)+a$. Then

$$
\begin{aligned}
x + (y+(a+1)) &= x+((y+a)+1) & \text{P4} \\
&= (x+(y+a))+1 & \text{P4} \\
&= ((x+y)+a)+1 & \text{assumption, =E} \\
&= (x+y)+(a+1) & \text{P4}.
\end{aligned}
$$

2. $\text{PA} \vdash \forall x \forall y(x+y=y+x)$. Hint: you'll need to use induction twice.

3. $PA \vdash 0 \neq 1$
4. $PA \vdash 1 + 1 \neq 1$
5. $PA \vdash \forall x \forall y \forall z (x + z = y + z \rightarrow x = y)$
6. $PA \vdash \forall x \forall y \forall z (x \cdot (y \cdot z) = (x \cdot y) \cdot z)$
7. $PA \vdash \forall x \forall y (x \cdot y = y \cdot x)$

Definition

In subsequent sections, we will move on to yet more sophisticated theories. However, when our theories become sophisticated, it becomes all the more important that we clearly express concepts and the relations between them. Thus, we take a quick detour to discuss how we can define new concepts from old ones.

There are many misconceptions about what it means to be logical. You might, for example, have thought that the logical person is the one who demands evidence before believing something. However, logic has nothing at all to say about which premises you should accept. What's more, the logical person makes suppositions that are in no way demanded by the evidence that she possesses. She does so because we humans cannot expect to receive the truth passively—we have to seek it actively.

Another misconception about logic is that good reasoning takes place against a fixed background scene of language—or, in philosophical terms, with a fixed repertoire of concepts. To the contrary, logic is concerned not just with good reasoning with a fixed set of concepts but also with best practices for constructing new concepts. To make the contrast more clear, deduction takes place within the framework of a fixed language. There is no way that deductively valid inference could reach a conclusion that mentions a new concept—that is, a concept that is not mentioned in the premises. For example, you couldn't validly infer a sentence with the relation symbol *Rxy* from sentences with predicates *Fx* and *Gx*.

Let's call the kind of reasoning we've been discussing earlier in this book *horizontal reasoning*, since it moves us from premises to conclusion in a single language. We now want to describe a kind of *vertical reasoning* that extends our language. If you've ever used a dictionary, then the main technique of vertical reasoning will be familiar to you: it's making definitions.

But we aren't concerned with the kind of definition that takes a word that's already in use and that spells out its meaning in terms of other words. We're concerned with the kind of definition that introduces a new term.

Consider, for example, the natural language predicates "x is a parent" and "x is female," as applied to persons. In this case, we can define a compound predicate

$$x \text{ is a parent } \wedge \ x \text{ is a female}$$

which can conveniently be abbreviated by "x is a mother." In other words, starting from predicates such as Gx and Fx, we can define a new compound predicate:

$$\phi(x) \equiv Gx \wedge Fx.$$

The left-hand side of the definition—that is, the thing being defined—is called the **definiendum**. The right-hand side of the definition consists of a formula in the antecedently established vocabulary, in this case, the vocabulary that consists of Gx and Fx. The right-hand side of the definition is called the **definiens**, that is, the thing in terms of which the new symbol is defined.

The quantifiers provide yet more sophisticated ways to formulate definitions. Suppose, for example, that instead of having a predicate for "x is a parent," we had a relation symbol Rxy for "x is a parent of y." Then we could define

$$
\begin{aligned}
\text{parent}(x) &\leftrightarrow \exists y Rxy \\
\text{child}(x) &\leftrightarrow \exists y Ryx \\
\text{grandparent}(x, z) &\leftrightarrow \exists y (Rxy \wedge Ryz) \\
\text{sibling}(x, z) &\leftrightarrow \exists y (Ryx \wedge Ryz)
\end{aligned}
$$

Exercise 7.13. Translate the following sentences into predicate logic notation. Restrict yourself to the following vocabulary: Fx for "x is female," Pxy for "x is a parent of y, and Lxy for "x loves y." Assume that we're only talking about people, so you don't need a predicate symbol for "is a person." You'll want to define new relations and predicates out of the ones we've supplied (e.g., "y is a child" can be symbolized as $\exists x Pxy$).

1. Every woman who has a daughter loves her daughter.
2. Every person loves their parent's children.
3. Everybody loves their own grandchildren.
4. Everybody loves their nieces and nephews.
5. No man loves children unless he has his own.
6. Everybody is loved by somebody.
7. Everybody loves a lover. (Hint: A lover is anyone who loves somebody.)

This kind of defining maneuver can be very powerful when used with genuine formal theories like Peano arithmetic. For example, let $<$ be a binary relation symbol, which we will write in infix notation. Define $x < y$ to be the formula $\exists z(x + (z + 1) = y)$. Then it can be shown that $x < y$ satisfies the axioms for a strict linear ordering, and knowing that, we can bring all of our knowledge about linear orderings to bear in our reasoning about arithmetic.

Exercise 7.14. Prove the following sequents.

1. PA $\vdash \forall x(\neg(x < x))$
2. PA $\vdash \forall xyz((x < y \land y < z) \to x < z)$
3. PA $\vdash \forall xy(x < y \lor x = y \lor y < z)$

Predicates and relations aren't the only things that can be defined. We can also define new terms (names and function symbols). For example, if I know your name (suppose it's "a"), and I have a function symbol $\mathsf{mom}(x)$ that I use to talk about the mother of x, then I have a name for your mother: $\mathsf{mom}(a)$. In other words, a name plus a function symbol gives a new name. We're very familiar with this maneuver in the case of arithmetic. In our formulation of Peano arithmetic above, we only had two names: 0 and 1. But now we can use the addition symbol to define names of new numbers (e.g., $2 = 1 + 1, 3 = 2 + 1$, etc.).

More generally, we can define terms from formulas, so long as we ensure that those formulas have the right features. For example, suppose that I have a language with a relation symbol Rxy for "y is the biological mother of x." (Note the order of variables: child comes first, then mother.) There are two particular facts about biological motherhood that will be relevant here:

$$\forall x \exists y R x y \qquad (Rxy \wedge Rxz) \to y = z.$$

The first fact is that everyone has a biological mother. The second fact is that everyone has at most one biological mother. Under these conditions, we say that Rxy is a **functional relation**, and we can define a new function symbol f by the condition

$$f(x) = y \leftrightarrow Rxy.$$

More generally, if $\phi(x_1, \ldots, x_n, y)$ is any formula with $n + 1$ free variables, and if T is a theory that implies that $\phi(x_1, \ldots, x_n, y)$ is a functional relation, then we permit T to be extended by means of a definition

$$f(x_1, \ldots, x_n) = y \leftrightarrow \phi(x_1, \ldots, x_n, y).$$

In the special case of $n = 0$, to say that T implies that $\phi(y)$ is a functional relation means that $T \vdash \exists! y\, \phi(y)$. In that case, we're permitted to define a new name c by the formula

$$c = y \leftrightarrow \phi(y).$$

The reason for the restriction on the definition of terms is so that definitions don't lead to bad logic. For example, suppose that an evil logician tried to pull a fast one on you by doing the following:

Let's write $\phi(x)$ to mean that x is omnipotent, omniscient, and omnibenevolent. Now define a name a by $\forall x(x = a \leftrightarrow \phi(x))$. Now, it's a theorem of predicate logic that $\exists x(x = a)$, and a quick argument shows that $\exists x \phi(x)$. Therefore, God exists.

No matter your opinion about theology, you shouldn't let this argument pass. The problem was letting the evil logician define the name a without first showing that there is a unique ϕ.

A similar problem would arise if you tried to define a name when it has not previously been proven that at most one thing satisfies the definiens. For example, suppose that you decided to define the name a by

$$\forall x((x = a) \leftrightarrow \text{even}(x)),$$

where the predicate even ranges over whole numbers. This definition would then entail that there is just one even number. So, one should only define a name in terms of a predicate if one has shown that the predicate is uniquely instantiated.

If making definitions doesn't add new information, then what really is the point of making them? One might ask in reply: if deducing consequences from a set of premises doesn't lead to genuinely new information, then what's the point of doing that? We won't try to solve these philosophical puzzles here. It's enough to point out that both deducing and defining are essential components of a logical lifestyle.

Exercise 7.15. The following series of exercises is intended to show how defining new concepts can facilitate reasoning. We begin with a spartan language that has only one binary function symbol ∘. We then impose three axioms:

B1. $\forall x \forall y \forall z(x \circ (y \circ z) = (x \circ y) \circ z)$
B2. $\forall x \forall z \exists! y(x \circ y = z)$
B3. $\forall x \forall z \exists! w(w \circ x = z)$

The theory given by B1–B3 is sometimes called **autosets**, because it describes a collection of things that act upon themselves. The exercises show that the theory of autosets is equivalent to **group theory**.

Recall here that ∃! is an abbreviation for the compound phrase "there exists a unique." From these axioms, one can directly prove the following sentence

$\exists! y \forall x (x \circ y = x = y \circ x)$.

But a direct proof is hideously complex. Another way the result can be proven is by first proving

$\exists! y \forall x (x \circ y = x)$

and then introducing a name e for this unique y. One can then prove that $\forall x (x = e \circ x)$, thus completing the proof. The following steps will lead you through the process.

1. Prove that $\forall x \forall z ((x \circ z = x) \rightarrow \forall y (y \circ z = y))$.
2. Prove that $\exists! y \forall x (x \circ y = x)$.
3. Define a name e for the unique y whose existence you just proved.
4. Prove that $\forall x (x = e \leftrightarrow (x \circ x = x))$.
5. Since $\forall x \exists! y (x \circ y = e)$, define a function symbol $^{-1}$ such that $\forall x (x \circ x^{-1} = e)$.
6. Prove that $\forall x (x^{-1} \circ x = e)$. [Hint: use $(x^{-1} \circ x) \circ (x^{-1} \circ x) = x^{-1} \circ x$.]
7. Prove that $\forall x (e \circ x = x)$.

Exercise 7.16. The following exercises ask you to define new relations and then to prove that these relations have certain nice properties.

1. Let F and G be predicates, and define

   $\phi(x, y) \equiv Fx \wedge Gy$.

   Show that $\phi(x, y)$ is symmetric, that is, $\forall x \forall y (\phi(x, y) \rightarrow \phi(y, x))$.
2. Let Rxy be a binary relation, and define

   $\phi(x, y) \equiv \forall w (Rwx \rightarrow Rwy)$.

   Show that $\phi(x, y)$ is transitive, that is, $\forall x \forall y \forall z ((\phi(x, y) \wedge \phi(y, z)) \rightarrow \phi(x, z))$.

3. Let F be a predicate, and define

$$\phi(x,y) \equiv Fx \leftrightarrow Fy.$$

Show that $\phi(x,y)$ is an equivalence relation, that is, reflexive, symmetric, and transitive.

Set Theory

The next theory we develop is of deep foundational importance. In fact, it is currently believed that *all* of mathematics rests on the foundation of set theory.

At the beginning of the twentieth century, some logicians hoped to show that all of mathematics can be derived from pure logic. I say "hoped" because the point of such a derivation would be to explain away the mystery of our certainty of the truths of mathematics. As we have seen, logical truths purchase certainty at the price of vacuity. For example, you can be certain that $P \vee \neg P$, but it doesn't exclude any possibilities. So, if math could be derived from logic, then mathematical truths (such as $1 + 1 = 2$) would not exclude any possibilities.

To make a long story short, the reduction of math to pure logic didn't quite work. However, it almost worked. A consensus emerged that to get all of mathematics, you only need to add a few axioms that describe properties of **sets** of things. In this section, we'll present a piece of this theory of sets. Besides its intrinsic interest for the foundations of mathematics, the theory of sets is of special interest to logicians, because it's a great reference point for checking our knowledge of basic logical facts. Most particularly, we can use set theory to construct the analogue of truth tables for quantifier logic, allowing us to show that certain sequents cannot be proven.

There are many different ways that we could formalize the theory of sets. The most common way these days is to formulate a theory with a single relation symbol $\in$ and whose objects (i.e., the things the quantifiers are supposed to range over) are supposed to be sets. From that spartan basis, one can then construct things like sets of ordered pairs, subsets of ordered pairs, and even functions (seen as a certain kind of subset of ordered pairs).

We find it more convenient, however, to take both sets and functions between sets as primitive, undefined notions. We could do this by using two predicates "is a set" and "is a function," but we'll usually just indicate whether something is a set or a function by means of using a different style of variables: we'll use capital letters such as A, B, X, Y for sets and lowercase letters such as f, g, h, . . . for functions. The notation $f : A \rightarrow B$ is shorthand for "A and B are sets and f is a function from A to B." The set A is said to be the **domain** of f, and the set B is said to be the **codomain** of f.[5]

As with any theory, the theory of sets tries to formalize an intuitive idea. Here the intuitive picture is something like the following: The two ovals are sets A and B, and the dots inside the ovals are their elements. Hence, A consists of elements a, b, c, d, and B consists of elements $1, 2, 3, 4$. We use the notation "$a \in A$" to indicate that a is an element of A. (Thus, $\in$ is a binary relation symbol, written in infix notation.) The arrows from elements in A to elements in B constitute a function $f : A \rightarrow B$, which consists of an assignment of each element in A to some element in B.

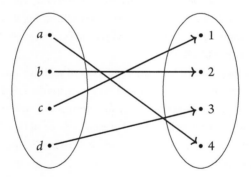

The following axiomatization of set theory prioritizes clarity over rigor. We have attempted to write the axioms in such a way that they are easy to understand, but so that it's possible for the interested reader to determine how they might be fully regimented in first-order logic.

---

5. To be clear, the symbols f, g, h here are not function symbols but variables that range over the type of thing that we intuitively think of as functions. If we were to fully formalize this theory, it would have function symbols d_0 for the domain of a function, d_1 for the codomain of a function, and i for the identity function of a set.

S1. Extensionality The first axiom provides the condition under which two sets are equal, namely, when they contain the same elements.

$$\forall A \forall B (A = B \leftrightarrow \forall x(x \in A \leftrightarrow x \in B)).$$

Similarly, two functions are equal if and only if they agree on all inputs.

$$\forall f \forall g (f = g \leftrightarrow \forall x(f(x) = g(x))).$$

S2. Comprehension The second axiom provides a method of building new sets from old sets. It tells us that if we already have a set A, and if we can describe a property $\phi(x)$ of elements of A (using the language of set theory), then there is a set B of things that contains just those elements. We sometimes write this set B as $\{x \in A \mid \phi(x)\}$, read as "the x in A such that $\phi(x)$." The meaning of this axiom will be clearer after we see which sorts of properties $\phi(x)$ can be described in the language of set theory.

S3. Empty Set The third axiom declares the existence of a set with no elements.

$$\exists A \forall x(x \notin A).$$

There will be a couple more axioms to come, but these first three will suffice to prove some interesting basic facts about sets and functions. Consider the following claim and proof.

Proposition 7.1. *There is only one empty set, that is $\exists! A \forall x(x \notin A)$.*

Proof. The empty set axiom says that there is at least one empty set, so we only need show that there is at most one. Suppose, then, that A and B are empty sets. That is, $\forall x(x \notin A)$ and $\forall x(x \notin B)$. We will show first that $\forall x(x \in A \rightarrow x \in B)$. Since $\forall x(x \notin A)$, we have $a \notin A$. Hence, by negative paradox, if $a \in A$, then $a \in B$. Since a was arbitrary, $\forall x(x \in A \rightarrow x \in B)$. A similar argument shows that $\forall x(x \in B \rightarrow x \in A)$. By extensionality, $A = B$. □

This proof is fully compliant with the inference rules you learned earlier in this book. You could, in fact, write it out in its full glory, with dependency numbers, citations of rules, and so on. However, it's slightly more pleasant for human beings to read and write proofs with words. Moreover, there's an art to saying just the right words to convince your reader that the proof really does work. One of the goals of this section is to help you hone your skill as a writer of clear and rigorous arguments.

It can be a lot easier to use set theory if we define some new relation and function symbols. We begin by using the fact we proved above—that there is a unique empty set—to define a name "$\emptyset$" with the condition

$$\forall A\big(A = \emptyset \leftrightarrow \forall x(x \notin A)\big).$$

We now define a binary relation symbol $\subseteq$ (written in infix notation) that is intended to capture the idea of one set being contained in another.

Definition. For sets A and B, we say that A is a **subset** of B, written $A \subseteq B$, just in case $\forall x(x \in A \rightarrow x \in B)$. More formally,

$$\forall A \forall B\big(A \subseteq B \leftrightarrow \forall x(x \in A \rightarrow x \in B)\big).$$

Keep in mind that the containment relation $\subseteq$ is very different from the elementhood relation $\in$. For most purposes in this book, you can think of the elementhood relation $\in$ as standing between some a that is *not* a set and some A that *is* a set. For example, you can think of yourself as an element or member of the set of people who have read this sentence. In contrast, the relation $\subseteq$ can only hold between two sets. Since you are not a set, you cannot stand in the relation $\subseteq$ to anything else.[6]

We illustrate the definition of subset by showing that the empty set $\emptyset$ is a subset of every other set.

Proposition 7.2. $\forall B(\emptyset \subseteq B)$.

---

6. For the advanced reader: We are intentionally maintaining a naive distinction between sets and nonsets. If one really adopted ZF set theory as their "theory of everything," then everything would be a set.

Proof. Let B be an arbitrary set. Since $\forall x(x \notin \emptyset)$, negative paradox gives $\forall x(x \in \emptyset \rightarrow x \in B)$. By the definition of $\subseteq$, it follows that $\emptyset \subseteq B$. Since B was an arbitrary set, it follows that $\forall B(\emptyset \subseteq B)$. $\qquad\square$

Exercise 7.17. Prove the following results.

1. $A \subseteq A$.
2. If $A \subseteq B$ and $B \subseteq C$, then $A \subseteq C$.
3. If $A \subseteq B$ and $B \subseteq A$, then $A = B$.

Recall that when a theory T implies that a relation $\phi(x, y, z)$ is functional, then we may define a binary function symbol, say $\cap$, by

$$(x \cap y = z) \leftrightarrow \phi(x, y, z).$$

Consider, then, the following relation, definable in the theory of sets:

$$\phi(A, B, C) \equiv \forall x(x \in C \leftrightarrow (x \in A \wedge x \in B)).$$

To see that ϕ is functional, suppose that $\phi(A, B, C)$ and $\phi(A, B, D)$. A quick argument shows then that $\forall x(x \in C \leftrightarrow x \in D)$, and hence by extensionality, $C = D$. Therefore, ϕ is functional, and we may define

$$(A \cap B = C) \leftrightarrow \phi(A, B, C).$$

In other words,

$$\forall x(x \in A \cap B \leftrightarrow (x \in A \wedge x \in B)).$$

We call $A \cap B$ the **intersection** of A and B.

Exercise 7.18. Prove the following results.

1. $A \cap A = A$.
2. $A \cap \emptyset = \emptyset$.

3. $A \subseteq B$ if and only if $A \cap B = B$.
4. $C \subseteq A \cap B$ if and only if $C \subseteq A$ and $C \subseteq B$.

Similar to the definition of intersection, we can also define a **union** of sets. Here, the relevant relation is

$$\phi(A, B, C) \leftrightarrow \forall x(x \in C \leftrightarrow (x \in A \lor x \in B)).$$

Since ϕ is functional, we may define a function symbol $\cup$ with the feature

$$\forall x(x \in A \cup B \leftrightarrow (x \in A \lor x \in B)).$$

Exercise 7.19. Prove the following results.

1. $A \cup A = A$.
2. $A \cup \emptyset = A$.
3. $A \subseteq B$ if and only if $A \cup B = B$.
4. $A \cap (B \cup C) = (A \cap B) \cup (A \cap C)$.

We need one more function on sets, namely, the **relative complement** of two sets. The idea here is that $A \backslash B$ should consist of all those elements in A that are *not* in B. Thus, the defining condition is

$$\forall x(x \in A \backslash B \leftrightarrow (x \in A \land x \notin B)).$$

It is frequently useful to speak as if a set A has an absolute complement A^c, that is, the set of all things that are not in the set A. Mathematicians know that it's dangerous to talk about "the set of all things such that …," but for many practical purposes, we can take some large set X as the background domain, and then we can think of A^c as the relative complement of A in X.

Exercise 7.20. Let $A^c = X \backslash A$, and prove the following:

1. $(A \cup B)^c = A^c \cap B^c$.
2. $(A \cap B)^c = A^c \cup B^c$.

3. $A \cup A^c = X$.

4. $A \cap A^c = X$.

The construction we perform now is not exactly a definition; in one sense, it should be considered a new axiom.

S4. Cartesian Products There is a construction process that takes two sets A, B as input and that produces a new set $A \times B$ as output. The set $A \times B$ is called the **Cartesian product** of A and B. Each element of this new set $A \times B$ can be written in the form $\langle a, b \rangle$ with the identity condition:

$$\langle a, b \rangle = \langle c, d \rangle \leftrightarrow a = c \wedge b = d.$$

Note that the order in $\langle a, b \rangle$ matters; that is, it is not necessarily the case that $\langle a, b \rangle = \langle b, a \rangle$. Accordingly, an element of the form $\langle a, b \rangle$ is called an **ordered pair**.

We define $\pi_1 : A \times B \to A$ to be the function that takes each ordered pair $\langle a, b \rangle$ to its first component a. Similarly, we define $\pi_2 : A \times B \to B$ to be the function that takes each ordered pair $\langle a, b \rangle$ to its second component b.

It's not difficult to see that if A and B are finite sets, then the number $|A \times B|$ of elements in $A \times B$ is $|A| \cdot |B|$, where $|A|$ is the number of elements in A, and $|B|$ is the number of elements in B. In fact, something like that result continues to hold even when A and B are infinite. However, that more general result depends on developing a notion of different sizes of infinity, and that's a subject for a more advanced book.

Exercise 7.21. Show that if A has two elements and B has two elements, then $A \times B$ has four elements.

Exercise 7.22. Show that $\emptyset \times A = \emptyset$.

Predicate logic makes heavy use of **relation symbols**, such as Rxy. But what is a relation? In the world of sets, we can think of a **relation** as a kind of set—namely, a subset of $A \times B$. That might seem like a strange thing to say. After all, if I asked you to give me an example of a relation, you might suggest the relation of being a parent, the relation of being a sibling, or the relation of being taller than. In what sense are these relations like a subset of $A \times B$?

Every relation has two aspects: an **intension** and an **extension**. The former, the intension, is a bit mysterious and difficult to define, but basically it's supposed to be the essence or meaning of the relation—what makes it the particular relation that it is. The latter, the extension, is easier to define: the extension of a relation is just the set of ordered pairs that stand in that relation. So, for example, the extension of the relation "has been married to" consists of all pairs of people who have been married to each other, including

⟨Donald, Marla⟩,   ⟨Donald, Ivana⟩,   ⟨Donald, Melania⟩.

So far, we've just been talking about binary relations, that is, those that hold between two things. There are, however, n-ary relations for every natural number n. The unary relations more frequently go under the name of **properties**. Just like other relations, a property has an intension and an extension. Thus, the extension of a property is simply the set of those things that possess the property.

Interestingly, properties with distinct intension can have the same extension. A famous example used by W.v.O. Quine are the properties "x is a living creature with a heart" and "x is a living creature with kidneys."[7] Obviously, having a heart is not the same thing as having kidneys. However, any living creature has a heart if and only if it has kidneys. Therefore, these two properties have the same extension.

It's surprisingly useful to classify relations into different kinds. Here, we'll talk about two special kinds of relations: equivalence relations and functional relations.

Equivalence Relations

We frequently have several names for the same thing. If a and b are names for the same thing, then we would say "a is identical to b," or in short

7. See Quine, "Two dogmas of empiricism." *The Philosophical Review* 60, 20–43 (1951).

"$a = b$." As we saw before, the equality relation has a peculiar logic. For example, we take it for granted that $a = a$ (which is certainly not the case for every relation). We also showed that if $a = b$, then $b = a$ and that if $a = b$ and $b = c$, then $a = c$. While the equality relation has these features, it's not the only relation with them. For example, consider the relation R where $\langle a, b \rangle \in R$ just in case a is the same height as b. Then $\langle a, a \rangle \in R$ (i.e., everyone is the same height as themselves); if $\langle a, b \rangle \in R$, then $\langle b, a \rangle \in R$ (being the same height as is symmetric); and if $\langle a, b \rangle \in R$ and $\langle b, c \rangle \in R$, then $\langle a, c \rangle \in R$ (being the same height as is transitive). These facts show that R is an equivalence relation.

A relation R on $A \times A$ is said to be an **equivalence relation** just in case it is

reflexive For all $a \in A$, $\langle a, a \rangle \in R$.
symmetric For all $a, b \in A$, if $\langle a, b \rangle \in R$, then $\langle b, a \rangle \in R$.
transitive For all $a, b, c \in A$, if $\langle a, b \rangle \in R$ and $\langle b, c \rangle \in R$, then $\langle a, c \rangle \in R$.

The simplest example of an equivalence relation is the equality relation $R = \{\langle a, a \rangle \mid a \in A\}$. Another equivalence relation is the relation of having the same value for a certain quantity. For example, "x is the same height as y" is an equivalence relation on the set of people.

Exercise 7.23.

1. Let R be an equivalence relation, and let $[a]$ be the set of all things related to a, that is,

   $$[a] = \{b \mid \langle a, b \rangle \in R\}.$$

   Show that either $[a] = [b]$ or $[a] \cap [b] = \emptyset$.
2. Suppose that R and S are equivalence relations. Show that $R \cap S$ is an equivalence relation.
3. Let $\phi \equiv \psi$ be the interderivability relation in propositional logic. Show that $\equiv$ is an equivalence relation.

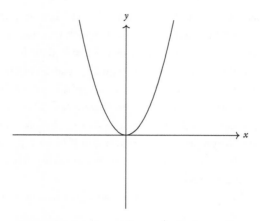

Figure 7.1. Graph of the function $f(x) = x^2$. The parabola is the set of ordered pairs $\langle x, x^2 \rangle$.

Functional Relations

There are several different ways to think of what a **function** is. First, a function can be thought of as a *rule* that assigns elements of one set to elements of another set. Second, a function can be conceived of as a *graph*, that is, a set of ordered pairs in a plane. You might remember that for a graph to be a function, it has to have the feature that any vertical line intersects it in only one point. In other words, the graph of a function has the feature that if both $\langle a, b \rangle$ and $\langle a, c \rangle$ occur in the graph, then $b = c$.

Many familiar functions are not really functions in the strict sense. Consider, for example, the inverse function $\frac{1}{x}$. This operation isn't defined at 0, and so it isn't really a function on all real numbers (i.e., its domain set is not the set of all real numbers). We require that a function is defined on all elements of its domain set, that is, for all x in the domain, there is an $f(x)$ in the codomain.

A relation R on $A \times B$ is said to be a **functional relation** just in case it satisfies

existence For all $a \in A$, there is a $b \in B$ such that $\langle a, b \rangle \in R$.
uniqueness If $\langle a, b \rangle \in R$ and $\langle a, c \rangle \in R$, then $b = c$.

Any function $f : A \to B$ gives rise to a functional relation called its graph:

$$\text{graph}(f) = \{\langle x, f(x) \rangle \mid x \in X\}.$$

By the extensionality axiom, there is a one-to-one correspondence between functions and functional relations, that is, each function corresponds to precisely one functional relation, and if two functions are distinct, then they correspond to distinct relations.

Since functions are relations, functions have both an intension and an extension. You may already have observed that fact (i.e., that a single function can be expressed in various ways). Consider, for example, the following functions:

$$f(x) = x^2 - 1, \qquad g(x) = (x + 1)(x - 1).$$

Here we might say that f and g have different intensions, since they provide different recipes for calculating an output. Nonetheless, these two recipes always produce the same output; hence, f and g have the same extension.

Functions, like relations, have an **arity**, that is, a number of inputs. Unlike relations, however, functions always have a single output. A function like $f(x) = x^2 - 1$ is unary (i.e., it takes one input). In contrast, the addition function is binary (i.e., its input is two numbers). In the limiting case, a 0-ary function has no inputs and one output. Such a function is called a **point** or an **element**, that is, it is an element in a set.

Since points are a special case of functions, which is a special case of a relation, it also follows that a point has both an intension and an extension. To see what's going on here, it may be easier to think of a point as a name. Then the intension of a name is its connotation, and the extension of a name is its denotation.[8]

If f is a function from A to B, and g is a function from B to C, then we may define a function $g \circ f$ from A to C by setting

$$(g \circ f)(x) = g(f(x)), \qquad \forall x \in A.$$

8. For further investigation of this issue, see Gottlob Frege's discussion of "morning star" and "evening star."

Exercise 7.24. Show the rather trivial fact that $h \circ (g \circ f) = (h \circ g) \circ f$, whenever f, g, and h have domains and codomains that align in the right way.

Exercise 7.25. Suppose that $R = \text{graph}(f)$ and $S = \text{graph}(g)$. Show that

$$\text{graph}(g \circ f) = \big\{ \langle x, z \rangle \mid \exists y (\langle x, y \rangle \in R \wedge \langle y, z \rangle \in S) \big\}.$$

Exercise 7.26.

1. Consider the function $f(x) = x^3$ on real numbers. Is f one-to-one? Is f onto?
2. Give an example of a functional relation that can be described in the vocabulary of a typical ten-year-old child.
3. Show that if $g \circ f$ is one-to-one, then f is one-to-one.
4. Give an example of functions g and f where $g \circ f$ is one-to-one, but g is not one-to-one.

Given a function $f : X \to Y$, there's a natural way to define a couple of other functions. First of all, we define an **inverse image** function f^{-1} that maps subsets of Y to subsets of X. In particular,

$$(x \in f^{-1}(A)) \leftrightarrow (f(x) \in A).$$

In other words,

$$f^{-1}(A) = \{ x \in X \mid f(x) \in A \}.$$

The set $f^{-1}(A)$ is called the **inverse image** or **preimage** of A under f. We now show that inverse image preserves intersections.

Proposition 7.3. $f^{-1}(A \cap B) = f^{-1}(A) \cap f^{-1}(B)$.

Proof. We string together a series of biconditionals.

$$x \in f^{-1}(A \cap B) \leftrightarrow f(x) \in A \cap B$$
$$\leftrightarrow f(x) \in A \wedge f(x) \in B$$

$$\leftrightarrow x \in f^{-1}(A) \wedge x \in f^{-1}(B)$$
$$\leftrightarrow x \in f^{-1}(A) \cap f^{-1}(B). \qquad \qquad \square$$

Whereas the preimage mapping f^{-1} takes subsets of Y to subsets of X, the **image** mapping moves in the opposite direction. Here we abuse notation by using f again for the image mapping, which applies to subsets of X instead of to elements of X. We define

$$f(A) = \{y \in Y \mid \exists x(x \in A \wedge f(x) = y)\}.$$

That is, $f(A)$ consists of those elements in Y that are in the range of A under the mapping f. In general, it is not the case that $f(A \cap B) = f(A) \cap f(B)$. Suppose, for example, that $A \cap B = \emptyset$ and that f is a function such that $f(A) = f(B) = Y$. Then $f(A \cap B) = f(\emptyset) = \emptyset$, but $f(A) \cap f(B) = Y$.

Exercise 7.27. Prove the following for arbitrary sets A, B, and function $f : A \to B$.

1. $f^{-1}(A \cup B) = f^{-1}(A) \cup f^{-1}(B)$.
2. If $A \subseteq B$, then $f^{-1}(A) \subseteq f^{-1}(B)$.
3. $f(A \cup B) = f(A) \cup f(B)$.
4. If f is a one-to-one function, then $f(A \cap B) = f(A) \cap f(B)$.

Exercise 7.28. Show that if $f : A \to B$ is one-to-one, and A is nonempty, then there is a function $g : B \to A$ such that $g \circ f$ is the identity function on A.

Axioms S1–S4 tell us what sets must be like, but they don't say much about which sets exist, other than the empty set. Our next axiom ensures us of the existence of a set whose elements form an infinite progression. You know this set under the common description: $0, 1, 2, \ldots$ (i.e., the **natural numbers** N). The key property of N is that it has an origin 0 and a successor function $s(x) = x + 1$ that enumerates all its elements.

S5. Infinity There is a set N, with element $0 \in N$, and a function $s : N \to N$ such that s is one-to-one, but not onto, and every element of N can be reached by a finite number of applications of s to 0.

Successive applications of s allow us to name all of the elements in N:

$$1 = s(0), 2 = s(s(0)), \ldots.$$

We can then use the comprehension axiom to define all the finite and cofinite subsets of N, such as

$$\{x \in N \mid x = 2 \vee x = 4\}, \qquad \{x \in N \mid x \neq 3\}.$$

It follows, then, that for each natural number n, there is a set S_n with exactly n elements. As a convenient shorthand, we will write $\{a_1, \ldots, a_n\}$ for the set

$$\{x \in N \mid x = a_1 \vee \cdots \vee x = a_2\}.$$

Then extensionality entails that duplicate items can be removed from a set, for example, $\{a, a, b\} = \{a, b\}$.

The structure of the natural numbers N makes it possible to define an addition function $+$ and a multiplication function $\cdot$. For example, we set $x + 0 = x$, and $x + s(y) = s(x + y)$. It can be shown that $+, \cdot, 0, 1$ satisfy the Peano axioms for arithmetic. Thus, there is a clear sense in which the theory PA can be translated into the theory of sets. This translation provides the desired reduction of at least one important part of mathematics (namely, arithmetic) to set theory.

For the comprehension axiom, one might think it would be simpler just to say that for any formula $\phi(x)$, there is a set $\{x|\phi(x)\}$ of all things that satisfy x. But that idea leads immediately to problems, as was noted by Bertrand Russell. Consider, for example, the following predicate:

$$\phi(x) \equiv x \notin x,$$

and let $A = \{x \mid \phi(x)\}$. In other words, A is the set of all sets that do not contain themselves.

Exercise 7.29. Show that if $A \in A$, then $A \notin A$. Then show that if $A \notin A$, then $A \in A$. Conclude that the assumption that A exists leads to a contradiction.

It turns out, then, not to be so easy to formulate a theory of sets that is both **consistent** and powerful enough to serve as a foundation for mathematics.

8
Models

THE PRIMARY GOAL OF THIS CHAPTER is to teach you how to *prove* that an argument is invalid. The idea here is like truth tables, but the method more closely resembles what one actually does in real-life scenarios, especially in the sciences.

A typical (scientific) theory is applicable in many different situations. For example, Darwin's theory of evolution applies to early human history, but it also applies to populations of fruit flies or to cancer cells. Similarly, a theory about economic bubbles might apply to the housing bubble in the United States in the early 2000s and also to the tulip crisis of 1637 in Holland. So, scientific thinking involves both abstract theory and the application of that theory to specific situations—or, to be more precise, application to more concrete descriptions of situations. We'll say that the concrete description is a **model** of the abstract theory.[1]

For our purposes, the primary utility of model building is that we can use it to show that an argument is invalid. For, if one can build a model where the premises of an argument are true, but its conclusion is false, then that argument is invalid. What, then, are the rules for model building, and how can we tell whether or not sentences are true in a model? To get answers to

---

1. Warning: The English verb "to model" is used in two almost opposite ways. First, one can model a concrete thing by constructing an abstract representation of it. Second, one can model an abstract idea or theory by constructing a more concrete instance of it. In this chapter, we will be concerned exclusively with the second sense of modeling.

these questions, let's begin with a famous example where model building played a crucial role.

For most of Western history, Euclidean geometry was taken to be the paradigm example of certain knowledge. Sitting in a dark room, you can use Euclidean geometry to deduce, with complete logical rigor, that in any triangle, the sum of the internal angles is 180 degrees. Then if you go outside and measure triangles, you will find again and again that the prediction of Euclidean geometry is correct: the internal angles always add up to 180 degrees.

It seems almost like a miracle that Euclidean geometry—discovered more than two thousand years ago—could be so certain. This kind of thought led many people throughout history to investigate the source of our knowledge of the axioms of Euclidean geometry. Some of these investigations were of a philosophical nature, and others were focused on mathematical questions, such as: is it possible to boil down the number of axioms of Euclidean geometry so that we're left with just a few axioms that are obviously true?

We won't go into details here, but just think about it this way. Some of the axioms of Euclidean geometry seem to be self-evidently true. For example, between any two points, there is a line, or similarly, any two right angles are equal to each other. Let's write Γ for the collection of these uncontroversial axioms.

However, Euclidean geometry also depends on the following, less obvious, axiom:

> Parallel postulate: for any line x, and for an point p not on x, there is a unique line y such that $p \in y$ and such that y is parallel to x.

Let's write P for the parallel postulate. Because P is not obviously true on its face, many mathematicians spent a lot of time trying to prove that it follows from the uncontroversial axioms. That is, they tried to show that $\Gamma \vdash P$. I'm sorry to say that some of these mathematicians spent their whole lives trying to prove this little sequent and died without having found an answer. In fact, nobody ever managed to prove it.

But then something amazing happened. In the nineteenth century, an obscure Russian mathematician named Nikolai Lobachevsky decided that he would try for a proof. Being a clever logician, Lobachevsky realized that all he had to do was to prove that Γ and $\neg P$ imply a contradiction. So, he assumed the uncontroversial axioms and the *negation* of the parallel postulate, and he got busy working his way toward a contradiction. Lobachevsky proved many things that seemed absurd. For example, he proved that the internal angles of a triangle are strictly less than 180 degrees. However, he never got a literal contradiction, that is, he never got a sentence ϕ and also its negation $\neg\phi$.

After a while, it dawned on Lobachevsky that he had proven so many things that these consequences amounted to the description of a new mathematical universe. In other words, he had described a model M in which the uncontroversial axioms Γ are true, and the parallel postulate P is false. This model M is a non-Euclidean universe, which means that our universe isn't necessarily Euclidean. Therefore, the method of modeling is responsible for history's most famous example of showing that we don't know something that we thought we knew.

Logical Grammar

The intuitive ideas of interpretations and models are really interesting and suggestive. These ideas have proven to be extremely useful in many domains of knowledge, from mathematics to economics and philosophy. However, as we've described them so far, these ideas are too vague to *prove* anything interesting about them and, a fortiori, to use them to prove anything about the system of logic we've developed in this book.

The tool we develop here is the notion of an **interpretation** of a predicate logic language into the theory of sets. For this we assume that we have a fairly firm grasp of what is true or false in the universe of sets. Thus, in order to show that a sequent $\phi \vdash \psi$ is not valid, we will show that ϕ and ψ can be interpreted as set-theoretic statements such that ϕ is obviously true, and ψ is obviously false.

To this end, we first need a precise description of the family of predicate logic sentences. Suppose that Σ is a fixed predicate logic signature. That is, Σ consists of function symbols and relation symbols. We'll also assume that Σ comes with an equality symbol. We then define the set of Σ -**terms** as follows:

- Each variable $x, y, z, \ldots$ is a Σ-term.
- If $f \in \Sigma$ is an n-ary function symbol, and $t_1, \ldots, t_n$ are Σ-terms, then $f(t_1, \ldots, t_n)$ is a Σ-term.

When no confusion can result, we'll just say "term" instead of "Σ-term." The special case of a 0-ary function symbol is called a **name** or a **constant symbol**.

This definition of terms should agree with the intuitions you have already developed. For example, if Σ comes with a binary function symbol $\circ$, then the terms include expressions such as $x \circ y$ and $(x \circ y) \circ z$. If Σ comes with a name 1 and a binary function symbol $+$, then the terms include expressions such as $1 + 1$ and $(1 + 1) + (1 + 1)$. Semantically speaking, the terms will be interpreted as functions and, in the special case of names, will be interpreted as points.

We define the set of Σ-**formulas** as follows:

- If t_1 and t_2 are terms, then $t_1 = t_2$ is a formula.
- If R is an n-ary relation symbol and $t_1, \ldots, t_n$ are terms, then $R(t_1, \ldots, t_n)$ is a formula.
- If ϕ and ψ are formulas, then $\phi \vee \psi$, $\phi \wedge \psi$, $\phi \to \psi$, and $\neg\phi$ are formulas.
- If ϕ is a formula that does not contain the quantifiers $\forall x$ or $\exists x$, then $\forall x \phi$ and $\exists x \phi$ are formulas.

A few comments on this definition of formulas. First, to be more rigorous, we might want to define simultaneously the notion of a formula and the notion of the variables that occur freely in that formula. However, we will operate for now on a more intuitive level. Basically, a variable occurs **freely** in a formula if that variable hasn't been bound by a quantifier at any stage of construction. So, for example, in the formula $x = y$, the variables x and y both occur freely. However, in the formula $\forall x(x = y)$, the variable x has been bound, and only y occurs freely.

Second, the quantifier clause of our definition is clumsy. It would be simpler to allow formulas like $\forall x(Px \to \exists x Qx)$, but that is not permitted by our quantifier clause. The reason for the more restrictive clause is simply to encourage the student to use perspicuous notation. While there is no reason in theory to ban sentences such as $\forall x(Px \rightarrow \exists x Qx)$, it's better to use a variant such as $\forall x(Px \rightarrow \exists y Qy)$ in which it's clear that the first quantifier applies only to the first occurence of x.

We now define a predicate logic **sentence** to be a formula in which no variables are free. Thus, $\exists x Rax$ is a sentence, but $\exists x Ryx$ is not a sentence since y is free. Our proofs will always and only involve sentences. If you ever have a step in a proof that has a formula rather than a sentence, then you've misapplied one of the inference rules.[2]

Interpretation Formalized

An **interpretation** of the symbols in Σ consists of four things:

1. Some fixed set M, which we call the **domain** or **universe** of the interpretation. For technical reasons, the domain M must be a nonempty set.[3]

2. An assignment of each n-ary relation symbol $R \in \Sigma$ to some subset R^M of $M \times \cdots \times M$. The set R^M is called the **extension** of R in M.

3. An assignment of each constant symbol $c \in \Sigma$ to some element $c^M \in M$.

4. An assignment of each n-ary function symbol $f \in \Sigma$ to some function f^M from $M \times \cdots \times M$ to M.

There will always be many different ways that the symbols in Σ could be interpreted. There is so much freedom here it can be dizzying. How should one choose the set M from among the untold number of conceivable sets? Fortunately, it doesn't make any difference which particular set you choose. All that matters are structural facts, namely, the size of the set, the size of the extensions of the relation symbols, and the relations between the extensions of the relation symbols. For many cases, you'll be able to tell whether a sentence is consistent or inconsistent by looking at interpretations in finite sets. For some sentences, you'll need an infinite set (e.g., the natural

---

2. The most elegant proof systems allow sequents with free variables. But baby steps....

3. This requirement has bothered many logicians, including Bertrand Russell. It can be avoided by using an alternative to classical logic such as free logic or coherent logic.

numbers). For the exercises in this book, you'll never need a set bigger than the natural numbers.

Once the symbols in Σ have been assigned to relevant set-theoretic items, there is a straightforward recipe for extending the assignment to all terms and formulas built on Σ. As with valuations (i.e., rows in truth tables), the assignment grows, from the inside out, starting with the assignments to the function and relation symbols and then applying set-theoretic operations corresponding to the connectives and quantifiers.

Let's begin by looking at the case of a formula $\phi(x)$ in which only the variable x occurs. In this case, we'll define $\phi(x)^M$ to be a subset of M, which can be thought of as follows:

$\phi(x)^M$ is the set of all $a \in M$ such that $\phi(x)$ is true when x takes value a.

The definition of $\phi(x)^M$ is inductive. In particular, we first define $\phi(x)^M$ when $\phi(x)$ is an atomic formula. Then we extend the definition to complex formulas.

If we temporarily ignore function symbols, then an atomic formula that contains only the variable x is either of the form $x = x$ or of the form $R(x, \ldots, x)$.

- Since $(x = x)^M$ should be the set of all M that are equal to themselves, it should be all of M.
- As for $R(x, \ldots, x)^M$, since R^M is defined to be a subset of $M \times \cdots \times M$, we can define $R(x, \ldots, x)^M$ to be the set of all $a \in M$ such that $\langle a, \ldots, a \rangle \in R^M$. More formally,

$$R(x, \ldots, x)^M = \{a \in M \mid \langle a, \ldots, a \rangle \in R^M\}.$$

Now that we have a definition of $\phi(x)^M$ for an atomic formula $\phi(x)$, we extend the definition to Boolean combinations of formulas. In particular,

$$(\phi \wedge \psi)^M = \phi^M \cap \psi^M \qquad (\phi \vee \psi)^M = \phi^M \cup \psi^M$$

$$(\neg\phi)^M = M \backslash \phi^M \qquad (\phi \rightarrow \psi)^M = (M \backslash \phi^M) \cup \psi^M$$

These definitions are fairly intuitive. For example, $(\phi \wedge \psi)^M$ is true of some a just in case both ϕ^M and ψ^M are true of a. For the case of $\phi \to \psi$, we use the intuitive equivalence with $\neg\phi \vee \psi$ and the previous definitions.

Finally, we need to extend the interpretation to formulas that are built up with quantifiers—and here we run into a little challenge. If $\phi(x)$ has a free variable x, then $\exists x \phi(x)$ no longer has a free variable, and so it doesn't make much sense to think of $\forall x \phi(x)$ as a set of things. Instead, we want to think of $\forall x \phi(x)$ as simply being true or false. The obvious thing to say here is that $(\exists x \phi(x))^M$ is true when $\phi(x)^M \neq \emptyset$, and $(\exists x \phi(x))^M$ is false when $\phi(x)^M = \emptyset$. Similarly, $(\forall x \phi(x))^M$ is true when $\phi(x)^M = M$, and $(\forall x \phi(x))^M$ is false when $\phi(x)^M \neq M$.

Example. Suppose that F and G are predicate symbols. Let $M = \{1, 2, 3\}$, let $F^M = \{1, 2\}$, and let $G = \{2, 3\}$. We can then compute

$$
\begin{aligned}
(Fx \wedge Gx)^M &= (Fx)^M \cap (Gx)^M = \{2\} \\
(Fx \vee Gx)^M &= (Fx)^M \cup (Gx)^M = M \\
\exists x (Fx \wedge Gx)^M &= \mathsf{true} \\
\forall x (Fx \wedge Gx)^M &= \mathsf{false}
\end{aligned}
$$

Example. Consider the sentence Fc. Let M be an interpretation with domain $\{1, 2\}$ where $F^M = \{1\}$ and $c^M = 2$. Then Fc is false in M. Let N be an interpretation just like M except that $c^N = 1$. Then Fc is true in N.

There are two primary reasons to build interpretations: to show that a collection of sentences is consistent and, derivatively, to show that a sequent cannot be proven. In propositional logic, a sentence ϕ is consistent just in case there is some valuation v such that $v(\phi) = 1$. In predicate logic, a sentence ϕ is consistent just in case there is some interpretation M such that ϕ^M is true. In propositional logic, a sequent $\phi \vdash \psi$ is provable if and only if every valuation that makes ϕ true also makes ψ true. In predicate logic, a sequent $\phi \vdash \psi$ is provable if and only if for any interpretation M, if ϕ^M is true, then ψ^M is true. To show, then, that a sequent cannot be proven, it suffices to produce an interpretation that makes its premises true and its conclusion false.

Definition. A **counterexample** to a sequent $\phi \vdash \psi$ is an interpretation M such that ϕ^M is true, but ψ^M is false.

A counterexample is a concrete illustration of the failure of an argument to preserve truth. That is, a counterexample to an argument is a formalization of the notion of a situation, or state of affairs, in which the premises are true and the conclusion is false.

Example. It is intuitively clear that $\forall x(Fx \vee Gx)$ doesn't imply $\forall xFx \vee \forall xGx$. We'll now construct a formal counterexample. Let $M = \{1, 2\}$, let $F^M = \{1\}$, and let $G^M = \{2\}$. Then,

$$(Fx \vee Gx)^M = (Fx)^M \cup (Gx)^M = \{1\} \cup \{2\} = M,$$

hence $(\forall x(Fx \vee Gx))^M$ is true. Since $2 \notin F^M$, it follows that $(\forall xFx)^M$ is false. Similarly, $(\forall xGx)^M$ is false, and hence $(\forall xFx \vee \forall xGx)^M$ is false. Therefore, M shows that $\forall x(Fx \vee Gx)$ does not imply $\forall xFx \vee \forall xGx$.

You might wonder: how did we know to choose this interpretation? Well, I'm sorry to say that there is no algorithm for finding predicate logic interpretations.[4] In this way, predicate logic differs markedly from propositional logic, where the truth table method provides a surefire method for finding the interpretation you want. Nonetheless, with practice, a human being can become quite good at sniffing out the relevant interpretations. For example, can I think of a situation where everything is F or G, but it's not true that everything is F, and it's not true that everything is G? What immediately comes to my mind here, as a counterexample, is even and odd numbers. Every number is either even or odd, but it's not true that every number is even, and it's not true that every number is odd. So, I could have chosen domain $M = \{1, 2, \dots\}$, and let F^M be odd numbers and G^M be even numbers. But then I realized that two numbers were enough to show that the argument is invalid, and that's why I chose $M = \{1, 2\}$ with $F^M = \{1\}$ and $G^M = \{2\}$.

4. The technical claim here is that predicate logic is **undecidable**.

There's another approach that is sometimes helpful, but it's not guaranteed to succeed. In particular, you can start to get a feel for whether or not an argument is valid by looking at what it says about small domains. For example, if you take a domain $M = \{a, b\}$ with two elements, then an existential sentence $\exists x \phi(x)$ says that $\phi(a) \vee \phi(b)$, and a universal sentence $\forall x \psi(x)$ says that $\psi(a) \wedge \psi(b)$. In some cases, you'll get lucky by looking at small domains, and you'll be able to see directly how to build a counterexample. In the example above, $\forall x(Fx \vee Gx)$ says that $(Fa \vee Ga) \wedge (Fb \vee Gb)$, and $\forall xFx \vee \forall xGx$ says that $(Fa \wedge Ga) \vee (Fb \wedge Gb)$. Then a simple truth table test shows that the valuation $v(Fa) = v(Gb) = 1$ and $v(Ga) = v(Fb) = 0$ makes the first sentence true and the second sentence false. From this, we see that $F^M = \{a\}$ and $G^M = \{b\}$ give a counterexample to the argument.[5]

Exercise 8.1. For each of the following sequents, provide a counterexample to show that it is invalid.

1. $\exists xFx \vdash Fc$
2. $Fc \vdash \forall xFx$
3. $\exists xFx \wedge \exists xGx \vdash \exists x(Fx \wedge Gx)$
4. $\forall xFx \rightarrow \forall xGx \vdash \forall x(Fx \rightarrow Gx)$
5. $\forall x(Fx \rightarrow Hx) \vdash \exists xFx \vee \neg \exists xHx$
6. $\forall x(Fx \rightarrow Gx) \vdash \exists x(Fx \wedge Gx)$
7. $\exists x(Fx \wedge Gx), \exists x(Gx \wedge Hx) \vdash \exists x(Fx \wedge Hx)$
8. $\vdash \forall xFx \vee \forall x\neg Fx$
9. $\exists x(Fx \rightarrow Gx), \exists x(Gx \rightarrow Hx) \vdash \exists x(Fx \rightarrow Hx)$
10. $\exists x(Fx \rightarrow Gx) \vdash \exists xFx \rightarrow \exists xGx$

Exercise 8.2. Suppose that ϕ and ψ are formulas where the only free variable is x. Show that $(\phi \rightarrow \psi)^M = M$ iff $\phi^M \subseteq \psi^M$.

Let's now expand the definition of an interpretation to cover propositional constants as well. An interpretation assigns a propositional constant a truth value, either true (1) or false (0). But now we have to think about

---

5. There is, in fact, an algorithm for determining the validity of arguments that use only unary predicate symbols. See p. 237.

how to extend an interpretation to formulas that contain both predicate symbols and propositional constants. Here we adopt the following definitions:

P^M is false	P^M is true
$(\phi \wedge P)^M = \emptyset$	$(\phi \wedge P)^M = \phi^M$
$(\phi \vee P)^M = \phi^M$	$(\phi \vee P)^M = M$
$(P \rightarrow \phi)^M = M$	$(P \rightarrow \phi)^M = \phi^M$
$(\phi \rightarrow P)^M = M \backslash \phi^M$	$(\phi \rightarrow P)^M = M$

In general, you should try to think of something like $(\phi \rightarrow P)^M$ as the collection of things such that if they are ϕ, then P. So, if P^M is true, then that holds for every individual. However, if P^M is false, then it only holds for those individuals that are not ϕ.

Example. Consider the sentences $\exists x(Fx \rightarrow P)$ and $\forall x(Fx \rightarrow P)$. Let M be an interpretation with domain $\{1, 2\}$ where $F^M = \{1\}$ and P^M is false. Then,

$$(Fx \rightarrow P)^M = M \backslash (Fx)^M = \{2\}.$$

Therefore, $\exists(Fx \rightarrow P)$ is true, while $\forall x(Fx \rightarrow P)$ is false.

Exercise 8.3. For each of the following sequents, provide a counterexample to show that it is invalid.

1. $\forall xFx \rightarrow P \vdash \forall x(Fx \rightarrow P)$
2. $\exists x(Fx \rightarrow P) \vdash \exists xFx \rightarrow P$

Interpretations Generalized

The previous discussion explained how to interpret formulas with one free variable. Now we need to deal with the general case. Roughly speaking, if $\phi(x_1, \ldots, x_n)$ is a formula with n free variables, then we would like for $\phi(x_1, \ldots, x_n)^M$ to be a collection of n-tuples of elements of M.

At this point, however, we have a difficult choice to make between intuitiveness and rigor. On the one hand, we can give an intuitive definition of $\phi(x_1, \ldots, x_n)^M$, but this definition is not completely rigorous. On the other hand, we can give a mathematically precise definition of $\phi(x_1, \ldots, x_n)^M$ but only after introducing some nonintuitive technical auxiliaries. We'll first give the intuitive definition and use it to solve some problems. At the end of the chapter, we'll give a more rigorous definition.

For the intuitive definition, we extend an interpretation M to all atomic formulas as follows. First, for a term t with n-free variables, we define t^M as an n-place function of those variables. For example, if f is a binary function symbol, then $f(x, x)$ is a term with one free variable, and we define $f(x, x)^M$ to be the function that takes input a and returns output $f^M(a, a)$. As a special case of a term, for a variable x_i, we define x_i^M to be the function that picks out the relevant component a_i. In particular, $x_i^M(a_1, \ldots, a_n) = a_i$.

Now for an atomic formula $R(t_1, \ldots, t_m)$, we define $R(t_1, \ldots, t_m)^M$ to be the set of n-tuples $\langle a_1, \ldots, a_n \rangle$ such that the m-tuple

$$\langle t_1^M(a_1, \ldots, a_n), \ldots, t_m^M(a_1, \ldots, a_n) \rangle$$

is in R^M. Finally, for an equality $t_1 = t_2$ of terms, we define $(t_1 = t_2)^M$ to be the set of $\langle a_1, \ldots, a_n \rangle$ such that $t_1^M(a_1, \ldots, a_n) = t_2^M(a_1, \ldots, a_n)$. In the special case of constant symbols, we say that $(c = d)^M$ is true just in case $c^M = d^M$.

This definition extends straightforwardly to Boolean combinations of formulas. Then, for quantified formulas, we extend as follows:

- If $\phi(x_1, \ldots, x_n, y)^M$ is already defined, then we let $(\exists y \phi(x_1, \ldots, x_n, y))^M$ be the set of $\langle a_1, \ldots, a_n \rangle$ such that there is some $b \in M$ such that $\langle a_1, \ldots, a_n, b \rangle \in \phi(x_1, \ldots, x_n, y)^M$. In the special case where $n = 0$, then $(\exists y \phi(y))^M$ is true when there is a $b \in \phi(y)^M$, and $(\exists y \phi(y))^M$ is false when there is no $b \in \phi(y)^M$.
- If $\phi(x_1, \ldots, x_n, y)^M$ is already defined, then we let $(\forall y \phi(x_1, \ldots, x_n, y))^M$ be the set of $\langle a_1, \ldots, a_n \rangle$ such that no matter which $b \in M$ is chosen, $\langle a_1, \ldots, a_n, b \rangle \in \phi(x_1, \ldots, x_n, y)^M$.

Example. Let $M = \{a_1, a_2\}$, and let $R^M = \{\langle a_1, a_1 \rangle, \langle a_2, a_2 \rangle\}$. Then $(\exists y R (x, y))^M$ is the set of $a \in M$ such that $\langle a, b \rangle \in R^M$ for some $b \in M$. Hence, $(\exists y R(x, y))^M = M$, and it follows that $(\forall x \exists y R(x, y))^M$ is true.

Example. Suppose again that R is a binary relation symbol. Let $M = \{1, 2\}$ and let R^M be the standard interpretation of "less than," namely, $R^M = \{\langle 1, 2 \rangle\}$. In this case,

$$(Rxx)^M = \{a \in M \mid \langle a, a \rangle \in R^M\} = \emptyset.$$

If we had instead interpreted R as "less than or equal," then we would get

$$(Rxx)^M = \{a \in M \mid \langle a, a \rangle \in R^M\} = M.$$

Example. We will show that $\forall y \exists x Rxy$ does not imply $\exists x \forall y Rxy$. Let $M = \{a, b\}$ and let $R^M = \{\langle a, a \rangle, \langle b, b \rangle\}$. Then, $(\exists x Rxy)^M$ is the set of $y \in M$ that occur on the right-hand side of some pair in R^M, that is, everything in M. Hence, $(\forall y \exists x Rxy)^M$ is true. In contrast, $(\forall y Rxy)^M$ is the set of $x \in M$ such that $\langle x, y \rangle \in R^M$ for all $y \in M$. There is no such $x \in M$; hence, $(\forall y Rxy)^M$ is the empty set, and $(\exists x \forall y Rxy)^M$ is false.

Example. Consider the numerical claim $\exists x \exists y (x \neq y)$, which is supposed to say that there are at least two things. Since $(x = y)^M$ is the set of $\langle a, a \rangle \in M \times M$, it follows that $(x \neq y)^M$ is the set of $\langle a, b \rangle \in M \times M$ such that $a \neq b$. Hence, $(\exists y (x \neq y))^M$ is the set of $a \in M$ such that there is some $b \in M$ with $a \neq b$. If M has only a single element, then there are no such $a \in M$, and if M has at least two elements, then every $a \in M$ is not equal to some $b \in M$. Thus, $(\exists x \exists y (x \neq y))^M$ is true iff $(\exists y (x \neq y))^M$ is nonempty iff M has at least two elements.

One of the primary functions of modeling in the sciences is to explore the possibilities that are consistent with a theory. What's more, scientists have a set of rules for how such possibilities must be described—and these rules correspond roughly, with some idealization, to the axioms of set theory. Hence, we'll say that a possibility relative to a theory is just an interpretation in which that theory's axioms are true, that is, it's a model of the theory.

Definition. If T is a theory, then an interpretation M is said to be a **model** of T just in case all of the axioms of T are true in M.

Example. Consider the theory T with a single axiom:

$$\exists x \exists y \left((x \neq y) \wedge \forall z((x = z) \vee (y = z)) \right).$$

Then, a model of T is any set that contains exactly two elements.

Example. We now consider an extended example. Let T be the theory of autosets from exercise 7.15. Here the signature Σ has a single binary function symbol $\circ$, and T has three axioms that jointly say that $\circ$ gives a transitive left and right action. (To say that the action is transitive means that from a fixed x, any z can be reached by means of acting on x with some y. In other words, from any starting point, you can reach any other point.)

Consider now an interpretation of Σ with domain $\{0, 1\}$. We need to interpret $\circ$ as a function from $M \times M$ to M, and we'll do this by explicitly writing out a multiplication table:

$\circ$	0	1
0	0	1
1	1	0

In other words,

$$\circ^M = \{ \langle 0, 0, 0 \rangle, \langle 0, 1, 1 \rangle, \langle 1, 0, 1 \rangle, \langle 1, 1, 0 \rangle \}.$$

It's easy to check that this interpretation satisfies the associativity and left-right action axioms. Hence, M is a model of the theory T, that is, M is an autoset.

In exercise 7.15, you were asked to prove that $T \vdash \exists! x(x \circ x = x)$. Here, we put T before the turnstile $\vdash$ as shorthand for the axioms of T. By the soundness of our proof rules (which we haven't proven yet, but which we promise is true), $\exists!x(x \circ x = x)$ is true in all models of T, in particular in M. Fortunately, we can see exactly what in M makes that sentence true: the element $0 \in M$ is the unique idempotent.

In exercise 7.15, you also showed that

$$T \vdash \forall x \exists! y \forall z (z \circ x \circ y = z).$$

Intuitively speaking, this unique y is the inverse x^{-1} of x, and we could (if we wanted) define a corresponding unary function symbol i. It's not hard to see, then, that in M, this unary function symbol is interpreted as the identity function, that is, 0 and 1 are both their own inverses.

Exercise 8.4. Present a model of T with domain $M = \{0, 1, 2\}$. (Hint: interpret $\circ$ as addition, where $2 + 1 = 1 + 2 = 0$ and $2 + 2 = 1$.) Identify the unique idempotent in M and the inverse operation i on M.

Exercise 8.5. Show that the theory of autosets does not imply that $\forall x \forall y (x \circ y = y \circ x)$.

Diagramming Interpretations

The goal of this section is heuristic in the sense of helping you find interpretations. We won't offer you an algorithm, but we will offer you some pictures that should help improve your intuitions. In particular, for sentences that involve a binary relation symbol, say R, we can think of an interpretation as a sort of diagram with nodes and arrows. With practice, you can start to see that particular sentences correspond to particular geometric configurations, and then you can use your geometric intuition to help find interpretations.

We showed previously that $\forall y \exists x Rxy$ does not imply $\exists x \forall y Rxy$. The counterexample we gave was completely mathematically rigorous but perhaps not very intuitive. We can capture the idea of the counterexample with the following simple picture. Think of an arrow between nodes as indicating that the relation R holds between them. Then, the first sentence

$\forall y \exists x R x y$ says that each node has an arrow coming into it—which is true in this picture. The second sentence $\exists x \forall y R x y$ says that there is a node that has arrows going out to every other node—which is false in this picture. Thus, we can see quickly from the picture that the first sentence does not imply the second.

Some sentences have particularly nice geometric interpretations. For example, the sentence Raa says that a bears the relation R to itself, which means that there is an arrow looping from a back to itself (as in the upper left of figure 8.1). Thus, in order for $\forall x R x x$ to be true, every node in the diagram must have an arrow coming back to itself. The sentence $Rab \rightarrow Rba$ says that if there is an arrow from a to b, then there is an arrow coming back from b to a. That could be true for two reasons: first, there may be an arrow from a to b and also an arrow back from b to a (as in the upper right of figure 8.1). Second, $Rab \rightarrow Rba$ would be true if there were no arrow from a to b. Generalizing, the sentence $\forall x(Rxy \rightarrow Ryx)$ says that the relation R is symmetric; pictorially, it says that for any two nodes a, b, if there is an arrow from a to b, then there is an arrow back from b to a. Finally, the sentence $(Rab \wedge Rbc) \rightarrow Rac$ says that if there are arrows from a to b and from b to c, then there is an arrow from a to c. Pictorially, the sentence is true if and only if any two-step path corresponds to a one-step path (as in the bottom of figure 8.1). The transitivity axiom $\forall x \forall y \forall z((Rxy \wedge Ryz) \rightarrow Rxz)$ asserts that this condition holds for all two-step paths.

Suppose now that you're given sentences $\phi_1, \ldots, \phi_n$, and you want to determine if these sentences are consistent. If these sentences only use the relation symbol R, then you can establish consistency by drawing a relevant arrow diagram. Consider, for example, the sentences that say that the relation R is antireflexive $[\forall x \neg Rxx]$, transitive, and total $[\forall x \forall y(Rxy \vee Ryx)]$. You might begin by drawing a single node a with no arrows. But then the totality axiom fails. Thus, we need to add at least one other node

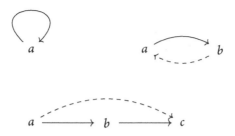

Figure 8.1. Visual representation of properties of Rxy.

b, and we need an arrow in one of the two directions. Without loss of generality, we put in an arrow from a to b. Since there's only one arrow, the diagram trivially satisfies transitivity. Since no node has an arrow to itself, the diagram satisfies irreflexivity. And by construction, the diagram satisfies totality. Therefore those sentences are consistent.

Exercise 8.6. Prove that if the relation R is antireflexive and total, then there are at least two things.

Suppose now that we add the sentence that says that the relation R is entire, that is, $\forall x \exists y Rxy$. Pictorially speaking, the relation R is entire only if each node in the diagram has an arrow coming out. Of course, that fails in the previous diagram; hence, it doesn't validate the sentence $\forall x \exists y Rxy$. What's more, we couldn't fix up that diagram simply by adding an arrow back from b to a. For in that case, we would have $Rab \wedge Rba$, and since we're requiring transitivity, we would have to put in an arrow from a to itself, which is banned by the irreflexivity diagram.

We now sketch an informal argument that no finite diagram can make those four sentences true. Suppose for reductio ad absurdum that there is a diagram with m nodes that makes these sentences true. The entirety axiom says that for each a_n, there is an a_{n+1} such that $Ra_n a_{n+1}$. We apply this axiom sufficiently many times so that we have a list $a_1, \ldots, a_{m+1}$ of nodes. We now show that this list has no repeated nodes. If $i < j$, then transitivity implies that $Ra_i a_j$, and irreflexivity implies that $a_i \neq a_j$. Hence, all elements $a_1, \ldots, a_{m+1}$ are distinct, in contradiction with the assumption that the diagram has only m nodes. Obviously, this argument works for any number m; hence, there is no finite diagram that makes all of these sentences true.

Of course, it doesn't follow (yet) that these sentences are *inconsistent*, for there might be an infinite diagram that makes them all true. I suspect, in fact, that you may already be thinking of an example, say the natural numbers $N = \{1, 2, \ldots\}$, with R interpreted as "less than or equal." Clearly, $\phi_1, \ldots, \phi_4$ are true under this interpretation, and so these sentences are consistent.

Exercise 8.7. For each of the following sentences, provide one interpretation in which it is true and one interpretation in which it is false.

1. $\forall x \forall y (Rxy \rightarrow Ryx)$
2. $\forall x \forall y \exists z (Rxz \land Ryz)$
3. $\exists x \forall y (Ryx \rightarrow Ryy)$
4. $\forall x (\exists y Ryx \rightarrow \forall z Rzx)$
5. $\exists x \exists y (Rxy \leftrightarrow \neg Ryy)$

Exercise 8.8. Is the following sentence consistent or not? If it is, describe an interpretation in which it is true.

$\forall x \exists y \forall z (\neg Rxx \land Rxy \land (Ryz \rightarrow Rxz)).$

Example. Let R be a binary relation symbol, and let T be the theory of partially ordered sets formulated with R. That is, T says that the relation R is reflexive, antisymmetric, and transitive. Not surprisingly, a model of T is called a partially ordered set, and there are many of these. First of all, take any set M and let $R^M = \{\langle a, a \rangle \mid a \in M\}$. Then, M is a partially ordered set—although a rather boring one. In contrast, consider the set $N = \{0, 1, 2, \ldots\}$ of natural numbers, and let $R^M = \{\langle a, b \rangle \mid a \leq b\}$. Then, N is a partially ordered set.

Exercise 8.9. Write down at least two sentences that are true in the model N of natural numbers but not consequences of the theory of partially ordered sets.

Interpretation Rigorized

The way we defined interpretations suffers from some (fairly innocuous) mathematical imprecision. In particular, we didn't define ϕ^M for an arbitrary formula ϕ. Instead, we defined $\phi(x_1, \ldots, x_n)^M$ but without explaining how to understand the notation $\phi(x_1, \ldots, x_n)$. In this section, we fix that problem, but only at the cost of introducing a new complication.

First we define two new things.

Definition. Let $x_1, \ldots, x_n$ be a duplicate-free list of variables. If all the free variables of the term t occur in the list $x_1, \ldots x_n$, then we say that $t(x_1, \ldots, x_n)$ is a **term in context**.

Definition. If all of the free variables of the formula ϕ occur in the list $x_1, \ldots, x_n$, then we say that $[x_1, \ldots, x_n : \phi]$ is a **formula in context**.

We sometimes abbreviate the list $x_1, \ldots, x_n$ by $\vec{x}$, so that $[\vec{x} : \phi]$ is a formula in context. We also use a dash "$-$" to indicate an empty list of variables, so that $[- : \phi]$ is a formula in context when ϕ is a sentence. We will soon define $[\vec{x} : \phi]^M$, but first let's explain the intuitive idea we're trying to express:

$[\vec{x} : \phi]^M$ is the set of n-tuples $\vec{a}$ in $M \times \cdots \times M$ such that ϕ is true when x_i is assigned to a_i.

If a variable x_i is not free in ϕ, then it serves as a "dummy" in this definition. For example, if p is a predicate symbol, then $[x_1, x_2 : p(x_1)]^M$ is the set of $\langle a_1, a_2 \rangle$ such that $a_1 \in p^M$. We also adopt the convention that the product of zero copies of M is a one-point set **1**. Hence, $[- : \phi]^M$ will be a subset of **1**, either the entire set, and we say that $[- : \phi]^M$ is true, or the empty set, and we say that $[- : \phi]^M$ is false.

Let M be an interpretation. We first define $t(\vec{x})^M$, where $t(\vec{x})$ is a term in context.

- Suppose that t is a variable x_i. Then, $t(x_1, \ldots, x_n)^M$ is the function that takes an n-tuple $\langle a_1, \ldots, a_n \rangle$ and returns the ith entry a_i.
- Suppose that c is a constant symbol. Then, $t(\vec{x})^M$ is the function that takes an n-tuple $\vec{a}$ and returns the element $c^M \in M$.

- Suppose that t is a term of the form $f(t_1, \ldots, t_m)$, where $t_i(\vec{x})^M$ has already been defined. Then, $t(\vec{x})^M$ is the composite function that assigns $f^M(b_1, \ldots, b_m)$ to $\vec{a}$, where $b_i = t_i(\vec{x})^M(\vec{a})$.

Now we define $[\vec{x} : \phi]^M$, where $[\vec{x} : \phi]$ is a formula in context.

- For the tautology $\top$, we define $[\vec{x} : \top]^M$ to be $M \times \cdots \times M$.
- Let t_1 and t_2 be terms. Then, $[\vec{x} : t_1 = t_2]$ is the set of $\vec{a}$ such that

$$t_1(\vec{x})^M(\vec{a}) = t_2(\vec{x})^M(\vec{a}).$$

- Let $t_1, \ldots, t_m$ be terms, and let R be an m-ary relation symbol. Then, $[\vec{x} : R(t_1, \ldots, t_m)]^M$ is the set of $\vec{a}$ such that

$$\langle t_1(\vec{x})^M(\vec{a}), \ldots, t_m(\vec{x})^M(\vec{a}) \rangle \in R^M.$$

For the inductive clauses, we look at a formula in context $[\vec{x} : \phi]$, where for any proper subformula ψ of ϕ and any context $\vec{y}$ of ψ, $[\vec{y} : \psi]^M$ has already been defined.

- For Boolean combinations:

$$
\begin{aligned}
{[\vec{x} : \phi \wedge \psi]}^M &= [\vec{x} : \phi]^M \cap [\vec{x} : \psi]^M \\
{[\vec{x} : \phi \vee \psi]}^M &= [\vec{x} : \phi]^M \cup [\vec{x} : \psi]^M \\
{[\vec{x} : \neg\phi]}^M &= [\vec{x} : \top]^M \backslash [\vec{x} : \phi]^M \\
{[\vec{x} : \phi \rightarrow \psi]}^M &= [\vec{x} : \neg\phi \vee \psi]^M.
\end{aligned}
$$

- For the quantifiers, we wish to define $[\vec{x} : \exists y\phi]^M$, where we assume that $[\vec{x}, y : \phi]^M$ has already been defined. In this case, we let $[\vec{x} : \exists y\phi]^M$ be the set that results from projecting out the last coordinate of $[\vec{x}, y : \phi]^M$. In other words, $[\vec{x} : \exists y\phi]^M$ consists of n-tuples $\langle a_1, \ldots, a_n \rangle$ such that there is a $b \in M$ with $\langle a_1, \ldots, a_n, b \rangle \in [\vec{x}, y : \phi]^M$. Similarly, for the universal quantifier, $[\vec{x} : \forall y\phi]^M$ consists of n-tuples $\langle a_1, \ldots, a_n \rangle$ such that $\langle a_1, \ldots, a_n, b \rangle \in [\vec{x}, y : \phi]^M$ for all $b \in M$.

Example. We show that $[x_1, x_2 : p(x_1)]^M = [x : p(x)]^M \times M$. It's clear that $[x : p(x)]^M = p^M$. Now, if t is the variable x_1, then $t(x_1, x_2)^M$ is the function that takes a pair $\langle a_1, a_2 \rangle$ and returns a_1. Hence, $[x_1, x_2 : p(x_1)]^M$ is the set of $\langle a_1, a_2 \rangle \in M \times M$ such that $a_1 = t(x_1, x_2)^M (a_1, a_2) \in p^M$.

Exercise 8.10. Describe the sets $[x, y : x = y]^M$ and $[x : x = x]^M$.

Summary

For the purposes of this book, the primary use of interpretations is to show that a sequent cannot be proven. Sometimes you'll want to know that for its own sake, and sometimes you'll want to know that so that you can avoid a bad strategy in trying to prove something else. In doing real science, one often goes back and forth between searching for a proof and searching for possible counterexamples. In particular, becoming convinced that there is no counterexample can frequently lead to the discovery of a proof.

Thinking about interpretations can also help find proofs in formal logic. Consider, for example, the sentence $\exists x \forall y (Fx \rightarrow Fy)$, which many students find to be one of the most challenging tautologies that involves only monadic predicates. Let's see, then, why this sentence has to be true in every interpretation. The key thing to observe is that in every interpretation M, either everything is F, or something is not F. Suppose first that $F^M = M$. Then, for any element $b \in M$, we have $b \in F^M$. If we pretend that b is a name, then we can say that Fb is true in M, in which case the conditional $Fa \rightarrow Fb$ is trivially true,[6] no matter what a is. Since b was an arbitrary element of M, $\forall y (Fa \rightarrow Fy)$ is also true, and hence $\exists x \forall y (Fx \rightarrow Fy)$ is true. Now suppose that there is an $a \in M$ such that $\neg Fa$. Then, for any $b \in M$, it trivially follows that $Fa \rightarrow Fb$,[7] and hence that $\forall y (Fa \rightarrow Fy)$, and so finally that $\exists x \forall y (Fx \rightarrow Fy)$. In both cases, whether F^M is empty or not, $\exists x \forall y (Fx \rightarrow Fy)$ is true. Hence, that sentence is true in every interpretation and is therefore provable from no premises at all.

Exercise 8.11. Try to construct a similar proof to show that $\forall x \forall y (Fx \rightarrow Fy)$ is always true. Where does it break down?

---

6. Positive paradox.
7. Negative paradox.

9

A Theory about Propositional Logic

IN CHAPTER 7, WE TALKED ABOUT how to formulate theories in predicate logic. Now here's a weird idea: how about we formulate a theory (in predicate logic) about propositional logic? Think of it this way. Suppose that you travel far back in time, to a time when human beings didn't know how to reason with quantifiers—they only knew how to reason with the propositional connectives "and," "or," and so on.[1] Your job is to describe the rules of the "game" that these early, propositional-logical humans like to play.

If you think that the scenario we've just described is strange or silly, then just think of it as a warmup for the real job: looking in the mirror, that is, reasoning about how we reason. Obviously, good human thinking isn't exhausted by propositional logic; at the very least, it also involves inferences with quantified statements. Hence, we'll want eventually to have a theory about predicate logic. We'll turn to that in chapter 10, and we'll restrict ourselves in this chapter to propositional logic.

So, to return to our simplified and fictional setup: we want a theory T that describes propositional logic. To build T, we first need to decide on a vocabulary (i.e., on relation symbols, function symbols, names, etc.) that

---

1. As far as I know, nobody believes that's how human thinking actually evolved.

can be used to describe propositional reasoning. For this, we'll make use of set theory. We will assume that there is a nonempty set Σ, which we'll call the *atomic sentences*. To be clear, the things in Σ aren't *our* atomic sentences—that is, they aren't part of our language. Instead of using the sentences in Σ, we are talking *about* them. We also assume that there is another set containing the symbols $\wedge$, $\vee$, $\rightarrow$, $\neg$, and perhaps some parentheses. Again, don't think of those symbols as the logical connectives we use; instead, they are the logical connectives that are used by the people we are studying. Finally, we assume that there is a basic operation on symbols called "concatenation."

We then notice that the people we are studying treat some strings of symbols differently than others. We then hypothesize that there is a feature of strings, which we might call "sentencehood," and we introduce a predicate symbol $\mathsf{sent}(\phi)$ to our language that we will use to describe which things are sentences. (Here we're using Greek letters, such as ϕ, as our variables.) Here, then, is our theory about the grammar of propositional logic:

- Any symbol in the set Σ is a sentence.
- For any string ϕ of symbols, if ϕ is a sentence, then so is the string $\neg\phi$.
- If ϕ and ψ are sentences, then $\phi \vee \psi$ is a sentence.
- If ϕ and ψ are sentences, then $\phi \wedge \psi$ is a sentence.
- If ϕ and ψ are sentences, then $\phi \rightarrow \psi$ is a sentence.

All of these axioms seem obviously correct, but they are not yet sufficient, for they don't entail some other things we know—for example, that our test subjects do *not* count gibberish strings as sentences. To capture that additional claim, we draw upon a little bit of set theory to say that the set of sentences is like the set of natural numbers—namely, all of its elements result from a finite number of applications of the construction methods to the atomic sentences.

We can give a visual representation of the construction of a sentence by means of the notion of a **parse tree**. In such a tree, each node corresponds to a formula. The initial nodes must be atomic sentences, and new nodes can be constructed from old ones using the propositional connectives.

Thus, for example, given nodes ϕ and ψ, we can construct new nodes as follows:

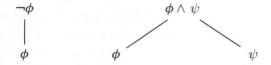

Here's one example of a full parse tree:

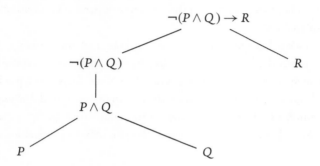

Parse trees are useful in many ways. First, a parse tree allows us to define the notion of a *subformula* of a formula ϕ: namely, any formula that occurs in the parse tree of ϕ. Second, a parse tree provides a nice visual representation of how the truth value of a sentence ϕ is computed from the truth value of its atomic subformulas. Indeed, each node of a parse tree can be considered a logic circuit: a negation node is the **not** circuit that flips a bit, a conjunction node is the **and** circuit that gives output 1 only if both inputs are 1, and so on. Third, a parse tree makes it obvious what the *main connective* of a sentence is: it's the connective at the root node of the parse tree. Finally, parse trees give a nice visual picture of what happens during *substitution*. Consider the simple case of the substitution $F(P) = Q \rightarrow R$ and $F(Q) = R \wedge \neg R$ applied to the sentence $\phi \equiv P \rightarrow Q$. The parse tree of $F(\phi)$ results from simply pasting the trees for $F(P)$ and $F(Q)$ to the nodes for P and Q in the parse tree of $P \rightarrow Q$.

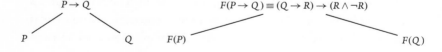

Induction on the Construction of Sentences

In chapter 7, we saw that the set N of natural numbers is defined so as to license the method of "proof by induction." This method says, roughly, that if you can prove that 0 is ϕ, and if you can prove that whenever n is ϕ then so is $n + 1$, then it follows that all natural numbers are ϕ. We will now see that this method of proof can be adapted to the set of sentences of propositional logic—giving us a powerful tool for proving that something or other is true for all sentences.

Let Σ be a fixed set of atomic sentences. For simplicity, we'll first consider a simple case where $\Sigma = \{P\}$, and where Δ is the set of sentences that are built with the $\neg$ and $\vee$ connectives. If you think of the set of sentences on analogy to the natural numbers N, then the sentence P is the 0, and the connectives $\neg$ and $\vee$ are like the successor function. In the case of the set N of natural numbers, each number $n \in N$ is the result of applying the successor function s to 0 some finite number of times. In the case of the set Δ of sentences, each sentence $\phi \in \Delta$ results from taking a certain number of copies of P and applying the connectives $\neg$ and $\vee$ a finite number of times. This definition of the set Δ thus licenses the following extension of the method of proof by induction.

Induction on the Construction of Sentences

(1)	Atomic sentences have property X.	base case
(2)	If ϕ and ψ have property X, then $\phi \vee \psi$ has property X.	induction $\vee$
(3)	If ϕ has property X, then $\neg\phi$ has property X.	induction $\neg$
(C)	Every sentence in Δ has property X.	conclusion

What we have here is a family of inference rules, one for each property X that can be described in our meta-theory of propositional logic. We haven't been completely precise in telling which properties of sentences can be articulated. However, as a general rule, the only relevant properties are the *purely syntactic* properties, for example, "the main connective of ϕ is $\wedge$," or "ϕ has three left parentheses."

We'll now use induction to show that every sentence in Δ is provably equivalent to one of the four in the diamond:

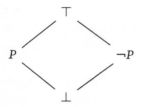

Here, $\top$ is shorthand for some tautology (e.g., $P \vee \neg P$) and $\bot$ is shorthand for some contradiction (e.g., $P \wedge \neg P$) and to say that ϕ and ψ are **provably equivalent** just means that $\phi \dashv\vdash \psi$.

Proposition 9.1. *Every sentence in Δ is provably equivalent to one of the four in the diamond above.*

Before we start the official proof, observe that if ϕ and ψ are provably equivalent, then so are $\neg\phi$ and $\neg\psi$. Indeed, suppose we're given proofs $\phi \vdash \psi$ and $\psi \vdash \phi$. Then, we can obtain proofs of $\neg\phi \vdash \neg\psi$ and $\neg\psi \vdash \neg\phi$ by using the (derived) contrapositive rule. Similarly, if ϕ and ϕ' are provably equivalent, and ψ and ψ' are provably equivalent, then so are $\phi \vee \psi$ and $\phi' \vee \psi'$.

Exercise 9.1. Prove that if $\phi \dashv\vdash \phi'$ and $\psi \dashv\vdash \psi'$, then $(\phi \vee \psi) \dashv\vdash (\phi' \vee \psi')$.

Proof. $\boxed{\text{base case}}$ Obviously P is equivalent to itself; hence, it's equivalent to one of the four sentences in the diamond.

$\boxed{\text{induction } \neg}$ Suppose that ϕ is equivalent to one of the four in the diamond. If ϕ is equivalent to $\top$, then $\neg\phi$ is equivalent to $\bot$. If ϕ is equivalent to P, then $\neg\phi$ is equivalent to $\neg P$. And so on.

induction $\vee$ Suppose that ϕ and ψ are each equivalent to some sentence in the diamond. If ϕ is equivalent to $\bot$, then $\phi \vee \psi$ is equivalent to ψ. If ϕ is equivalent to $\top$, then $\phi \vee \psi$ is equivalent to $\top$. Similar conclusions hold if ψ is equivalent to $\top$ or $\bot$. If ϕ and ψ are equivalent to each other, then $\phi \vee \psi$ is equivalent to ϕ. Finally, if ϕ is equivalent to $\neg \psi$, then $\phi \vee \psi$ is equivalent to $\top$. $\square$

We've seen how to use proof by induction to show that something is true for every sentence in the set Δ of sentences containing only the connectives $\vee$ and $\neg$. This method can now be extended to the set of *all* sentences, only we need to add inductive steps for the other two connectives, $\wedge$ and $\to$.

    (4) If ϕ and ψ have property X, then   induction $\wedge$
         $\phi \wedge \psi$ has property X.
    (5) If ϕ and ψ have property X, then   induction $\to$
         $\phi \to \psi$ has property X.

We will now use induction to prove that every sentence (whose only atomic sentence is P) is equivalent to one of the four in the diamond. We have already shown that every sentence in Δ is equivalent to one of the four in the diamond. Thus, it will suffice—by the transitivity of logical equivalence—to show that every sentence is equivalent to a sentence in the set Δ.

Proposition 9.2. *Every sentence is provably equivalent to a sentence in the set Δ.*

Proof. Let's say that a sentence ϕ has property X just in case ϕ is provably equivalent to a sentence in the set Δ. We will use induction on the construction of formulas to prove that every sentence has property X. Before we begin, note that if ψ has property X, and $\phi \dashv\vdash \psi$, then ϕ has property X.

base case   Since $P \in \Delta$, P has property X.

induction ∨ and ¬   If ϕ and ψ have property X, then $\neg\phi$ and $\phi \vee \psi$ obviously have property X.

induction ∧   Suppose that both ϕ and ψ have property X. Then, $\phi \wedge \psi \dashv\vdash \neg(\neg\phi \vee \neg\psi)$, and the latter obviously has property X. Therefore, $\phi \wedge \psi$ has property X.

induction →   Suppose that both ϕ and ψ have property X. Then, $\phi \rightarrow \psi \dashv\vdash \neg\phi \vee \psi$, and the latter obviously has property X. Therefore, $\phi \rightarrow \psi$ has property X.

This completes the inductive steps, and so it follows that every sentence has property X.   □

Exercise 9.2. Let Θ be the set of sentences whose only atomic sentence is P and whose only connectives are $\neg$ and $\wedge$. Show that every sentence is provably equivalent to a sentence in Θ.

Exercise 9.3. Let Γ be the set of formulas defined as follows:

- $P \in \Gamma$.
- If $\phi \in \Gamma$ and $\psi \in \Gamma$, then $\phi \vee \psi \in \Gamma$.
- Every element of Γ arises from a finite number of the previous steps.

Use mathematical induction to show that for all $\phi \in \Gamma$, $\phi \vdash P$.

Truth Functions

In chapter 5, we introduced truth tables as a tool for deciding whether arguments are valid or not. It's time now to think more theoretically about what truth tables are and what they can do.

Each one of our connectives $\neg$, $\wedge$, $\vee$, and $\rightarrow$ has an associated truth table. Therefore, these connectives are **truth-functional**, that is, the truth value of an output sentence, say ¬φ, is completely determined by the truth value of the input sentence φ. Now, you might wonder: how in the world could a connective *not* be truth-functional? Well, consider for example, the connective "Donald Trump said that…." This phrase is a bona fide propositional connective because for any declarative sentence φ, you can set it in the blank, and the output is a new sentence: "Donald Trump said that φ." However, even the most blind defender of Trump wouldn't want to say that this connective is truth-functional, for there is surely at least one false sentence φ such that "Donald Trump said that φ" is true and at least one false sentence ψ such that "Donald Trump said that ψ" is false. Therefore, the connective cannot determine the output truth value simply on the basis of the input truth value.

The "Donald Trump said that …" connective has not been studied carefully by philosophers. However, there are other non-truth-functional connectives that have been. One of philosophers' favorites is the connective "It is necessarily true that…." As long as there are some truths that are not necessarily true, then this connective is not truth-functional. And since philosophers have long been interested in necessary truths, they have taken particular interest in non-truth-functional connectives. They study these connectives in a subject called **modal logic**.

Our focus here, however, is on truth-functional connectives. We can now raise the question: are there other truth-functional connectives besides ¬, ∨, ∧, →? Well, immediately we know the answer is yes, for we also have the connective ↔, which doesn't have the same truth table as any of those latter three. However, you might be quick to point out that the truth table for ↔ can be simulated by using both the ∧ and → connectives. Let's distinguish, then, between connectives that can be expressed in terms of ¬, ∨, ∧, → and those that cannot be so expressed. We can then rephrase the question as follows: are there any truth-functional connectives that cannot be expressed in terms of the ones we already have?

It might sound at first like that question is impossibly difficult to answer. But let's start by thinking about how many possible truth functions there could be. (Here, a **truth function** is simply a function that takes truth

values as inputs and returns truth values as outputs. Since our truth values
are 0 and 1, a truth function is a function from the set $\{0, 1\}$ to itself.)
For this, we need to do some basic calculation. Starting with the case of
unary truth functions (i.e., those that take one input), there are precisely
four functions from $\{0, 1\}$ to itself: the identity function, the function that
exchanges 0 and 1, the function that maps both elements to 0, and the
function that maps both elements to 1. And clearly we can express those
four functions in terms of combinations of connectives (e.g., the constant
0 function is expressed by $P \wedge \neg P$).

Now, for binary truth functions (i.e., those with two inputs), we already
have many more possibilities. Each function from $\{0, 1\} \times \{0, 1\}$ to $\{0, 1\}$
corresponds to a division of the former set into two parts: those elements that get assigned 0 and those elements that get assigned 1. Since
the former subset is the complement of the latter, each such function
is uniquely determined by the subset of elements to which it assigns 1.
Hence, there is a one-to-one correspondence between binary truth functions and subsets of $\{0, 1\} \times \{0, 1\}$, that is, elements of the powerset of
$\{0, 1\} \times \{0, 1\}$.

If a set X has $|X|$ elements, then X has $2^{|X|}$ subsets. In the case at hand,
$\{0, 1\} \times \{0, 1\}$ has four elements, hence 2^4 subsets; consequently, there are
$2^4 = 16$ binary truth functions. Thus, there are thirteen more truth functions besides those represented by $\wedge$, $\vee$, and $\rightarrow$. It might seem, then,
we're very far indeed from being able to express all binary truth functions.
But in fact, the opposite is true. In figure 9.1, we display sixteen sentences
that have distinct truth tables.

Since we have equivalences:

$$P \rightarrow Q \equiv \neg P \vee Q \qquad \text{and} \qquad P \wedge Q \equiv \neg(\neg P \vee \neg Q),$$

any sentence is equivalent to a sentence whose only connectives are $\vee$ and
$\neg$, and each of the sixteen truth functions can be expressed in terms of
these connectives. Similarly, each of these sixteen truth functions can be
expressed just with $\neg$ and $\wedge$. If every truth function can be expressed in
terms of a set Γ of connectives, then we say that Γ is **expressively complete** or **expressively adequate**. Thus, we just sketched proofs that $\{\neg, \vee\}$
and $\{\neg, \wedge\}$ are expressively complete.

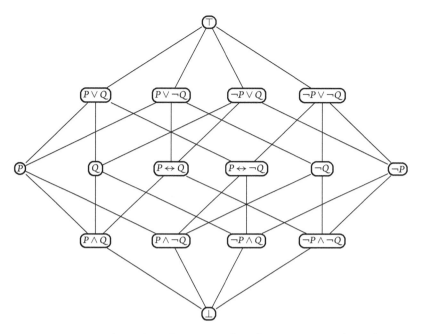

Figure 9.1. Horizontal rows have the same number of 1s. A connecting line indicates logical implication going upward.

Amazingly, there is a single truth function that is itself expressively complete. The corresponding connective is called "nand" and is usually symbolized by ↑. The truth table for $P \uparrow Q$ is, by definition, the same as that for $\neg(P \wedge Q)$.

$P\,Q$	$P \uparrow Q$
1 1	1 **0** 1
1 0	1 **1** 0
0 1	0 **1** 1
0 0	0 **1** 0

To show that the set {↑} is expressively complete, it will suffice to show that it can reproduce the truth tables for ¬ and ∨. After some trial and error, we find that the following definitions work:

P	P ↑ P
1	1 **0** 1
0	0 **1** 0

P Q	(P ↑ P) ↑ (Q ↑ Q)
1 1	1 0 1 **1** 1 0 1
1 0	1 0 1 **1** 0 1 0
0 1	0 1 0 **1** 1 0 1
0 0	0 1 0 **0** 0 1 0

Exercise 9.4. Give a formula using only P, Q, and ↑ that has the same truth table as $P \wedge Q$.

If any truth function can be expressed by the ↑ connective, then, why, you might wonder, don't we use it, instead of the redundant collection $\{\neg, \vee, \wedge, \rightarrow\}$ of four connectives? The answer, in short, is that we face a trade-off between simplicity and naturality, where the latter is a function of what we are familiar with. For most of us, it's fairly natural to reason in terms of "and" and less natural to reason in terms of "nand." Why that is, we don't pretend to know. Nonetheless, you now know that if somebody has the concept of "nand," then they can express any other truth-functional concept.

It can be more difficult to show that a set of connectives is *not* expressively complete. For example, suppose that we want to show that the set $\{\vee\}$ is not, by itself, truth-functionally complete. The way we would approach this is to start trying to express some of the truth tables, to get a feeling of what we *cannot* do. With the connective $\vee$, we can write $P \vee P$, which is equivalent to P again. We can also write $P \vee Q$. But it seems that we get stuck at that point. If we write longer disjunctions, say $P \vee (P \vee Q)$, we quickly realize that we haven't expressed anything new. That is, we get stuck with truth functions that are true whenever P and Q are true. That realization then gives us an idea: perhaps we can prove that every truth function that can be expressed with just $\vee$ has this feature, that is, that it's true whenever P and Q are true. That idea provides the intuition behind the following proof.

To make this proof a bit more clear, we need a slight change of terminology. Instead of talking about a row of a truth table, let's talk about a **valuation**. To be precise, a valuation v assigns each atomic sentence (in this case, P and Q) either 0 or 1. If we follow the truth table recipe, then a valuation naturally extends to assign every sentence either 0 or 1. For example, if $v(\phi) = 1$ and $v(\psi) = 1$, then $v(\phi \vee \psi) = 1$. The claim above, then, is that if v is a valuation such that $v(P) = 1$ and $v(Q) = 1$, then $v(\phi) = 1$ for any sentence whose only connective is $\vee$.

Proposition 9.3. *The set* $\{\vee\}$ *is not truth-functionally complete.*

Proof. Let Γ be the set of sentences built only with the connective $\vee$. Let v be the valuation that assigns 1 to every atomic sentence. We show that for every sentence $\phi \in \Gamma$, $v(\phi) = 1$. Our argument proceeds by induction on the construction of Γ. By definition, for ϕ an atomic sentence in Γ, we have $v(\phi) = 1$. Furthermore, if $v(\phi) = 1$ and $\phi(\psi) = 1$, then $v(\phi \vee \psi) = 1$. Therefore, $v(\phi) = 1$ for all $\phi \in \Gamma$. It follows that there is no sentence in Γ that is logically equivalent to $P \wedge \neg P$, and $\{\vee\}$ is not truth-functionally complete. $\square$

Exercise 9.5. Show that the set $\{\wedge\}$ is not truth-functionally complete.

Exercise 9.6. Consider sentences built out of the atomic sentences P and Q. In this case, there are four valuations v_1, v_2, v_3, v_4. Let's say that a sentence ϕ is an *even* just in case ϕ is true for either zero, two, or four valuations. Show that if ϕ is even, then $\neg \phi$ is even. Show that if ϕ and ψ are even, then $\phi \leftrightarrow \psi$ is even.

Exercise 9.7. Is the set $\{\neg, \leftrightarrow\}$ truth-functionally complete?

A Theory of What Can Be Proven

In the previous sections, we developed a theory about the grammar and semantics of propositional logic. In this section, we develop a theory about proofs, that is, about what can and cannot be proven with the inference rules for propositional logic. To this end, we introduce into *our* language— that is, the language we are using to describe propositional logic—a relation symbol $\vdash$, which we write in infix notation, taking an argument on the left and an argument on the right. (Technically, the symbol ⊢ ambiguously represents several different relation symbols, one for each finite number of sentences that can occur on the left. But we'll brush this complication under the rug.)

The inference rules for propositional logic provide an **inductive definition** of the set of valid sequents, that is, of the extension of the relation ⊢. The base case here is the rule of assumptions: for any formula ϕ, the sequent $\phi \vdash \phi$ is valid. Each of the other inference rules is a recipe for constructing a new valid sequent from one, two, or three old ones. Since the extension of ⊢ is defined inductively, it follows that we can prove things about all sequents by means of an induction schema. Here, the induction schema looks like this:

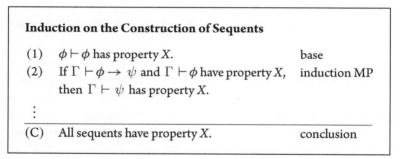

Induction on the Construction of Sequents

(1) $\phi \vdash \phi$ has property X.   base

(2) If $\Gamma \vdash \phi \rightarrow \psi$ and $\Gamma \vdash \phi$ have property X,   induction MP
      then $\Gamma \vdash \psi$ has property X.

⋮

(C) All sequents have property X.   conclusion

As you can see, a proof by induction on the construction of sequents will involve *many* inductive steps—one for each inference rule. But what kinds of things might we want to show about the collection of all sequents? There are two things about the collection of sequents that we've already assumed and used. First, we assumed that sequents couldn't be messed up by find-and-replace operations. That is, for any sequent $\phi \vdash \psi$, if you perform a uniform substitution of sentences for propositional constants, then you get another valid sequent $F(\phi) \vdash F(\psi)$. Second, we assumed that truth tables can detect when a sequent cannot be proven. In other words, we assumed that for any valid sequent $\phi \vdash \psi$, the truth table for ϕ and ψ will have no row in which ϕ is true and ψ is false. It's time now to prove that these two assumptions are true.

In order to set up these proofs, it will be helpful to imagine two different languages, with different atomic sentences. Let Σ be one list of atomic sentences, and let Σ' be another list of atomic sentences. We call Σ the **signature** of the one language, whereas Σ' is the signature of the second language. (If it helps you to remember, you could think of Σ' as having atomic sentences that have a prime symbol, say P', Q', R'.) We then let both languages build their sentences from their respective atomic sentences using the logical connectives $\neg$, $\wedge$, $\vee$, $\rightarrow$.

Now let's imagine what might count as a **translation** between languages Σ and Σ'. Keep in mind that a good translation between languages need not be word-for-word. For example, it's doubtful that there is a single English word that could translate the German word *Zeitgeist* or a single English word that could translate the Danish word *hygge*. (I've hear that there are many more interesting examples from languages such as Hindi, Urdu, and Mandarin.) So, we shouldn't require that a translation from Σ to Σ' has to match an atomic sentence in Σ with an atomic sentence in Σ'. Instead, we will allow that an atomic sentence in Σ be reconstrued as *any* sentence of Σ'.

Definition. Let Σ and Σ' be propositional signatures. A **reconstrual** F from Σ to Σ' is a function that takes atomic sentences of Σ to sentences of Σ'.

A reconstrual $F : \Sigma \rightarrow \Sigma'$ extends naturally to a function from *all* sentences of Σ to sentences of Σ'. We define

$$F(\neg\phi) = \neg F(\phi),$$
$$F(\phi \wedge \psi) = F(\phi) \wedge F(\psi),$$
$$F(\phi \vee \psi) = F(\phi) \vee F(\psi),$$
$$F(\phi \rightarrow \psi) = F(\phi) \rightarrow F(\psi).$$

To get a feel for how this extension works, let's look at a specific example. Suppose that $\Sigma = \{P, Q\}$, $\Sigma' = \{R, S\}$ and that we define the reconstrual F by $F(P) = R \wedge S$ and $F(Q) = \neg S$. Then,

$$F(\neg P \vee Q) = \neg F(P) \vee F(Q) = \neg(R \wedge S) \vee \neg S.$$

While a translation F can run between distinct languages, it can also run from a language back to itself. This kind of thing happens, in fact, quite frequently in the sciences. For example, a few decades ago, some clever economists figured out that some of the differential equations of physics could be applied to financial markets. Their proposal amounted to a translation from the language of physics into the language of economics—and since both are part of our total language, a translation from our language back into itself.

Within propositional logic, we can use this notion of translating a language into itself to make sense of the idea of a substitution instance of a sentence. In short, a substitution instance of a sentence ϕ is any sentence to which ϕ could be translated. (It can be helpful here to continue thinking of translations to other languages. In that case, a sentence in our language can have substitution instances in many other different languages.)

Definition. A substitution instance of ϕ is any sentence of the form $F(\phi)$, where $F : \Sigma \rightarrow \Sigma'$ is a reconstrual.

The key idea here is that a substitution instance of a sentence has the *same form* as that sentence. One confirmation that we've got the notion right is that any substitution instance of a tautology is still a tautology. (Here, we are using "tautology" in its semantic sense: a sentence that is true relative to every valuation.)

Proposition 9.4. *If ϕ is a tautology, then any substitution instance of ϕ is also a tautology.*

Proof. Suppose that ϕ is a tautology and that $F(\phi)$ is a substitution instance of ϕ. Let v be an arbitrary valuation. We need to show that $v(F(\phi)) = 1$. Consider the valuation w defined by $w(P) = v(F(P))$ for each atomic sentence P. Since ϕ is a tautology, $w(\phi) = 1$. In addition, since w and $v \circ F$ agree on atomic sentences, and both commute with all the sentence connectives, it follows that $w = v \circ F$. Therefore, $v(F(\phi)) = (v \circ F)(\phi) = w(\phi) = 1$. Since v was an arbitrary valuation, it follows that $F(\phi)$ is a tautology. $\qquad\square$

Proposition 9.5. *If ϕ is a contingent sentence, then ϕ has a tautologous substitution instance.*

Proof. Suppose that ϕ is contingent, and let $P_0, \ldots, P_n$ be a list of the atomic sentences that occur in ϕ. Since ϕ is contingent, there is a valuation v such that $v(\phi) = 1$. Let F be an arbitrary contradiction, and let T be an arbitrary tautology. For $i = 0, \ldots, n$, define $f(P_i) = T$ if $v(P_i) = 1$, and $f(P_i) = F$ if $v(P_i) = 0$. We claim, then, that $f(\phi)$ is a tautology. Let w be an arbitrary valuation. For each atomic sentence P_i, if $v(P_i) = 1$, then $v(P_i) = w(T) = w(f(P_i))$, and if $v(P_i) = 0$, then $v(P_i) = w(F) = w(f(P_i))$. Thus, v and $w \circ f$ agree on all atomic sentences. Since v and $w \circ f$ are truth-functional, they agree on all sentences, hence on ϕ. Therefore, $w(f(\phi)) = v(\phi) = 1$. Since w was an arbitrary valuation, $f(\phi)$ is a tautology. $\square$

Exercise 9.8. Give a tautologous substitution instance of the sentence $P \to (Q \wedge R)$.

Exercise 9.9. Follow the outlines of the previous proof to show that if ϕ is a contingent sentence, then ϕ has an inconsistent substitution instance.

We're now ready for the main show. The substitution meta-rule says that if you take a valid proof and perform uniform substitution, then the result is still a valid proof. We now prove that fact.

Substitution theorem. *Let $F : \Sigma \to \Sigma'$ be a reconstrual. If $\phi_1, \ldots, \phi_n \vdash \psi$, then $F(\phi_1), \ldots, F(\phi_n) \vdash F(\psi)$.*

Proof. We prove the result by induction on the construction of sequents. (We will prove the inductive steps for $\wedge$ I, CP, and $\vee$ E and leave the other steps to the reader.)

$\boxed{\text{base case}}$ The rule of assumptions gives not only $\phi \vdash \phi$ but also $F(\phi) \vdash F(\phi)$.

$\boxed{\text{induction } \wedge \text{I}}$ Suppose that $\phi_1, \ldots, \phi_n, \psi_1, \ldots, \psi_n \vdash \phi \wedge \psi$ results from an application of $\wedge$ I to $\phi_1, \ldots, \phi_n \vdash \phi$ and $\psi_1, \ldots, \psi_n \vdash \psi$, and suppose that the result holds for these latter two sequents. That is, $F(\phi_1), \ldots, F(\phi_n) \vdash F(\phi)$ and $F(\psi_1), \ldots, F(\psi_n) \vdash F(\psi)$. By conjunction introduction, we have

$$F(\phi_1), \ldots, F(\phi_n), F(\psi_1), \ldots, F(\psi_n) \vdash F(\phi) \wedge F(\psi).$$

Since $F(\phi) \wedge F(\psi) = F(\phi \wedge \psi)$, it follows that

$$F(\phi_1), \ldots, F(\phi_n), F(\psi_1), \ldots, F(\psi_n) \vdash F(\phi \wedge \psi).$$

induction CP   Suppose that $\phi_1, \ldots, \phi_n \vdash \psi \rightarrow \chi$ is derived by CP from $\phi_1, \ldots, \phi_n, \psi \vdash \chi$. Now assume that the result holds for the latter sequent, that is, $F(\phi_1), \ldots, F(\phi_n), F(\psi) \vdash F(\chi)$. Then, CP yields

$$F(\phi_1), \ldots, F(\phi_n) \vdash F(\psi) \rightarrow F(\chi).$$

Since $F(\psi) \rightarrow F(\chi) = F(\psi \rightarrow \chi)$, it follows that

$$F(\phi_1), \ldots, F(\phi_n) \vdash F(\psi \rightarrow \chi).$$

induction RAA   Suppose that $\phi_1, \ldots, \phi_n \vdash \neg \psi$ is derived by RAA from $\phi_1, \ldots, \phi_n, \psi \vdash \chi \wedge \neg \chi$, and assume that the result holds for the latter sequent, that is, $F(\phi_1), \ldots, F(\phi_n), F(\psi) \vdash F(\chi \wedge \neg \chi)$. By the properties of F, $F(\chi \wedge \neg \chi) = F(\chi) \wedge \neg F(\chi)$, which is also a contradiction. Thus, RAA yields $F(\phi_1), \ldots, F(\phi_n) \vdash \neg F(\psi)$. Since $\neg F(\psi) = F(\neg \psi)$, it follows that $F(\phi_1), \ldots, F(\phi_n) \vdash F(\neg \psi)$, which is what we wanted to prove.

induction $\vee$ E   Suppose that $\phi, \psi_1, \psi_2 \vdash \chi$ results from an application of $\vee$ E to the following three sequents:

$$\phi \vdash \theta_1 \vee \theta_2 \qquad \psi_1, \theta_1 \vdash \chi \qquad \psi_2, \theta_2 \vdash \psi$$

and assume that the result holds for the latter three sequents, that is,

$$F(\phi) \vdash F(\theta_1 \vee \theta_2) \qquad F(\psi_1), F(\theta_1) \vdash F(\chi)$$
$$F(\psi_2), F(\theta_2) \vdash F(\psi).$$

Since $F(\theta_1 \vee \theta_2) = F(\theta_1) \vee F(\theta_2)$, an application of $\vee$ E yields

$$F(\phi), F(\psi_1), F(\psi_2) \vdash F(\chi).$$

As mentioned before, we leave the remaining steps to the interested reader. With those steps completed, it follows that for any sentences $\phi_1, \ldots, \phi_n, \psi$, if $\phi_1, \ldots, \phi_n \vdash \psi$, then $F(\phi_1), \ldots, F(\phi_n) \vdash F(\psi)$. $\square$

The previous proposition immediately yields the following corollary.

Proposition 9.6. *If ϕ is provable, then any substitution instance of ϕ is also provable.*

We're now ready to prove the **soundness** of the inference rules for propositional logic. The proof is essentially another version of the proof of the substitution theorem, except that we map sentences to the numbers 0 and 1 instead of to other sentences.

Soundness theorem. *For any valuation v, if $\phi_1, \ldots, \phi_n \vdash \psi$, then* $\min\{v(\phi_1), \ldots, v(\phi_n)\} \leq v(\psi)$.

In the statement of the theorem, "min" treats the premises $\phi_1, \ldots, \phi_n$ as forming a conjunction: the minimum of $v_1(\phi_1), \ldots, v(\phi_n)$ is the same as $v(\phi_1 \wedge \cdots \wedge \phi_n)$.

Proof. The proof is by induction on the construction of sequents. We will just show a couple of cases and leave the others to the reader.

$\boxed{\text{induction MP}}$ Suppose that $\phi_1, \phi_2 \vdash \chi$ results from MP applied to $\phi_1 \vdash \psi \to \chi$ and $\phi_2 \vdash \psi$. Suppose also that $v(\phi_1) \leq v(\psi \to \chi)$ and $v(\psi_1) \leq v(\psi)$. If $\min\{v(\phi_1), v(\phi_2)\} = 0$, then we're done. If $\min\{v(\phi_1), v(\phi_2)\} = 1$, then $v(\psi \to \chi) = 1$ and $v(\psi) = 1$, from which it follows that $v(\chi) = 1$. In either case, $\min\{v(\phi_1), v(\phi_2)\} \leq v(\chi)$.

$\boxed{\text{induction CP}}$ Suppose that $\phi \vdash \psi \to \chi$ is derived by CP from $\phi, \psi \vdash \chi$, and assume that the result holds for the latter sequent, that is,

$\min\{v(\phi), v(\psi)\} \le v(\chi)$. Either $v(\psi) = 0$ or $v(\psi) = 1$. If $v(\psi) = 0$, then $v(\psi \to \chi) = 1$ and we're done. If $v(\psi) = 1$, then the above gives $v(\chi) = 1$, and hence $v(\psi \to \chi) = 1$. In either case, $v(\phi) \le v(\psi \to \chi)$.   □

This fulfills the promise we made in chapter 5 that the truth table method provides a reliable test for when a sequent cannot be proven. In particular, if there is a row in the truth table where ϕ is assigned 1 and ψ is assigned 0, then the sequent $\phi \vdash \psi$ cannot be proven. Similarly, if there is a row in the truth table where ψ is assigned 0, then $\vdash \psi$ cannot be proven.

Exercise 9.10. Prove the steps of the soundness theorem for the $\vee$ I and $\vee$ E rules.

Exercise 9.11. Show that if ϕ is inconsistent, then any substitution instance of ϕ is inconsistent. Here we mean "inconsistent" in the semantic sense of being assigned 0 by all valuations.

Exercise 9.12. Show that if ϕ is a contingent sentence, then ϕ has a contradictory substitution instance.

Disjunctive Normal Form

What we want to do next is to prove the **completeness** theorem: if an argument is truth preserving, then it can be proven with our inference rules. That's actually a nontrivial theorem that was only discovered in the early twentieth century. So, to get there, we're going to need to do some work. We'll start with something that might seem to be nothing but boring syntactic bookkeeping. We define a particular kind of form a sentence can take. Then we show that every sentence is provably equivalent to one with this particular kind of form.[2] It turns out, however, that this fact is quite useful—in particular, because sentences in this form wear their inferential

---

2. It's at this point where it becomes crucial that we have *enough* inference rules. If we didn't have enough rules, then not every sentence would be provably equivalent to one in this form.

relations on their sleeves. (It's as if these sentences have an address that shows where they live in logical space.)

Definition. A sentence ϕ is in **disjunctive normal form (DNF)** just in case it is a disjunction of conjunctions of literals (atomic and negated atomic sentences).

For example, the following sentences are DNF:

$$P \qquad P \wedge \neg Q \qquad (P \wedge \neg Q) \vee (\neg P \wedge Q)$$

We can define the family of DNF formulas inductively as follows:

- All conjunctions of literals (atomic and negated atomic sentences) are DNF.
- All disjunctions of DNF formulas are DNF.

The disjunctive normal form theorem will show that every propositional logic sentence is provably equivalent to a DNF sentence. That result can be proven in a couple of different ways, and it's useful in a couple of different ways. On the one hand, one can prove the DNF theorem directly by establishing a bunch of sequents and then using mathematical induction to generalize to all sentences. In that case, the DNF theorem is useful as a step along the way to proving the completeness theorem for propositional logic. On the other hand, if one has established the completeness theorem by some other means, then it gives a quick proof of the DNF theorem. In what follows, we'll first sketch the argument from completeness to the DNF theorem. Then we'll sketch a direct proof of the DNF theorem.

Suppose first that if two sentences have the same truth table, then they are provably equivalent. (This supposition is a direct consequence of the completeness theorem.) Now given a sentence ϕ, we will construct a DNF sentence ϕ' from the truth table for ϕ. If ϕ is always false (i.e., it has 0 in all rows of the main column), then let ϕ' be the sentence $P \wedge \neg P$. Otherwise, for each row i in which ϕ is true, let ψ_i be the conjunction of all the atomic sentences that are assigned true in that row, along with the negations of all the atomic sentences that are assigned false in that row. Note that ψ_i is true on row i of the truth table and false on every row $j \neq i$. Finally, let ϕ' be the disjunction of all the ψ_i that we have just constructed.

It's obvious that ϕ' is DNF. So we just need to show that ϕ and ϕ' have the same truth table. Suppose that we set them side by side, and consider row i of the truth table. If ϕ is true on row i, then one of the disjuncts of ϕ' is ψ_i, which is true on row i. Hence, ϕ' is true on row i. Conversely, if ϕ' is true on row i, then the disjunct ψ_i appears in it, and by construction, ϕ is true on row i. Thus, we have shown that ϕ and ϕ' have the same truth table. If we assume completeness, it follows that ϕ and ϕ' are provably equivalent.

This somewhat abstract argument can be illustrated by means of an example. Consider the sentence $\phi \equiv (P \to R) \to (Q \wedge R)$. If you write out the full truth table of ϕ, you'll find that it's true in rows 1, 2, 4, and 5 and false in all other rows. Thus, the above recipe yields the sentence

$$(P \wedge Q \wedge R) \vee (P \wedge Q \wedge \neg R) \vee (P \wedge \neg Q \wedge \neg R) \vee (\neg P \wedge Q \wedge R).$$

It's pretty easy to see here that $\phi' \vdash \phi$. If one performed a big disjunction elimination, then the first and fourth disjuncts immediately yield $Q \wedge R$, and positive paradox yields ϕ. The second and third disjuncts yield $P \wedge \neg R$, hence $\neg(P \to R)$, and then ϕ by negative paradox. Since ϕ' is a disjunction, it's a bit more difficult to see that $\phi \vdash \phi'$. However, you'll recall that ϕ entails $\neg(P \to R) \vee (Q \wedge R)$, which in turn entails $(P \wedge \neg R) \vee (Q \wedge R)$. This last formula is actually in DNF, and although not strictly identical to ϕ', it's not hard to see how it's related to ϕ'.

Making liberal use of known equivalences, we can rewrite ϕ' as

$$(P \wedge \neg R \wedge Q) \vee (P \wedge \neg R \wedge \neg Q) \vee (Q \wedge R \wedge P) \vee (Q \wedge R \wedge \neg P)$$
$$\dashv\vdash [(P \wedge \neg R) \wedge (Q \vee \neg Q)] \vee [(Q \wedge R) \wedge (P \vee \neg P)]$$
$$\dashv\vdash (P \wedge \neg R) \vee (Q \wedge R).$$

This example shows that DNF equivalent forms are not generally unique.

We now turn to the argument for the DNF theorem. Actually, it's easiest to prove something stronger, for which we need another definition.

Definition. A sentence is in **conjunctive normal form (CNF)** just in case it's a conjunction of disjunctions of literals.

DNF theorem. *Every sentence ϕ is provably equivalent to a sentence ϕ^d in disjunctive normal form and to a sentence ϕ^c in conjunctive normal form.*

Proof. We argue by induction on the construction of sentences.

- Each atomic sentence is both in DNF and in CNF.
- Suppose that ϕ is equivalent to ϕ^c and to ϕ^d. Then, $\neg\phi$ is equivalent to $\neg\phi^d$, which has the form $\neg(\psi_1 \vee \cdots \vee \psi_n)$. By DeMorgan's rule, the latter is equivalent to $\neg\psi_1 \wedge \cdots \wedge \neg\psi_n$. By another application of DeMorgan's rule, each $\neg\psi_i$ is equivalent to a disjunction of literals. Putting everything together, $\neg\phi^d$ is equivalent to a CNF sentence. A similar argument shows that $\neg\phi$ is equivalent to $\neg\phi^c$, which is equivalent to a DNF sentence. Therefore, $\neg\phi$ is equivalent to sentences in both CNF and DNF.
- For disjunction and conjunction, we first note that $\vee$ trivially preserves the family of DNF sentences, and $\wedge$ trivially preserves the family of CNF sentences. Thus, if ϕ and ψ are sentences that satisfy the hypothesis of the theorem, then $\phi \vee \psi$ is equivalent to a DNF sentence. It's also equivalent to $\neg(\neg\phi \wedge \neg\psi)$, which is equivalent to a CNF sentence. A similar argument shows that $\phi \wedge \psi$ is equivalent to DNF and CNF sentences.
- For conditionals, we have $\phi \to \psi \dashv\vdash \neg\phi \vee \psi$. By the previous two steps, if ϕ and ψ satisfy the hypotheses of the theorem, so does $\neg\phi \vee \psi$.

$\square$

Exercise 9.13. Go back through the proof of the DNF theorem and identify each provable equivalence that was cited. Now identify which inference rules are needed to prove those equivalences. Are any of the primitive rules of inference not needed for the proof to go through?

What use is it that every sentence is equivalent to a DNF sentence? For one, it gives us a quick way of understanding all the different possible logical relations between sentences. Consider, for example, the case of all sentences whose only atomic sentence is P. In this case, the only literals are P and ¬P, and every elementary conjunction is equivalent to P, ¬P, or P ∧ ¬P. Consequently, the DNF formulas are equivalent to P, ¬P, P ∧ ¬P, or P ∨ ¬P. That is, every sentence is logically equivalent to one of these four sentences.

Furthermore, if two sentences ϕ, ψ are in DNF, then it can be quite easy to see whether or not $\phi \vdash \psi$. In short, $\phi \vdash \psi$ just in case ϕ contains a conjunction that is as long as some conjunction in ψ. Consider, for example, the two DNF formulas:

$$Q \wedge P \qquad Q \vee (\neg Q \wedge \neg P)$$

A quick inspection shows that $\phi \vdash \psi$, since $Q \wedge P \vdash Q$ by conjunction elimination and $Q \vdash \psi$ by disjunction introduction.

We saw above that if ϕ is a sentence containing only P, then ϕ is equivalent to one of the four sentences P, ¬P, ⊤, ⊥. If you took some time writing out formulas in DNF, you'd also see that for sentences containing both P and Q, there are $16 = 2^4$ possibilities. (The possibilities are the four consistent elementary conjunctions,

$$P \wedge Q \quad P \wedge \neg Q \quad \neg P \wedge Q \quad \neg P \wedge \neg Q,$$

and all possible disjunctions of those.) In general, if there are n atomic sentences, then there are 2^{2^n} possible sentences up to logical equivalence. Unsurprisingly, 2^{2^n} is also the number of distinct truth functions on n inputs. (Each distinct sentence corresponds to a distinct truth-function.)

Practically speaking, it's doubtful that you'll ever need to transform a sentence into DNF or CNF. In fact, you can have a computer do that task for you. But how, you might wonder, could you write a program to convert sentences to DNF? On the one hand, you could program the computer first to compute a truth table and then to use the rows of the truth table to construct a corresponding formula. On the other hand, you could program the computer to perform a series of syntactic manipulations on the relevant formula. Here's one sort of algorithm you could use:

- Replace all instances of $\phi \rightarrow \psi$ with $\neg\phi \vee \psi$.
- Whenever $\neg$ is prefixed to a conjunction or disjunction, use DeMorgan's equivalences to drive $\neg$ inward.
- Whenever $\wedge$ is applied to a disjunction, use distribution to transform to a disjunction of conjunctions.

In order to trust such an algorithm, you would want to prove that it will always terminate—after a finite number of steps—in a DNF formula.

Completeness

The claim here is that we have sufficiently many derivation rules to be able to prove everything that we want to prove—in particular, all truth-preserving arguments. Before we prove that, however, we can show already that we couldn't add any more inference rules—at least not if we want to maintain soundness. That is, if we add any more inference rules, then we'll be able to prove an argument that is *not* truth preserving.

We first need to be clear about what it would mean to add a "new" inference rule. For example, suppose that I proposed adding the following inference rule, namely, DeMorgan's rule:

$$\frac{\Gamma \quad \vdash \quad \neg(\phi \vee \psi)}{\Gamma \quad \vdash \quad \neg\phi \wedge \neg\psi}.$$

I might think myself very clever for coming up with a plausible new inference rule. The problem here, though, is that the rule isn't really new: it can be derived from the rules that we already have. Indeed, we've already proven that $\vdash \neg(\phi \vee \psi) \rightarrow \neg\phi \wedge \neg\psi$. So suppose now that you were given a derivation that begins with assumptions Γ and that ends with $\neg(\phi \vee \psi)$. Then, you could append the derivation of that conditional, perform a step of MP, and that would yield a proof of $\neg\phi \wedge \neg\psi$, depending on Γ. In other words, $\Gamma \vdash \neg(\phi \vee \psi)$ can always be converted to $\Gamma \vdash \neg\phi \wedge \neg\psi$.

A genuinely new derivation rule, then, would have to be a rule that permits a derivation of a sentence ϕ, without any remaining dependencies,

whereas ϕ previously was not derivable. In other words, $\not\vdash \phi$, where $\vdash \phi$
means that there is a derivation of ϕ using the previous rules.

Proposition 9.7. *If ϕ is not provable, then there is a substitution instance of
ϕ that is provably equivalent to $\bot$.*

Proof. To illustrate the idea behind the proof, we'll consider first the case
where the only atomic sentence in ϕ is P. If ϕ is not provable, then ϕ must
be provably equivalent to P, $\neg P$, or $\bot$. In the last case, the result is trivially
true. But if ϕ is equivalent to P, then the substitution $F(P) = \bot$ will do. If
ϕ is equivalent to $\neg P$, then the substitution $F(P) = \top$ will do.

For the general case, suppose that the atomic sentences in ϕ are
$P_1, \ldots, P_n$. By the DNF theorem, ϕ is equivalent to a disjunction of elementary conjunctions of the P_i. If ϕ is equivalent to a disjunction of all 2^n
distinct elementary conjunctions, then ϕ is provable. Since ϕ was assumed
not to be provable, at least one of those 2^n conjunctions doesn't occur in ϕ^d.
Without loss of generality, suppose that $P_1 \wedge \cdots \wedge P_n$ doesn't occur in ϕ^d.
Now let $F(P_i) = \top$ for $i = 1, \ldots, n$. Then each disjunct ψ that occurs in
ϕ^d contains $\neg P_j$ for some j, and since $F(\neg P_j) = \neg \top$, it follows that $F(\psi)$
$\vdash F(\neg P_j) \vdash \bot$. Therefore, $F(\phi) \vdash \bot$, and $F(\phi)$ is the desired substitution
instance of ϕ. $\qquad\square$

We can now show that if we added a new inference rule, then we could
prove anything whatsoever.[3] If there were a new inference rule, then we
could prove some sentence ϕ that was not previously provable. Impor-
tantly, it's not just that we could prove ϕ but that we could prove any
substitution instance $F(\phi)$ of ϕ. Since ϕ wasn't previously provable, there
is a substitution instance $F(\phi)$ of ϕ such that $\vdash F(\phi) \leftrightarrow \bot$. But then we
could prove $\bot$, and since $\bot \vdash \psi$ for all sentences ψ, we could prove
anything whatsoever.

We can now prove the completeness theorem. For this, we use the con-
venient notation $\phi \vDash \psi$ to mean that for any valuation v, if $v(\phi) = 1$, then

---

3. This result is usually called **Post completeness** in honor of the logician Emil Post (1897–
1954).

$v(\psi) = 1$. In other words, $\phi \vDash \psi$ means that the argument with premise ϕ and conclusion ψ is truth preserving.

Lemma. *If ϕ is not provable, then there is a valuation v such that $v(\phi) = 0$.*

Proof. Go through the preceding proof, replacing each case of $F(P) = \top$ with $v(P) = 1$, each case of $F(P) = \bot$ with $v(P) = 0$, and each case of $F(\phi) \equiv \bot$ with $v(\phi) = 0$. $\qquad\square$

Finite completeness theorem. *If $\phi \vDash \psi$, then $\phi \vdash \psi$.*

Proof. We argue for the contrapositive. Suppose that $\phi \nvdash \psi$. Then $\nvdash \phi \rightarrow \psi$. By the lemma, there is a valuation v such that $v(\phi \rightarrow \psi) = 0$. Therefore, $v(\phi) = 1$ and $v(\psi) = 0$, which means that $\phi \nvDash \psi$. $\qquad\square$

The finite completeness theorem tells you that if an argument is truth preserving, then there is a proof. But it doesn't give you a recipe for finding that proof. In that sense, completeness is a *nonconstructive* result: it shows $\exists x \phi(x)$ without producing some a such that $\phi(a)$. In the case of propositional logic, it's possible to redo the proof of completeness so that it really is constructive—that is, it takes the relevant truth table and builds a proof (that might be long and ugly). However, our goal here is not to give you a recipe for outsourcing the job of proving to a computer.

There's another really interesting thing we could prove about propositional logic, but it's significantly more mathematically demanding, since it deals with infinite sets. Imagine that we had a language with infinitely many atomic sentences $P_0, P_1, \ldots$, in which case there aren't just infinitely many distinct sentences, there are also infinitely many logically inequivalent sentences. Let's now suppose that Γ is any set of sentences, possibly an infinite set. We write $\Gamma \vDash \phi$ just in case any valuation that makes *all* the sentences in Γ true also makes ϕ true. We write $\Gamma \vdash \phi$ just in case there is a proof that begins with some finite number of sentences from Γ and that ends with ϕ. Now we can raise the question: does completeness continue to hold in this more general case?

The answer is yes, provided that we help ourselves to an additional assumption about sets of sentences. This assumption can be formulated in various ways; for example:

Compactness (C) If a set Δ of sentences is inconsistent, then some finite subset Δ_0 of Δ is already inconsistent. (Here, we are describing a semantic notion of inconsistency.)

Grow (G) If a set Γ of sentences does not imply $\bot$, then it's contained in a set Γ^* that is maximal with respect to this property. (Here, we are describing a syntactic notion of consistency.)

The **Grow** axiom makes a lot of sense. Imagine that your current state of belief was represented by the set Γ_0, and image that you are fortunate enough that your beliefs don't imply a contradiction. Then, the second assumption says that your set of beliefs could grow to the limit point Γ where you couldn't add any more without falling into contradiction. That idea doesn't just make sense, it seems obviously true.

We now show that **C** is equivalent to **G**. Suppose first that **C** is true, and let Γ be a set of sentences that does not imply $\bot$. Thus, no finite subset Γ_0 of Γ implies $\bot$. By the finite completeness theorem, every finite subset Γ_0 of Γ is semantically consistent. Therefore by **C**, Γ is semantically consistent, that is, there is a valuation v that assigns 1 to every sentence in Γ. Let Γ^* be the set of all sentences that are assigned 1 by v. If $\Gamma^* \vdash \bot$, then soundness would fail. Therefore, $\Gamma^* \nvdash \bot$. If $\phi \notin \Gamma^*$, then $v(\phi) = 0$ and $v(\neg\phi) = 1$. Hence, $\neg\phi \in \Gamma^*$, from which it follows that $\Gamma^* \cup \{\phi\} \vdash \bot$. Therefore, Γ^* is maximally consistent (in the syntactic sense).

Suppose now that **G** is true. We're going to show first that for any set Δ, if $\Delta \nvdash \bot$, then Δ is consistent. Suppose, then, that $\Delta \nvdash \bot$. By **G**, $\Delta \subseteq \Gamma$, where $\Gamma \nvdash \bot$, and if $\phi \notin \Gamma$, then $\Gamma \cup \{\phi\} \vdash \bot$. We claim, then, that Γ is the set of sentences that are assigned 1 by some valuation.

- We show that if $\Gamma \vdash \phi$, then $\phi \in \Gamma$. Suppose that $\Gamma \vdash \phi$. If $\Gamma \cup \{\phi\} \vdash \bot$, then $\Gamma \vdash \neg\phi$; hence, $\Gamma \vdash \bot$, contrary to what we assumed about Γ. Therefore, $\Gamma \cup \{\phi\} \nvdash \bot$, and by maximality, $\phi \in \Gamma$.

- We show that if $\Gamma \nvdash \phi$, then $\neg\phi \in \Gamma$. Suppose that $\Gamma \nvdash \phi$. If $\Gamma \cup \{\neg\phi\} \vdash \bot$, then $\Gamma \vdash \neg\neg\phi$, and hence, $\Gamma \vdash \phi$, contrary to our assumption. Therefore, $\Gamma \cup \{\neg\phi\} \nvdash \bot$, and by maximality, $\neg\phi \in \Gamma$.

- We show now that $\phi \wedge \psi \in \Gamma$ iff $\phi \in \Gamma$ and $\psi \in \Gamma$. If $\phi \wedge \psi \in \Gamma$, then $\Gamma \vdash \phi$ and $\phi \in \Gamma$. Similarly, $\Gamma \vdash \psi$ and $\psi \in \Gamma$. Conversely, if $\phi \in \Gamma$ and $\psi \in \Gamma$, then $\Gamma \vdash \phi$ and $\Gamma \vdash \psi$; therefore, $\Gamma \vdash \phi \wedge \psi$ and $\phi \wedge \psi \in \Gamma$.

- We show that $\phi \vee \psi \in \Gamma$ iff either $\phi \in \Gamma$ or $\psi \in \Gamma$. If $\phi \notin \Gamma$ and $\psi \notin \Gamma$, then $\neg\phi \in \Gamma$ and $\neg\psi \in \Gamma$, from which it follows that $\neg\phi \wedge \neg\psi \in \Gamma$. But then $\neg(\phi \vee \psi) \in \Gamma$, which means that $\phi \vee \psi \notin \Gamma$. Conversely, if $\phi \in \Gamma$, then $\Gamma \vdash \phi$, from which $\Gamma \vdash \phi \vee \psi$, and therefore, $\phi \vee \psi \in \Gamma$.

We can then define $v(\phi) = 1$ iff $\phi \in \Gamma$, and it follows that v is a well-defined valuation. Therefore, v assigns 1 to all sentences in Δ, and Δ is consistent.

By the previous argument, if Δ is inconsistent, then $\Delta \vdash \bot$. But if $\Delta \vdash \bot$, then $\Delta_0 \vdash \bot$ for some finite subset Δ_0 of Δ. By soundness, Δ_0 is inconsistent, which completeness the derivation of **C** from **G**.

Let's check now that **C** plus finite completeness implies general completeness. If $\Gamma \vdash \psi$, then $\Gamma \cup \{\neg\psi\}$ is inconsistent. By compactness, there is a finite subset $\{\phi_1, \ldots, \phi_n\}$ of Γ such that $\{\phi_1, \ldots, \phi_n, \neg\psi\}$ is inconsistent, and hence, $\phi_1, \ldots, \phi_n \vDash \psi$. By the finite completeness theorem, $\phi_1, \ldots, \phi_n \vdash \psi$, which means that $\Gamma \vdash \phi$.

Some day you might find another logic book that claims to prove compactness. Why, then, would we assume compactness, when it can be proven to be true? In this case, proofs of compactness assume not only the axioms of set theory but an additional axiom that goes under various names, such as "the axiom of choice" and "Hausdorff's maximal principle." Those latter axioms are like industrial-strength power tools, designed to crack some of the hardest mathematical puzzles. For an introductory book, we don't need such heavy-duty set-theoretic assumptions. Nonetheless, you might be interested to know that compactness for propositional logic is provably equivalent to some other well-known mathematical facts. First, if you take a course in abstract algebra, you'll learn that each Boolean ideal can be extended to a prime ideal (the Boolean prime ideal theorem). That fact is very similar to our "grow" axiom, and it is indeed provably equivalent to compactness. Similarly, if you take a course in graph theory, you might learn that in a tree T with infinitely many nodes, if each node has only finitely many children, then T has a branch of infinite length (König's lemma). That fact is also provably equivalent to compactness.

The compactness property can seem a bit paradoxical. Consider, for example, the following apparently valid argument with infinitely many premises.

There is more than one angel.
There are more than two angels.
$\vdots$

_____

There are infinitely many angels.

If this argument is valid, then compactness entails that the conclusion is a logical consequence of only finitely many of the premises. In particular, there is a largest natural number n such that the premise "there are more than n angels" implies the conclusion "there are infinitely many angels," which seems obviously wrong. The solution to this little puzzle is simply that propositional logic renders a false verdict about the structure of this argument. But that shouldn't be surprising; we already know that propositional logic provides only a partial picture of what makes arguments valid.

Exercise 9.14.

*1. Let T stand for the system of propositional logic with connectives $\neg$, $\wedge$, and with rules $\wedge$ I, $\wedge$ E, RAA, and DN. We write $\succ \phi$ to indicate that ϕ is provable in system T. Either prove or refute the following statement: for a sentence ϕ that contains only $\neg$ and $\wedge$, if $\vdash \phi$, then $\succ \phi$.

*2. In this exercise, you're asked to show that the RAA rule is redundant. Let T stand for the system of propositional logic that results from dropping the RAA rule, and write $\phi \succ \psi$ to indicate that the corresponding sequent is provable in system T. Show that if $\phi \vdash \psi$, then $\phi \succ \psi$. (Hint: prove that $P \rightarrow \neg P \succ \neg P$.)

3. Show that the DN introduction rule is redundant, that is, is derivable from the remaining rules in our system.

4. Show that MT is redundant, that is, is derivable from the remaining rules in our system.

*5. Show that the set of stage 0 rules of inference (i.e., those given in chapter 2) is incomplete. Hint: construct an alternate truth table for $\vee$, and show that the stage 0 rules are sound relative to that truth table.

*6. Give introduction and elimination rules for the nand connective $\uparrow$. Prove that your rules are sound relative to the truth table for $\uparrow$.

10

A Theory about Predicate Logic

IN THIS CHAPTER, WE SKETCH THE OUTLINES of a theory predicate logic—or what's usually called "metatheory of predicate logic." This theory began to be developed in the early twentieth century, and since then, it's given rise to a number of distinct subdisciplines of mathematics: proof theory, model theory, and recursion theory, among others. The metatheory of predicate logic is also the context for the proof of the famous incompleteness theorem of Kurt Gödel. Here we'll take up a sampling of metatheoretical topics, with focus on those that will help us become more proficient users of predicate logic.

Substitution

The aim of formal logic is to articulate the notion of a valid argument form. Once we know that a form is valid, we can use it again and again to generate new valid arguments. We generate these new valid arguments by taking the valid argument form and by *substituting* new content for old. The trick, however, is in explaining what counts as a legitimate substitution of content.

In propositional logic, the idea of substitution is simple: an elementary sentence such as p can be replaced by any sentence ϕ. In predicate logic, we'll have to be a bit more sophisticated. For example, suppose that we have a proof of the sequent $\vdash \forall x(Fx \lor \neg Fx)$. Suppose, in particular, that the last two lines of the proof look like this:

(8) $Fa \lor \neg Fa$
(9) $\forall x(Fx \lor \neg Fx)$

Intuitively, it didn't really matter that we used F here. Surely we could have used G instead. So, imagine that you perform a "find F and replace with G" on the above proof. Then, intuitively, the result should be a valid proof of $\vdash \forall x(Gx \lor \neg Gx)$.

However, the "find-and-replace" intuition is not sufficient here. For example, the validity of $\forall x(Fx \lor \neg Fx)$ doesn't depend on the fact that Fx is a simple formula (with no subformulas). We should be able to modify the proof of $\forall x(Fx \lor \neg Fx)$ to produce a structurally identical proof of $\forall x((Fx \land Gx) \lor \neg(Fx \land Gx))$. Nonetheless, this modification cannot be as simple as replacing instances of Fx with instances of $Fx \land Gx$, because the proof is likely also to contain formulas such as Fa, and that should be replaced with $Fa \land Ga$.

Similarly, it's of course possible to prove the sequent $\forall x \forall y Rxy \vdash \forall x Rxx$, and a structurally similar proof would result in the sequent

$$\forall x \forall y(Fx \land Gy) \vdash \forall x(Fx \land Gx).$$

To get the latter proof, we would need to substitute $Fx \land Gy$ for Rxy, $Fa \land Gb$ for Rab, and so on.

Now we will make this notion of substitution precise. In the first instance, we will think of a substitution as resulting from reconstruing the relation symbols of one vocabulary as formulas in another vocabulary.

Definition. A **reconstrual** F of Σ into Σ' is an assignment of each atomic formula $r(t_1, \ldots, t_n)$ of Σ to a formula $Fr(t_1, \ldots, t_n)$ of Σ'.

We implicitly require here that if the terms after r are changed, then the output formula Fr is changed in the same way. So, for example, if $r(x, y)$ is reconstrued as $p(x) \land q(y)$, then $r(z, z)$ must be reconstrued as $p(z) \land q(z)$.

A reconstrual F of Σ into Σ' extends naturally to all Σ-formulas. In particular, we stipulate that $F(\phi \land \psi) = F(\phi) \land F(\psi)$ and similarly for the other binary connectives. We also stipulate that $F(\neg\phi) = \neg F(\phi)$ and for the quantifiers $F(\forall x\phi) = \forall x F(\phi)$ and $F(\exists x\phi) = \exists x F(\phi)$.

Example. Consider the reconstrual F that takes $r(x, y)$ to $p(x) \wedge q(y)$. Then,

$$F(\forall z\, r(z, z)) = \forall z\, F(r(z, z)) = \forall z\, (p(z) \wedge q(z)).$$

Now consider the reconstrual G that takes $p(x)$ to $\forall y\, r(x, y)$. In this case, G must reconstrue $p(y)$ as a corresponding formula with free variable y. Since the formula $\forall y\, r(x, y)$ is equivalent to the formula $\forall z\, r(x, z)$, we set $G(p(y)) \equiv \forall z\, r(y, z)$.

Now we can define the notion of a substitution instance of a formula.

Definition. A **substitution instance** of a formula ϕ is any formula of the form $F\phi$, for some reconstrual F.

As was the case for propositional logic, substitution preserves provability.

Substitution theorem. *Let F be a translation of relation symbols to formulas. If $\phi \vdash \psi$, then $F\phi \vdash F\psi$. In particular, if ϕ is a tautology, then any substitution instance of ϕ is a tautology.*

The proof of this result is actually a simple induction on the construction of proofs—as it was in the case of propositional logic.

Exercise 10.1. Assume that you've already got a proof of the sequent $\forall x Fx \to P \vdash \exists x(Fx \to P)$. Use substitution to show that $\vdash \exists x(Fx \to \forall y Fy)$.

The substitution theorem continues to hold if Σ and Σ' both have the equality symbol and if we require that the reconstrual preserves equality. Unfortunately, the substitution theorem doesn't hold—without further tweaks—for signatures that contain function symbols or names. Indeed, it's a little bit complicated in the first place to decide what a function symbol (or name) should be reconstrued as. For example, if Σ has a name c, but Σ' has no names, then how could c be translated from Σ to Σ'?

One potential solution to this difficulty is to think of the name c in terms of the associated formula $\phi(x) \equiv (x = c)$. We can then ask whether $\phi(x)$ can be translated to some Σ' formula $F(\phi(x))$.

Definition. A reconstrual F of an n-ary function symbol f if a $(n + 1)$-ary formula $Ff(x_1, \ldots, x_n, y)$. A reconstrual F of a constant symbol c is a formula $Fc(y)$.

It is fairly intuitive, although somewhat tedious, to extend a reconstrual F to complex terms like $1 + 1$ or $\mathsf{father}(a)$. The key here is to remember that if n-ary terms are represented by $(n + 1)$-ary formulas, then complex terms can be represented by composing the formulas.

Example. Suppose that $f(y) = z$ is reconstrued as $\phi(y, z)$ and that $c = y$ is reconstrued as $\psi(y)$. Then, $f(c)$ can be thought of as the composite of the constant c function and the f function. In other words, $f(c) = z$ would be represented by

$$\exists y \left(\psi(y) \wedge \phi(y, z) \right),$$

which says that z is the unique thing related by ϕ to the unique thing that satisfies ψ.

A general term is of the form $f(t_1, \ldots, t_n)$, where f is an n-ary function symbol, and $t_1, \ldots, t_n$ are terms. In this case, the formula $f(t_1, \ldots, t_n) = z$ is equivalent to the following formula:

$$\exists y_1 \cdots \exists y_n \left((t_1 = y_1) \wedge \cdots \wedge (t_n = y_n) \wedge (f(y_1, \ldots, y_n) = z) \right).$$

Hence, if the terms $t_1, \ldots, t_n$ have been reconstrued as formulas, we can use the above formula as a guide for how to reconstrue the complex term $f(t_1, \ldots, t_n)$.

So now we have a general recipe for generating new substitution instances of formulas. However, the substitution theorem no longer holds in its original form. For example, $\phi \equiv \exists y(y = c)$ is a tautology, but if $Fc(y)$ is the formula $P(y)$, then $F\phi$ is the formula $\exists y Py$, which is not a tautology. Nonetheless, it's pretty simple to modify the statement of the substitution theorem so that we get something valid. In short, if f is a function symbol, then let Δ_f be the sentence $\forall x \exists! y Ff(x, y)$. Similarly, if c is a constant symbol, then let Δ_c be the sentence $\exists! y Fc(y)$. If we now let Δ be a list of all these sentences for the constant and function symbols that occur in ϕ and ψ, then we have the result: if $\phi \vdash \psi$, then $\Delta, F\phi \vdash F\psi$.

At this stage, it behooves us to ask whether we have found the most general notion of a validity-preserving substitution. For, in one important sense, we understand "validity in terms of form" only insofar as we understand which substitutions preserve validity. In the case at hand, there is good reason to think that there is an even more general notion of substitution, where individual variables can be replaced with multiple variables.[1]

Soundness

When you're first learning to use formal logic, it's perfectly reasonable to trust that the system of rules that you've been given is both safe and sufficiently strong. Think of it like this: if you buy a car from a reputable dealer, then you can trust that its wheels will stay on, that its engine will allow you to reach certain speeds, and so on. However, if you want to become an expert driver, then at some point, you'll have to learn some of the theory behind how cars work. In the same way, if you want to reach a higher level of logical expertise, then at some point, you'll have to learn some of the theory behind how logic works.

We'll first prove that the system of predicate logic that we developed in this book is **sound**. That is, we want to check that we can't prove just anything, and we hope even to reassure ourselves that the limits of what can be proven match fairly well with our intuitions of what should be provable.

---

1. See chapter 5 of Halvorson, *The Logic in Philosophy of Science*, Cambridge (2019).

For the proof of soundness, we'll need to make use of the following fact:

Proposition 10.1. *Suppose that M is an interpretation and that c is a name. Then, for any $a \in M$, there is an interpretation N such that $c^N = a$, and $\phi^N = \phi^M$ for all formulas ϕ in which the name c does not occur. In particular, if ϕ is a sentence in which c does not occur, then $M \vDash \phi$ iff $N \vDash \phi$.*

We won't argue in detail here for proposition 10.1, but it should be fairly obvious why it's true. In particular, the interpretation N is defined to agree with M on all symbols except for the name c, where N is defined so that $c^N = a$. The work of the argument comes in showing that $\phi^N = \phi^M$ for any formula ϕ in which the name c does not occur. To prove this rigorously, one could use induction on the construction of formulas. We leave the details to the reader.

Now on to the proof of soundness. We want to show that any line in a "correctly written" proof is soundness in the sense that for any interpretation M, if the dependencies of the line are true in M, then the sentence on the right-hand side of the line is also true in M. For this, it will suffice to show that the rule of assumptions produces sound lines and that all the other inference rules convert sound lines to sound lines. The case of the rule of assumptions is obvious, so we move on to the other inference rules.

First of all, let's note that the rules for the Boolean connectives convert sound lines to sound lines. To see this, you need to convince yourself, for example, that if ϕ and ψ are true in an interpretation M, then $\phi \wedge \psi$ is also true in M. We'll leave these steps to the reader.

Exercise 10.2. Prove the soundness of conditional proof.

We show now that the $\forall$ introduction rule converts sound lines to sound lines. Suppose that $\phi \vDash \psi(c)$, where the name c does not occur in ϕ. Now let M be an interpretation such that $M \vDash \phi$. We need to show that $M \vDash \forall x\, \psi(x)$, that is, we need to show that $\psi(x)^M = M$. Let a be an arbitrary element of M. Since c does not occur in ϕ, proposition 10.1 entails that there is an interpretation N such that $c^N = a$ and $N \vDash \phi$. Since $\phi \vDash \psi(c)$, it follows that $a = c^N \in \psi(x)^N$. Since c does not occur in $\psi(x)$, we have $\psi(x)^N = \psi(x)^M$, and therefore, $a \in \phi^M$. Since a was an arbitrary member of M, it follows that $\psi(x)^M = M$, and therefore, $M \vDash \forall x\, \psi(x)$.

Notice how the argument we just made uses the fact that the name c does not occur in $\psi(x)$, which is one of the restrictions on the use of the UI rule. If c had occurred in ψ, then we might have been able to generate an unsound line, as in the following:

1	(1)	$\forall x Rxx$	A	
1	(2)	Rcc	1 UE	
1	(3)	$\forall x Rxc$	2 UI	$\Leftarrow$ wrong
1	(4)	$\forall y \forall x Rxy$	3 UI	

Here, step 3 violates the restriction on the UI rule, for it applies $\forall x$ to the formula $\psi(x) \equiv Rxc$ in which c occurs. Moreover, lines 3 and 4 are unsound. For example, consider the interpretation M with domain $\{1, 2\}$ and where $R^M = \{\langle 1, 1 \rangle, \langle 2, 2 \rangle\}$ and $c^M = 1$.

Now we argue for the soundness of the EE rule. Suppose that $\phi \vDash \exists x\, \psi(x)$ and $\psi(c) \vDash \theta$, where c does not occur in ϕ or in $\psi(x)$. We need to show that $\phi \vDash \theta$. Let M be an interpretation such that $M \vDash \phi$; hence, $M \vDash \exists x\, \psi(x)$. Thus, there is an $a \in M$ such that $a \in \psi(x)^M$. Since c does not occur in $\psi(x)$, proposition 10.1 entails that there is an interpretation N that agrees with M on all formulas not containing c and such that $c^N = a$. Thus, $c^N \in \psi(x)^N$, which means that $N \vDash \phi(c)$. Since $\phi(c) \vDash \theta$, we also have $N \vDash \theta$, and since c does not occur in θ, $M \vDash \theta$. Finally, since M was an arbitrary interpretation, $\phi \vDash \theta$.

Exercise 10.3. Prove the soundness of the EI and UE rules.

Once we've proven that each inference rule converts sound lines to sound lines, then we know that every line in a (correctly written) proof will be sound. So, our rules of argument won't lead us astray. That's half of the battle. The other half of the battle is to find rules of argument that can get us where we want to go.

Completeness

Predicate logic interpretations can be used for the same purposes as truth tables were for propositional logic. In particular, the soundness and completeness theorems show that there's a proof of a sequent iff there is no counterexample to that sequent. In particular, since soundness holds, you can give a counterexample to demonstrate that a sequent cannot be proven. And since completeness holds, if you know that ψ is true in every model where ϕ is true, then you know that there is a proof of ψ from ϕ.

The completeness theorem for predicate logic tends not to be of great practical value. For one, it's often just as difficult (if not more so) to show that $\phi \vDash \psi$ than to show that $\phi \vdash \psi$. For another, even if you know that $\phi \vDash \psi$, and so there *is* some proof of ψ from ϕ, still that doesn't necessarily help you to see how to find that proof.

There's an in-principle reason why the completeness theorem is not of all that much practical utility: to reason about interpretations requires the full power of the theory of sets. Moreover, logicians have proven that there are trade-offs between power and tractability. Here, "tractability" is a semitechnical term that means, roughly speaking, how easy it is to use a theory. Since set theory is so powerful, it's not very tractable.

Thus, the value of the completeness theorem tends to be more conceptual than practical. It helps us to understand better what's going on in logic, even if for individual problems, it may not provide us a quicker route to a solution.

For a rigorous proof of the completeness theorem for predicate logic, you'll have to wait for a second course in logic. Here, we'll restrict ourselves to two things. First, we'll sketch the idea behind one version of the completeness theorem. Second, we'll explain how the completeness theorem for predicate logic differs from the famous *incompleteness* theorem that was proven by Gödel.

Suppose for simplicity that Σ is a signature without function symbols or names. That is, Σ only has relation symbols. Let ϕ be a Σ-sentence. We will sketch a proof of the following result:

If no contradiction can be derived from ϕ, then there is a model M of ϕ.

What's nice about this result is that it mimics what Lobachevsky did with non-Euclidean geometry (see page 157). Lobachevsky assumed a sentence ϕ, which implies the negation of Euclid's parallel postulate. Then, he started proving things from ϕ, never achieving a contradiction $\perp$. From the list of sentences he proved, Lobachevsky was essentially able to describe a model M in which ϕ is true.

Let's suppose further that ϕ has the following simple form: if it contains any quantifiers, then they all occur out in the front. You might think that this assumption greatly reduces the generality of our proof. But in fact, with a little work, you can show that any sentence ϕ is provably equivalent to one in the form we just described—which is called **prenex normal form**. So let's just assume that ϕ itself is in prenex normal form.

Let's suppose first that ϕ has the simple form $\exists x\,\psi\,(x)$, where no quantifiers occur in ψ. Then, take the instance $\psi\,(1)$, which contains no variables (free or bound). If $\psi\,(1) \vdash \perp$, then an instance of EE gives $\exists x\,\psi\,(x) \vdash \perp$, contrary to our assumption. Therefore, $\psi\,(1) \nvdash \perp$. By completeness for *propositional* logic, there is a valuation on the atomic sentences in $\psi\,(1)$ such that $v[\,\psi\,(1)] = 1$. Define an interpretation M by setting $M = \{1\}$, and for each relation symbol R that occurs in $\psi\,(1)$, let $\langle 1, \ldots, 1 \rangle \in R^M$ iff $v(R(1, \ldots, 1)) = 1$. It immediately follows that $M \vDash \psi\,(1)$ and hence $M \vDash \exists x\,\psi\,(x)$. Therefore, ϕ has a model.

Let's suppose now that ϕ has the form $\exists x \exists y\,\psi\,(x, y)$. It might be tempting then to try a repeat with the domain $M = \{1\}$, but that won't necessarily work. For example, the sentence $\exists x \exists y(Rxy \wedge \neg Ryx)$ has a model with two elements, but it has no model with one element. Thus, when ϕ begins with more than one existential quantifier, we should generate a new object for each existential quantifier. In this case, we can take the domain $M = \{1, 2\}$ and generate the instance $R(1, 2) \wedge \neg R(2, 1)$, giving $R^M = \{\langle 1, 2 \rangle\}$.

The cases we just considered are misleadingly simple. Indeed, those cases have the feature that the relevant model M is finite. We know, though, that there are consistent sentences that have no finite model. Interestingly, all such sentences share the feature that, when put into prenex normal form, they have a mix of existential and universal quantifiers. Thus, we need to consider how to generate a model from such sentences.

Consider first the sentence $\forall x \exists y (Rxy \wedge \neg Ryx)$. We begin by generating an instance $R(1, 2) \wedge \neg R(2, 1)$, choosing a new name 2 for the existence claim, since we don't know that it must be the same thing. However, this instance alone won't generate a model for ϕ, because when we introduce the new thing 2, we need to make sure that the original universal quantifier $\forall x$ also applies to it. So, we have to add a new object 3 and take another instance $R(2, 3) \wedge \neg R(3, 2)$. This situation repeats ad infinitum, so following our recipe will lead to a domain $M = \{1, 2, \ldots\}$ and a relation $R^M = \{\langle 1, 2 \rangle, \langle 2, 3 \rangle, \ldots\}$. In this particular case, we didn't actually need an infinite model—a model with two elements would have done. But what we do need is a general recipe that sometimes leads to our constructing an infinite model.

The procedure we have just sketched does, in fact, work quite generally to produce a model M for ϕ, so long as no contradiction can be derived from ϕ. It thus shows that the inference rules we gave you in this book are **completeness**, at least for arguments with finitely many premises. For the case of infinitely many premises, one must again invoke a new set-theoretic axiom (such as compactness).

Complete and Incomplete Theories

In compact symbolic form, the completeness theorem shows that if $\phi \vDash \psi$, then $\phi \vdash \psi$. What, then, is all this business about "incompleteness," as in **Gödel's incompleteness theorem**?

Definition. Let T be a theory formulated in signature Σ. We say that T is **complete** just in case for each Σ-sentence ϕ, either $T \vdash \phi$ or $T \vdash \neg\phi$.

Exercise 10.4. Let T be a consistent theory in propositional logic. Show that T is complete iff T has exactly one model.

It's important to note that the completeness of a theory is relative to the language in which the theory is formulated. For example, in an empty signature (with equality), the theory that says, "There is exactly one thing" is complete. However, in a signature with predicate symbol P, that same theory is incomplete—because it doesn't decide whether $\exists x Px$ is true or false.

One might think that incompleteness is a defect of a theory, since it seems to indicate that the theory hasn't yet given an answer to some relevant question. However, many theories in mathematics are intentionally incomplete, and their power comes precisely from the fact that there are many different ways for these theories to be true. For example, consider the theory of autosets, which we discussed briefly in chapter 7, and which (as we mentioned there) turns out to be equivalent to the so-called theory of groups, which is much loved by mathematicians. The theory of autosets has models of all sizes: a model with one element, a model with two elements, and so on. What's more, since the sentence "there are exactly n-elements" corresponds to a sentence in the language of autosets, it follows that the theory of autosets neither implies ϕ nor $\neg\phi$. Therefore, the theory of autosets—and hence the theory of groups—is incomplete. The word "incomplete" might sound bad, but mathematicians are quite happy with the incompleteness of the theory of groups. What's so interesting about groups is that there is a wide variety of them, with all sorts of different features.

Exercise 10.5. Let T be the theory with no axioms (besides tautologies) in a signature with only the equality symbol. Show that T is incomplete.

In 1931, Gödel published a proof of the incompleteness of arithmetic or, more precisely, of first-order Peano arithmetic.[2] Frequently, Gödel's remarkable result is paraphrased as showing that there is a true statement of arithmetic that is not provable. That way of speaking is licensed by the following simple result.

Proposition 10.2. *Let T be a consistent theory. Then the following three conditions are equivalent:*

---

2. Kurt Gödel, 1931, "Über formal unentscheidbare Sätze der Principia Mathematica und verwandter Systeme, I," *Monatshefte für Mathematik und Physik*, v. 38 n. 1, pp. 173–198.

1. T is complete.
2. For each model M of T, if $M \vDash \phi$, then $T \vdash \phi$.
3. For some model M of T, if $M \vDash \phi$, then $T \vdash \phi$.

Exercise 10.6. Prove this proposition.

If T is Peano arithmetic, then the set $N = \{0, 1, \ldots\}$ of natural numbers is a model of T. Gödel proved that there is a sentence ϕ in the language of arithmetic such that neither $T \vdash \phi$ nor $T \vdash \neg\phi$, which we now know is equivalent to the fact that there is a sentence ϕ such that $N \vDash \phi$ but $T \nvdash \phi$. In other words, there is a truth ϕ about N that does not follow from Peano arithmetic.

Now, you might raise the following objection to the supposed profundity of Gödel's theorem: although Peano arithmetic T is incomplete, can't we just keep adding new axioms until it's complete? In one sense, the answer is yes. In fact, there's an easy recipe for constructing a complete extension of T (if, in fact, N exists): let T^+ be the set of all sentences that are true in the model N. (Sometimes the theory T^+ is called **true arithmetic**.) Then, T^+ is obviously complete and extends T. Why not just take T^+ as a better theory than T?

The problem, in short, is that T^+ is essentially an ineffable theory. We know some consequences of T^+, but we possess no general recipe for generating *all* consequences of T^+. In fact, a fully precise statement of Gödel's theorem says that *no* effable theory about the natural numbers can be complete.

Exercise 10.7. Suppose that T has a model M such that $M \vDash \phi$, and T has a model N such that $N \vDash \neg\phi$. Show that T is incomplete.

Decidability

We concluded our discussion of completeness by saying that no "effable" theory about the natural numbers is complete. If Gödel actually proved such a claim, with mathematical rigor, then the word "effable" must have a precise mathematical meaning in this context. In fact, it does, although it usually goes by a more technical-sounding name, **recursively enumerable**.

Intuitively speaking, a recursively enumerable collection is a collection that can be generated step-by-step by applying some rule. In this book, you have encountered several paradigm examples of recursively enumerable collections.

- The set N of natural numbers is recursively enumerable: it is generated by applying the successor function $s : N \to N$ repeatedly to the number $0 \in N$.
- If Σ is a propositional logic signature, then the set of Σ-sentences is recursively enumerable. It is generated by applying the construction rules (corresponding to the connectives) repeatedly to the atomic sentences in Σ.
- If Σ is a propositional logic signature, then the set of provable sequents is recursively enumerable. It is generated by applying the inference rules repeatedly to instances of the rule of assumptions.

Based on these characterizations, it's also easy to see that the collection of predicate logic formulas is recursively enumerable, as is the set of provable sequents in predicate logic.

It does *not* follow from what we said here that every subset of a recursively enumerable subset is also recursively enumerable. To prime your intuition about this matter, think about subsets of the natural numbers. There is an uncountable infinity of subsets of the natural numbers, but only countably many recipes for generating subsets.

In the case of predicate logic, our theories T often have a finite number of axioms—and hence, they are automatically recursively enumerable, as is the set of all their consequences. However, a theory need not have only a finite number of axioms. For example, consider the theory T that has axioms:

$$\exists_{>1}, \exists_{>2}, \ldots, \exists_{>n}, \ldots$$

where $\exists_{>n}$ is the sentence that says that there are more than n things. This theory is sometimes called the **theory of infinite sets**, since its models are all infinite sets. Now, while the theory of infinite sets has an infinite number of axioms, intuitively, its set of axioms is recursively enumerable. Indeed, by writing the ellipsis after the first few axioms, I suggested a method of generating all of the infinitely many axioms of T.

Now return to the theory T^+ of true arithmetic, which consists of all sentences that are true in the model N of natural numbers. Gödel showed not only that Peano arithmetic is incomplete; he showed that no complete and consistent extension of Peano arithmetic can have a recursively enumerable set of axioms. In particular, T^+ is not recursively enumerable, that is, there is no rule that generates all and only the consequences of T^+.

The notion of a recursively enumerable set is investigated in the subfield of mathematical logic called **recursion theory**. This theory also covers the related notion of a **decidable set**, a notion with which you are now familiar.

Suppose that Σ is some fixed propositional logic signature, and let Γ be the set of all tautologous Σ-sentences. The set Γ is rather boring, in the following sense: you could program your computer so that for any input sentence ϕ, it will tell you whether or not $\phi \in \Gamma$. The algorithm is simple: have your computer write out a truth table for ϕ, and if all rows under the main column are 1, then the computer says Accept. Otherwise, it says Reject. Given this feature of the set Γ, we say that it is a **decidable set**.

What we just said also indicates that the set of valid propositional logic sequents is also a decidable set. (We already knew that it was a recursively enumerable set, since it is generated by applying a finite number of rules of inference.) Indeed, given a proposed sequent $\phi \vdash \psi$, just have the computer decide whether or not $\phi \rightarrow \psi$ is a tautology. If the computer says Accept, then the sequent is provable; if the computer says Reject, then the sequent is not provable.

Surprisingly, perhaps, the situation turns out to be different in predicate logic. Again, the set of valid predicate logic sequents is obviously a recursively enumerable set. Indeed, we were busy generating that set earlier in the book. Nonetheless, the set of valid predicate logic sequents is *not* a decidable set. That fact is known as Church's theorem, and its proof is far from trivial.[3] What it means for you, the practicing logician, is that

---

3. Named for Alonzo Church (1903–1995).

there is no mechanical method for checking whether or not a predicate logic sequent can be proven.

Compactness

Recall from our discussion of propositional logic that the full completeness theorem can be derived from the finite completeness theorem, if we allow ourselves a new set-theoretic axiom: compactness. One version of the compactness axiom seems counterintuitive: it says that if every finite subset of a set Γ of sentences is consistent, then Γ is consistent. Another version of the compactness axiom seems obviously true: it says that if a set Γ doesn't imply a contradiction $\bot$, then Γ can be grown to a maximal set Γ^* that doesn't imply a contradiction.

The compactness axiom also applies in the case of predicate logic, where it's perhaps even less controversial but is quite a bit more powerful in applications. Indeed, one can prove all sorts of interesting things about models using the compactness theorem. One can also use compactness to prove some interesting things about what cannot be said in first-order logic.

So long as we get to use the equality symbol $=$, first-order logic can make any finite numerical claim we wish. For example, we can say that there are less than n things, more than n things, or exactly n things. That is, for each of these claims, there is a predicate logic sentence ϕ that captures its precise sense. There cannot, however, be a predicate logic sentence ϕ that says, "There are infinitely many things." To be clear, there are—as we have already seen—predicate logic sentences that are only true in infinite domains (e.g., the sentence that describes a linear order without endpoints). However, those sentences must say something more than that there are infinitely many things. For if ϕ says that there are infinitely many things, then $\neg\phi$ says that there are finitely many things. But as we will now see, if a sentence ϕ has models of arbitrarily large finite size, then ϕ also has an infinite model.

Suppose that for each natural number n, ϕ has a model M_n that has more than n elements. Thus, $M_n \vDash \exists_{>n}$, where the latter sentence says, "There are more than n things." Now let Γ be the collection of all sentences: $\phi, \exists_{>1}, \exists_{>2}, \ldots$. We have just shown that every finite subset of Γ

is consistent. Therefore, by compactness, Γ itself is consistent, that is, Γ has a model M. However, M must be an infinite set, because for each n, $M \vDash \exists_{>n}$. Therefore, ϕ has an infinite model.

Interestingly, although first-order logic doesn't have a sentence ϕ that says that there are infinitely many things, it does have an infinite set T of sentences that together say there are infinitely many things. Indeed, the set $T = \{\exists_{>1}, \exists_{>2}, \dots\}$ has only infinite models. However, that fact in no way contradicts compactness, which says that if T is inconsistent, then some finite subset of T is inconsistent.

We've just shown, then, that first-order logic cannot say some things; in particular, it cannot say that there are infinitely many things. Perhaps even more interesting, first-order logic cannot distinguish between different sizes of infinity. To understand what's going on here, you'll have to take on faith that the size of the set of real numbers (i.e., decimal expansions) is strictly greater than the size of the set of natural numbers. That's a fact that one routinely proves in set theory. However, once again, if a first-order logic sentence ϕ has a model N that is the size of the natural numbers, then it has a model M of the size of the real numbers.

Suppose, indeed, that N is a model of ϕ. Whatever signature Σ the sentence ϕ is written in, we can expand it by adding a new name c_r for each real number r. Now let Γ be the set of sentences that includes ϕ and also the sentences $c_r \neq c_s$ for $r \neq s$. We claim, then, that each finite subset of Γ is consistent. Indeed, any finite subset Γ_0 of Γ contains only finitely many of the names c_r. Let M be an interpretation that agrees with N on the vocabulary in ϕ and that assigns each c^r to a distinct name in N. Clearly, then, $M \vDash \phi$, and M validates each sentence $c_r \neq c_s$ that occurs in Γ_0. Therefore, Γ_0 is consistent. By compactness, Γ is consistent, and it's clear that a model M of Γ must be as large as the real numbers. Therefore, ϕ has a model that is as large as the real numbers.

Consider next the case of linear orders. Suppose that $<$ is a binary relation symbol, and suppose that T is a theory that says that $<$ is a discrete linear order without endpoints. (The word "discrete" here means that each point has an immediate successor and an immediate predecessor.) The "standard" model of T is the integers, that is, all negative and positive whole numbers: $\{\dots, -2, -1, 0, 1, 2, \dots\}$. However, T also has nonstandard models, such as the "double integers," which we now describe. Take two copies M_1 and M_2 of the integers, and paste them together, declaring each number in the first copy is strictly smaller than each number in the second copy. Let M be the resulting interpretation. Then, it's straightforward to verify that M is also a model of T.

Now, suppose that you are a mathematician, and your job is to come up with a set of axioms that picks out the integers. If you see that your axioms T also permit the double integers, then you might reasonably conclude that you need a further axiom to rule out that case. So, what is the feature of the double integers that we would like to rule out? Well, the double integers have the following funny property: there are finite numbers a and b such that there are infinitely many numbers between a and b. (For example, let a be the 0 from the first copy of the integers, and let b be the 0 from the second copy of the integers.) Thus, it would make sense to try to add a new axiom that says

> Between any two numbers x and y, there are at most finitely many other numbers.

Is there a first-order logic sentence that can express that English language sentence? In short, the answer is no, for the following reason.

Suppose that $\phi(x, y)$ says that there are finitely many numbers between x and y. Then, $\phi(x, y)$ is consistent with there being n numbers between x and y and also with there being $n + 1$ numbers, and so on. In other words, for each n, $\phi(x, y)$ is consistent with the following statement:

> $\psi_n(x, y) \equiv$ There are more than n numbers between x and y.

However, this formula $\psi_n(x, y)$ can be expressed in first-order logic. Thus, a compactness argument shows that the entire set

$$\{\phi(c, d),\ \psi_1(c, d),\ \psi_2(c, d), \ldots\}$$

is consistent, where c and d are new names. But if there is no bound on the distance between c^M and d^M, then it cannot be correct to say that there are finitely many numbers between c^M and d^M. Therefore, the formula $\phi(x, y)$ doesn't express the fact that there are finitely many numbers between x and y.

We've just seen that first-order logic cannot express an axiom that says that there are finitely many numbers between any two other numbers. The problem, of course, is with that pesky word "finite." First-order logic can say things about specific finite numbers, but the amorphous concept of "finiteness" is beyond its grasp. If you wanted to speak that way, you'd have to use a language that is more expressive than the one we've developed in this book.

Let's look at one last case of something that first-order logic cannot express—this time close to home for anyone who has studied calculus. In more advanced applications of calculus, it becomes important to know that there are lots and lots of real numbers. In fact, every bounded subset S of real numbers has a least upper bound. (That's how we know that the irrational number π exists: let S be the subset of all rational numbers that are less than this theoretical number π. Since S has a least upper bound, π exists.) Stated symbolically, to say that y is an upper bound for S is expressed by the formula

$$\phi(x) \equiv \forall x (x \in S \rightarrow x \leq y).$$

Thus, to say that r is the least upper bound of S can be expressed by

$$\phi(r) \wedge \forall y (\phi(y) \rightarrow r \leq y).$$

Thus, first-order logic can say that r is a least upper bound, but what it cannot say directly is that *every* subset S has a least upper bound. Indeed, you should immediately be suspicious when you see a quantifier word, such as "every," precede a name for a subset S of the relevant domain. Such a locution is a signal that one is quantifying not just over points in the domain but also over subsets of the domain. In such cases, then, we are doing something that cannot be done in first-order logic.

The preceding considerations show, or at least indicate, that the study of the real number system $\mathbb{R}$ cannot proceed within the bounds of first-order logic. That might seem like a blow to the idea that logic forms the foundation for all human knowledge. However, the story is in fact more nuanced than that. As we saw in chapter 7, first-order logic can be used to axiomatize set theory. And as one learns in a class on mathematical analysis, set theory can be used to formulate the theory of real numbers, including the principle that each bounded subset has a least upper bound. Thus, the foundational aspirations of first-order logic are still alive and well.

11

Beyond Logic

SINCE LOGIC HAS NO CONTENT, you cannot have failed to learn the content of this book. We hope, though, to have shown you an example of how you can think more clearly, more rigorously, and more freely.

You might be disappointed. You might have hoped that logic would tell you what to to believe or how to behave. However, since logic only cares about form (and not content), it cannot possibly advise us on what to believe. At best, logic can help us to calculate the costs of our beliefs. And once again, it's up to you to decide what costs you are willing to pay.

Consider, for example, the following simple argument for God's existence.

> If God does not exist, then there are no moral rules.
> There are moral rules.
> Therefore, God exists.

This argument is valid. But so what? It doesn't tell you what to believe. Perhaps you don't believe the premises. Or perhaps you believe the premises, and upon discovering that they entail this conclusion, you'll decide to reject the premises. Logic does not tell you that you ought not do that. There's an old philosophers' saying: *one person's modus ponens is another person's modus tollens.* In other words, logic doesn't tell you whether to accept the premises and the conclusion or whether to reject one of the premises because you reject the conclusion.

What Next?

Did you just waste a class (or many hours, or both) on learning techniques that you'll never again use? Even if you never again write a formal proof, the work you've put into learning formal logic will not be wasted. Consider an analogy. A competitive athlete may spend hour upon hour performing exercises that she will never perform in competition. Of course, those exercises are not wasted time. The different individual exercises are like vectors that can be summed together to produce the desired outcome during competition. The individual component contributors to performance may be invisible, but if they weren't there, the performance would be undermined.

Your life is more important than any athletic competition, and your brain is one of your most important tools for winning in life (however you define that for yourself). You can think of formal logic as the brain's version of isolation exercises. By learning the individual inference rules and by using them again and again, you've built some exquisite mental muscles. In real life, you might never have occasion to employ these individual mental muscles in isolation. However, any time you need to think hard, fast, or clearly, these individual mental muscles will combine to enable you to perform at the highest possible level.

If you want to go further with formal logic, then I have good news for you: it's a thriving subject, with connections to many other fields of study, such as computer science. As for the study of logic itself, there are many different directions you could go from here, and I'll briefly discuss five of them.

First, you might wish to study **extensions of classical logic**. For philosophers, the most important of these extensions is **modal logic**, which studies intensional connectives such as "it is necessarily true that ..." usually symbolized with a box □.[1]

While modal logic has primarily found its audience among philosophers, other extensions of classical logic are of interest in the exact sciences.

---

1. For propositional modal logic, see J. C. Beall and B. van Fraassen, *Possibilities and Paradox*, Oxford (2003), or G. Forbes, *Modern Logic*, Oxford (1994). For quantified modal logic, see K. Konyndyk, *Introductory Modal Logic*, University of Notre Dame Press (1986), or T. Sider, *Logic for Philosophy*, Oxford (2010).

Here, we should mention higher-order logics (where one can quantify over subsets),[2] infinitary logics (where one can form infinite conjunctions or disjunctions of sentences), and the lambda calculus (where one adds an operator for forming names out of predicate phrases).[3]

Second, if you're feeling a bit more revolutionary, then you might be interested in studying **alternatives to classical logic**. These alternatives to classical logic can again be subdivided into two classes: fragments of classical logic and substructural logics. A fragment of classical logic is a logic that uses only some subset of the logical vocabulary or the inference rules. For example, **intuitionistic logic** drops the double-negation elimination rule and instead adopts an ex falso quodlibet rule. (In this case, excluded middle can no longer be proven.) The move to intuitionistic logic was initially motivated by an outlook in the philosophy of mathematics that has largely been discredited. However, intuitionistic logic is still an important tool for reasoning about mathematical structures that do not "live in" the universe of sets.[4] More generally, **coherent logic** drops the negation symbol and the universal quantifier and so is neutral between intuitionistic and classical logic.

A **substructural logic** is a logic that modifies some of the rules we tacitly adopted for manipulating dependency numbers. In particular, we tacitly assumed that lists of dependency numbers aggregate like sets, for example, the aggregate of "2" and "2, 3" is "2, 3," which is no different than "3, 2." In substructural logic, these identities are no longer assumed to hold. Already in the 1960s, some logicians argued that changes in the structural rules were the best solution to the paradoxes of material implication.[5] More recently, it has been observed that changes in the structural rules can yield logics that better represent the kind of reasoning used in quantum physics (e.g., quantum logic)[6] and in computer science (e.g., linear logic).[7]

2. https://plato.stanford.edu/entries/logic-higher-order

3. https://plato.stanford.edu/entries/lambda-calculus

4. S. Mac Lane and I. Moerdijk, *Sheaves in Geometry and Logic*, Springer (1994).

5. https://plato.stanford.edu/entries/logic-relevance

6. P. Gibbins, *Particles and Paradoxes: The Limits of Quantum Logic*, Cambridge (1987).

7. A. S. Troelstra, *Lectures on Linear Logic*, CSLI (1992). For a general overview, see G. Restall, *An Introduction to Substructural Logics*, Routledge (2000).

Third, this entire book has focused on a limiting case of good arguments, namely, those arguments where the premises provide decisive support for the conclusion (i.e., deductively valid arguments). So, it would make a lot of sense to now go on to study less-idealized cases, where the premises are only intended to provide some (less than decisive) support conclusion. One promising approach to this idea is to use the **probability calculus**, which offers various ways to measure the evidential support that premises provide for a conclusion.[8] More generally, various **inductive logics** have been proposed, although there has been some controversy among philosophers about whether the notion of inductive support can be properly formalized.[9]

Fourth, one could proceed from here to a more in-depth study of the metatheory of first-order logic. For example, in **proof theory**, one builds and studies elegant "sequent calculi." In fact, we intentionally chose the proof system in this book because it closely resembles the sequent calculus, and so anyone who learns this system is well prepared to move on to proof theory.[10] Going in a different metatheoretical direction, in **model theory**, one studies the relation between theories and their models, and it's here that one proves some of the most powerful results of metalogic.[11] For example, the Löwenheim-Skolem theorem shows that any theory with an infinite model also has a countably infinite model—which is deeply puzzling when applied to Zermelo-Fraenkel set theory, which entails that there is an uncountably infinite set.[12]

Fifth, you might wish to study particular theories within first-order logic. Of course, that's precisely what's done in many different parts of mathematics—for example, one studies group theory, or ring theory, or field theory, or …. However, some such theories are of special interest to logicians, most particularly Zermelo-Fraenkel set theory and Peano

8. Colin Howson and Peter Urbach, *Scientific Reasoning: The Bayesian Approach*, Open Court (2005).

9. Brian Skyrms, *Choice and Chance: An Introduction to Inductive Logic*, Cengage (1999).

10. A. S. Troelstra and H. Schwichtenberg, *Basic Proof Theory*, Cambridge (2000).

11. D. Marker, *Model Theory: An Introduction*, Springer (2002).

12. For a general overview of metatheory, see G. Hunter, *Metalogic: An Introduction to the Metatheory of Standard First Order Logic*, University of California Press (1996), or H. Enderton, *A Mathematical Introduction to Logic*, Academic Press (2001).

arithmetic. Set theory has itself become a massive field of study, and there are many good textbooks. As for the study of Peano arithmetic and Gödel's incompleteness theorem, we would point the interested reader to Burgess, Boolos, and Jeffrey, *Computability and Logic*, Cambridge (2007), or P. Smith, *An Introduction to Gödel's Theorems*, Cambridge (2013).

Sixth, and finally, you might want to study the network of all theories as they are related to each other via translations. Here we would (immodestly) point you to H. Halvorson, *The Logic in Philosophy of Science*, Cambridge (2019).

Resumé of Inference Rules

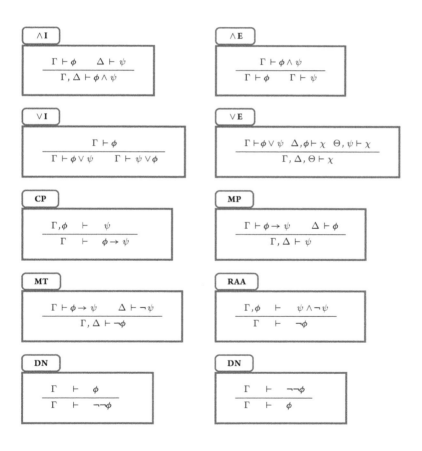

∧I

$$\frac{\Gamma \vdash \phi \quad \Delta \vdash \psi}{\Gamma, \Delta \vdash \phi \wedge \psi}$$

∧E

$$\frac{\Gamma \vdash \phi \wedge \psi}{\Gamma \vdash \phi \quad \Gamma \vdash \psi}$$

∨I

$$\frac{\Gamma \vdash \phi}{\Gamma \vdash \phi \vee \psi \quad \Gamma \vdash \psi \vee \phi}$$

∨E

$$\frac{\Gamma \vdash \phi \vee \psi \quad \Delta, \phi \vdash \chi \quad \Theta, \psi \vdash \chi}{\Gamma, \Delta, \Theta \vdash \chi}$$

CP

$$\frac{\Gamma, \phi \quad \vdash \quad \psi}{\Gamma \quad \vdash \quad \phi \rightarrow \psi}$$

MP

$$\frac{\Gamma \vdash \phi \rightarrow \psi \quad \Delta \vdash \phi}{\Gamma, \Delta \vdash \psi}$$

MT

$$\frac{\Gamma \vdash \phi \rightarrow \psi \quad \Delta \vdash \neg \psi}{\Gamma, \Delta \vdash \neg \phi}$$

RAA

$$\frac{\Gamma, \phi \quad \vdash \quad \psi \wedge \neg \psi}{\Gamma \quad \vdash \quad \neg \phi}$$

DN

$$\frac{\Gamma \quad \vdash \quad \phi}{\Gamma \quad \vdash \quad \neg \neg \phi}$$

DN

$$\frac{\Gamma \quad \vdash \quad \neg \neg \phi}{\Gamma \quad \vdash \quad \phi}$$

EI

$$\frac{\Gamma \quad \vdash \quad \phi(a)}{\Gamma \quad \vdash \quad \exists x \phi(x)}$$

EE

$$\frac{\Gamma \vdash \exists x \phi(x) \qquad \Delta, \phi(a) \vdash \psi}{\Gamma, \Delta \vdash \psi} \qquad \begin{array}{l} a \text{ does not occur} \\ \text{in } \Gamma, \Delta, \text{ or } \phi(x) \end{array}$$

UE

$$\frac{\Gamma \quad \vdash \quad \forall x \phi(x)}{\Gamma \quad \vdash \quad \phi(a)}$$

UI

$$\frac{\Gamma \quad \vdash \quad \phi(a)}{\Gamma \quad \vdash \quad \forall x \phi(x)} \qquad \begin{array}{l} a \text{ does not occur in} \\ \Gamma \text{ or } \phi(x) \end{array}$$

Useful Valid Argument Forms

hypothetical syllogism	$\phi \to \psi, \; \psi \to \chi$	$\vdash$	$\phi \to \chi$
prefixing	$\psi \to \chi$	$\vdash$	$(\phi \to \psi) \to (\phi \to \chi)$
suffixing	$\phi \to \psi$	$\vdash$	$(\psi \to \chi) \to (\phi \to \chi)$
permutation	$\phi \to (\psi \to \chi)$	$\vdash$	$\psi \to (\phi \to \chi)$
contraction	$\phi \to (\phi \to \psi)$	$\vdash$	$\phi \to \psi$
positive paradox	ψ	$\vdash$	$\phi \to \psi$
negative paradox	$\neg\phi$	$\vdash$	$\phi \to \psi$
ex falso quodlibet	$\phi, \neg\phi$	$\vdash$	ψ
weakening	$\neg\phi$	$\vdash$	$\neg(\phi \wedge \psi)$
disjunctive syllogism	$\phi \vee \psi, \neg\phi$	$\vdash$	ψ
excluded middle		$\vdash$	$\phi \vee \neg\phi$
commutation	$\phi \wedge \psi$	$\dashv\vdash$	$\psi \wedge \phi$
commutation	$\phi \vee \psi$	$\dashv\vdash$	$\psi \vee \phi$
association	$\phi \wedge (\psi \wedge \chi)$	$\dashv\vdash$	$(\phi \wedge \psi) \wedge \chi$
association	$\phi \vee (\psi \vee \chi)$	$\dashv\vdash$	$(\phi \vee \psi) \vee \chi$
material conditional	$\phi \to \psi$	$\dashv\vdash$	$\neg\phi \vee \psi$
material conditional	$\neg(\phi \to \psi)$	$\dashv\vdash$	$\phi \wedge \neg\psi$
contraposition	$\phi \to \psi$	$\dashv\vdash$	$\neg\psi \to \neg\phi$
DeMorgan	$\neg(\phi \vee \psi)$	$\dashv\vdash$	$\neg\phi \wedge \neg\psi$
DeMorgan	$\neg(\phi \wedge \psi)$	$\dashv\vdash$	$\neg\phi \vee \neg\psi$
distribution	$\phi \wedge (\psi \vee \chi)$	$\dashv\vdash$	$(\phi \wedge \psi) \vee (\phi \wedge \chi)$
distribution	$\phi \vee (\psi \wedge \chi)$	$\dashv\vdash$	$(\phi \vee \psi) \wedge (\phi \vee \chi)$
exportation	$\phi \to (\psi \to \chi)$	$\dashv\vdash$	$(\phi \wedge \psi) \to \chi$
duplication	ϕ	$\dashv\vdash$	$\phi \wedge \phi$

duplication	ϕ	$\dashv\vdash$	$\phi \vee \phi$
top	$\top$	$\dashv\vdash$	$\phi \vee \top$
top	ϕ	$\dashv\vdash$	$\phi \wedge \top$
bottom	ϕ	$\dashv\vdash$	$\phi \vee \bot$
bottom	$\bot$	$\dashv\vdash$	$\phi \wedge \bot$
self-undermining	$\phi \rightarrow \neg\phi$	$\dashv\vdash$	$\neg\phi$
biconditional	$\neg(\phi \leftrightarrow \psi)$	$\dashv\vdash$	$\neg\phi \leftrightarrow \psi$
biconditional	$\phi \leftrightarrow \psi$	$\dashv\vdash$	$(\phi \wedge \psi) \vee (\neg\phi \wedge \neg\psi)$
biconditional	$\phi \leftrightarrow \psi$	$\dashv\vdash$	$(\phi \rightarrow \psi) \wedge (\psi \rightarrow \phi)$
bicontraposition	$\phi \leftrightarrow \psi$	$\dashv\vdash$	$\neg\phi \leftrightarrow \neg\psi$

Useful Quantifier Equivalences

quantifier negation	$\neg\forall x\phi$	$\dashv\vdash$	$\exists x\neg\phi$	
quantifier negation	$\neg\exists x\phi$	$\dashv\vdash$	$\forall x\neg\phi$	
alpha	$\forall x\phi$	$\dashv\vdash$	$\forall y\phi[y/x]$	substitute y for x
alpha	$\exists x\phi$	$\dashv\vdash$	$\exists y\phi[y/x]$	substitute y for x
swoosh	$\forall x(\phi \wedge \psi)$	$\dashv\vdash$	$\forall x\phi \wedge \forall x\psi$	
swoosh	$\exists x(\phi \vee \psi)$	$\dashv\vdash$	$\exists x\phi \vee \exists x\psi$	
	$\forall x(\chi \rightarrow \phi)$	$\dashv\vdash$	$\chi \rightarrow \forall x\phi$	x not free in χ
	$\exists x(\chi \rightarrow \phi)$	$\dashv\vdash$	$\chi \rightarrow \exists x\phi$	x not free in χ
	$\forall x(\phi \rightarrow \chi)$	$\dashv\vdash$	$\exists x\phi \rightarrow \chi$	x not free in χ
	$\exists x(\phi \rightarrow \chi)$	$\dashv\vdash$	$\forall x\phi \rightarrow \chi$	x not free in χ
	$\forall x\forall y\phi$	$\dashv\vdash$	$\forall y\forall x\phi$	
	$\exists x\exists y\phi$	$\dashv\vdash$	$\exists y\exists x\phi$	

Truth Tables

ϕ	ψ	$\phi \wedge \psi$		
1	1	1	**1**	1
1	0	1	**0**	0
0	1	0	**0**	1
0	0	0	**0**	0

ϕ	$\neg\phi$	
1	**0**	1
0	**1**	0

ϕ	ψ	$\phi \vee \psi$		
1	1	1	**1**	1
1	0	1	**1**	0
0	1	0	**1**	1
0	0	0	**0**	0

ϕ	ψ	$\phi \rightarrow \psi$		
1	1	1	**1**	1
1	0	1	**0**	0
0	1	0	**1**	1
0	0	0	**1**	0

Validity Tests for Predicate Logic

In this appendix, we sketch an algorithm for testing whether arguments with only unary predicate symbols are valid. Note that it's enough to have an algorithm that tests for the consistency of sentences. Thus, we first describe an algorithm (algorithm A) that tests the consistency of quantifier-free sentences. We then describe algorithm B, which tests the consistency of simple monadic sentences (which have just one quantifier at the beginning). Finally, we describe algorithm C, which tests the consistency of Boolean combinations of simple monadic sentences.

Algorithm A

Use: To test for the consistency of a set of quantifier-free sentences.

Algorithm: For any set Γ of quantifier-free sentences, try to assign truth values to all of the elementary sentences that make up the sentences in Γ in such a way as to make all of the sentences in Γ true. If there is such an assignment, then the sentences in Γ are consistent. If not, then they are inconsistent.

To determine the extension of the predicates: if a given sentence is true, then put the object named into the extension of the predicate used in the sentence. So, for example, if Fa is false, then leave a out of the extension of F.

Algorithm B

Use: To test for the consistency of a set of simple monadic sentences (note: a sentence is simple monadic just in case the main operator of the sentence is a quantifier and it doesn't contain any other quantifiers or names within the scope of the main quantifier).

1. Take each sentence beginning with an existential quantifier and give an instance of the sentence such that each sentence contains a different arbitrary name.
2. Then, take each sentence beginning with a universal quantifier and produce an instance of the quantifier for each name used in step (1). If there are no sentences beginning with existential quantifiers, then you need only one instance of each universal sentence.
3. Take the list of instances and plug that set of sentences into algorithm A. If those sentences are consistent, then the set of simple monadic sentences is consistent. If not, then they aren't.

Algorithm C

Use: To test for the consistency of pure monadic sentences (note: a pure monadic sentence is a sentence that is a truth-functional combination of simple monadic sentences).

1. Take your pure monadic sentences and conjoin them into one giant sentence of the form $\phi \land \psi \land \chi$, and so on.
2. Treating the simple monadic sentences as elementary, put the entire giant sentence into **disjunctive normal form (DNF)**.
3. Drive in any negations that are on the outside of quantifiers.
4. You've now got a big disjunction of conjunctions, that is, a sentence of the form $(\phi \land \psi) \lor (\chi \land \theta)$, and so on, where each sentence letter is a simple monadic sentence. Take each disjunct one at a time and plug the simple monadic sentences into algorithm B. If any one disjunct is consistent, then the whole giant sentence is consistent, and the original set of pure monadic sentences is consistent. If none of them are consistent, then the whole thing is inconsistent.

Glossary

⊨ Semantic implication: whenever the sentences to the left of the double turnstile are true, the sentence to the right of the double turnstile is true   203

⊢ The relation of provability defined by the inference rules   12

antecedent The antecedent of a conditional is the sentence that occurs after "if"; for example, in "if it is raining then the sidewalk is wet," the sentence "it is raining" is the antecedent   16

atomic sentence An atomic sentence is a sentence that does not have any other sentence as a proper syntactic part. In propositional logic, atomic sentences are represented by capital letters such as $P, Q, R, \ldots$. In quantifier logic, the atomic sentences are either relation symbols applied to closed terms, such as Rab, or equalities between closed terms, such as $a = b$ 23, 52, 85, 178

biconditional A biconditional is a statement of the form "ϕ if and only if ψ." It asserts that ϕ is a necessary and sufficient condition for ψ 58

complete (1) A complete proof system is one that proves everything it should: if $\phi \vDash \psi$, then $\phi \vdash \psi$. (2) A theory T is complete just in case $T \vdash \phi$ or $T \vdash \neg\phi$, for every sentence ϕ in its language   196, 217

conditional A conditional sentence is one whose main connective is "if … then," symbolized by $\rightarrow$ 16

conjunct A conjunct is one of the two subformulas that are combined with $\wedge$ to form a conjunction   11 *consequent* The consequent of a conditional is the sentence that occurs after "then"; for example, in "if it is raining then the sidewalk is wet" the sentence "the sidewalk is wet," is the consequent   16

contingency A contingency is a sentence that is true in some situations and false in other situations   73

counterexample A counterexample to an argument is a formalization of the notion of a situation, or state of affairs, in which the premises are true and the conclusion is false   18, 71, 164

dependency number A number in the leftmost column of a proof that displays which assumptions are in force at a particular step in the proof   29

disjunction A disjunction is a sentence whose main connective is "or," symbolized by ∨   13

existential quantifier The symbol ∃ that plays the role of "some" or "there is"   88

expressively complete A collection of connectives is expressively complete if it can express all truth functions   185

inconsistency An inconsistency is a sentence that is false in all situations   72

interpretation An interpretation is an assignment of symbols to set-theoretic structures   161

main column Is the column in the truth table of a sentence corresponding to the main connective of that sentence   66

main connective For a propositional logic sentence ϕ, the last connective in the construction of ϕ 179

model A model of a theory is an interpretation in which all the theory's sentences are true   169

necessary condition In a conditional statement "if ϕ, then ψ," the consequent ψ is a necessary condition for ϕ 19

reconstrual A reconstrual assigns nonlogical symbols to corresponding syntactic structures. For example, a reconstrual assigns a predicate symbol to a formula with one free variable   52, 190

sequent A sequent consists of a list of sentences (premises), a turnstile ⊢, and another sentence (conclusion). It is the symbolic representation of a valid argument form   12, 29 *signature* A signature is a set of nonlogical symbols: propositional constants, relation, function, and constant symbols   190

sound A sound proof system is one that doesn't prove things it shouldn't: if $\phi \vdash \psi$, then $\phi \vDash \psi$ 194, 213

subformula A subformula of ϕ is any formula that occurs in the construction of ϕ 179

substitution When some nonlogical symbols are replaced with other suitable syntactic structures   179

substitution instance A substitution instance of a sentence is any other sentence that results from the first by a uniform replacement of nonlogical terms. That is, it is any sentence that could result from translating that sentence to another language   52, 191

sufficient condition In a conditional statement "if ϕ, then ψ," the antecedent ϕ is a sufficient condition for ψ 19

tautology A tautology is a sentence ϕ that is provable from no premises (i.e., $\vdash \phi$) or that is true merely in virtue of its form or that is true in all situations   73

translation A translation is a map from formulas to formulas, generated by a reconstrual of the nonlogical vocabulary in those formulas   52, 190

truth-functional A connective is truth-functional just in case its truth value is a function of the truth value of the relevant component sentences   183

universal quantifier The symbol $\forall$ that plays the role of "all" or "every"   87

valid An argument is valid just in case its premises provide decisive support for its conclusion, alternatively, if the truth of its premises guarantees the truth of its conclusion   5

variable A symbol such as x, which plays the role of an open term   87

Acronyms

Index